Making Progress in Primary Science, 2nd edition

This new and extensively revised edition of *Making Progress in Primary Science* is intended for all those involved in training teachers of primary school science, both preservice and on professional development courses. Its flexible, modular structure enables course leaders to tailor their course to participants' needs. The modules can be studied individually or as part of an extended programme and each module contains notes for facilitators, photocopiable workshop materials, activities for practitioners and suggestions for further reading.

Throughout the book, the focus is on the learning of science as an investigative process through which pupils develop an understanding of ideas. This is supported by modules on different aspects of teaching and learning in science, including:

- Building on children's own ideas
- How to ask and answer questions
- Managing practical work in the classroom
- Science for very young children
- Effective assessment, self-assessment and feedback
- Cross-curricular links
- ICT and science
- Science outside the classroom

Course leaders may also like to know that there is a companion *Study Book* available, which can be used by those participating on courses. It follows the same module structure and contains the same information as this book – making planning and delivering your course easier and less time consuming.

Wynne Harlen OBE is Visiting Professor at the Graduate School of Education, University of Bristol. **Chris Macro** was a Senior Lecturer in Primary Science at Edge Hill College of Higher Education and is now a part-time lecturer. **Kathleen Reed** is Education Adviser in the Learning and Development Directorate of Milton Keynes Council. **Mike Schilling** was Deputy Director of the Centre for Research in Primary Science and Technology at Liverpool University, and now works as a consultant.

Making Progress in Primary Science, 2nd edition

A handbook for professional development and preservice course leaders

**Wynne Harlen, Chris Macro,
Kathleen Reed and Mike Schilling**

RoutledgeFalmer
Taylor & Francis Group

LONDON AND NEW YORK

First published 2003 by RoutledgeFalmer
11 New Fetter Lane, London EC4P 4EE

Simultaneously published in the USA and Canada
by RoutledgeFalmer
29 West 35th Street, New York, NY 10001

RoutledgeFalmer is an imprint of the Taylor & Francis Group

Typeset in Palatino and Frutiger by
Keystroke, Jacaranda Lodge, Wolverhampton
Printed and bound in Great Britain by TJ International Ltd, Padstow, Cornwall

British Library Cataloguing in Publication Data
A catalogue record for this book is available from the British Library

Library of Congress Cataloging in Publication Data
Making progress in primary science : a handbook for professional development
and preservice course leaders/Wynne Harlen . . . [et al.]. — 2nd ed.
      p. cm.
   Includes bibliographical references and index.
   1. Science—Study and teaching (Elementary)—Handbooks, manuals, etc.
   I. Harlen, Wynne.
LB1585 .M285 2003
372.3′5—dc21   2002033309

ISBN 0–415–27673–X

Contents

This module gives participants direct experience of practical enquiry and this is used as a basis for reflection on what it involves. There is some consideration of how we learn through enquiry and the role of process skills in developing ideas. The implications of considering children's own ideas when teaching are discussed and there are opportunities to identify ways of accessing these ideas.

This module involves practical activity which is used to define enquiry skills and to enable participants to recognise them in practice. Approaches to developing both skills and ideas are considered.

In this module strategies for helping children to ask their own questions for enquiry are examined. There is also the opportunity to consider the type and wording of questions which encourage children to express their ideas and an examination of approaches to handling and categorising children's questions.

Here we consider how teachers manage practical work in the classroom in order to provide opportunities for children to develop the skills of enquiry and to develop concepts. There is an opportunity to reflect on how teaching is organised and to consider how resources and adult help are used.

In this module we consider how a curriculum for early years children based on experiential learning can develop skills and ideas. The teacher's role in planning for play is discussed and we look at how teachers can interact with children.

The aim of this module is to develop an understanding of the meaning, purposes and methods of assessment as applied to primary science. The characteristics of assessment and the relationship between formative and summative assessment are considered.

The aim of this module is to describe the development of enquiry skills in a way which can be used in assessing progress and handling the information formatively. The use of developmental criteria in the formative assessment of enquiry skills is considered by looking at evidence from practical and written work. Finally, there are activities which help participants to think about how developmental criteria can be related to levels of achievement used in summative reporting.

The aim of this module is to consider the extent to which there is sequence in the development of scientific concepts and the nature of the changes that indicate progress. The potential of children's written work for assessing progress in the understanding of concepts is discussed and the use of concept mapping is examined as a means of assessing progress in understanding.

Here we consider the reasons for and the importance of sharing learning goals with children and how goals of different kinds can be conveyed to children of various ages. There is some discussion of the ways of helping children to understand and use criteria for assessing the quality of their work and the different ways of involving children in self-assessment. Peer assessment is also considered.

This module is about giving feedback to children of the kind that will help their learning. The module activities are designed to enable participants to consider how feedback can be more effective and to make better use of the time spent marking. There is a consideration of how to give feedback which helps children to take the next steps in their learning and to think about the different kinds of responses which teachers make to children's work.

Here we think about how to plan more economically, using, on occasions, an integrated approach. The links between science and other subjects are considered as is planning so that children might see their learning in an holistic way. Links with other subjects are made but there is emphasis on identifying learning outcomes so that the integrity of the individual subjects is not lost.

The aim of this module is to consider how to identify criteria to ensure that planning is thorough and appropriate and recognises curriculum continuity.

There are opportunities to discuss how to cater for individual differences and to ensure progression in learning.

The aim of this module is to discuss how ICT can be used in the teaching and learning of science and it provides opportunities for participants to consider whether or not the use of ICT would be beneficial. There is some evaluation of software and an examination of the use of databases, spreadsheets and sensors.

Here we evaluate and compare CD-ROMs and consider how they might be used effectively. Some Internet sites are appraised and the learning opportunities are discussed. There is an examination of the way in which children use graphs and databases to analyse information and how they interpret data from sensors.

This module considers the science learning which might take place out of school. There is the opportunity to consider the local guidance in respect of school visits with particular reference to the legal aspects and the safety issues. Participants consider how the local environment, both natural and man-made, can provide a focus for scientific enquiry and examine research in order to think about how interactive science centres might be used.

This module considers the different ways in which science subject leaders can evaluate planning and practice within their schools. Work sampling and class-room observations are discussed and consideration is given to the methods of providing effective feedback. The role of governors and senior management teams is evaluated.

Preface

The first edition of this book was published in 1990 in response to the development of the National Curriculum for Science and the requirement for all primary school children to be taught science as part of the core curriculum in England and Wales. The original material was based on workshops developed and run to meet the sudden expansion of need for professional development in science in the wake of the new regulations. Within a few years the National Curriculum for Science had changed and some aspects of the material became out of date. However, those parts dealing with general and continuous aspects of teaching science in the primary school continued to be used by those providing initial teacher education and professional development.

Now, thirteen years on, four of the original authors have revisited *Progress in Primary Science* and *Making Progress in Primary Science, 2nd edition* is the result. The original intention of the material remains the same – to support active learning in teachers about active learning for children in their classrooms. However, the context now is very different from the situation in 1990. The curriculum has changed several times, becoming less prescriptive as teachers and schools have become more used to incorporating science into the curriculum. Curriculum programmes covering the requirements of the National Curriculum and its counterpart in other parts of the UK have been produced, and the optional Scheme of Work for Key Stages 1 and 2 has been published by the QCA and DfEE (as it then was).

Nevertheless, teachers face a considerable challenge in putting all this into practice: planning a programme that suits their particular pupils, adapting activities that enable individual pupils to use and develop their ideas and enquiry, or process, skills. A good deal of material, and all of the goals, of *Progress in Primary Science* remain highly relevant for primary teachers. In bringing the material up to date we have continued to give attention to practical work, planning, handling questions and to the teacher's role in providing for progression and continuity in the development of enquiry skills and conceptual understanding. We have added emphasis on assessment, the use of ICT, science in the early years, using out-of-school resources and in-school evaluation of provision for science.

Most significantly we have continued to use a modular format and an active approach in the material. Each of the sixteen modules provides activities and resource materials for workshop tasks to be undertaken in groups. These are designed to engage teachers and trainees in active learning, reinforcing the message about the value to learners at all levels of being involved in constructing their understanding.

We have also recognised that some teachers are unable to undertake organised professional development courses but still wish to continue their study of effective practice. Others may wish to have a more permanent record than their own notes of the topics studied in the modules. Thus we have produced a companion book, *Making Progress in Primary Science:*

A Study Book for Teachers and Student Teachers, which can be used for individual or group study and which contains all the activities and resources in the modules.

Wynne Harlen,
Chris Macro,
Kathleen Reed,
Mike Schilling

Acknowledgements

Thank you to the children and teachers at Thatto Heath Community Primary School, St Helens, Merseyside, and Legh Vale Community Primary School, Haydock, St Helens, Merseyside.

Thank you also to Joanne Edwards and Janet Skelton: PGCE trainees at Edge Hill College of Higher Education.

Figure 15.4, by S. Schwartzenberg © Exploratorium, www.exploratorium.edu

We would also like to thank Liverpool University Press for the use of illustrations from SPACE publications and Heinemann Education for the use of extracts from *Primary Science: Taking the Plunge*, 2nd edition.

General notes for facilitators

THE AIM: LEARNING ABOUT TEACHING THROUGH ENQUIRY

The modular material of *Making Progress in Primary Science* both advocates and exemplifies active learning through engagement with ideas, materials and emerging educational issues. It takes the form of workshops for practising or trainee teachers which encourage activity and the essential accompaniment to it, reflection and analysis. Reflection is both for clarification and reinforcement; it is not a passive matter and usually takes the form of reporting and discussing the processes and products of the workshop activities. The outcome of the work is that teachers and trainees become familiar with the meaning of learning science through enquiry and with the teacher's and pupils' roles in developing scientific understanding in this way.

In active enquiry learning, learners bring their experience and initial ideas to bear in trying to answer questions or understand new events and phenomena. It is the same for adults and for pupils in school. In science this means making sense of new experience and building understanding of scientific ideas through practical investigation, through sharing and exchanging ideas with others and through consulting reference sources including experts, books, the Internet and databases. By working in this way in this material on tasks at their own level, teachers develop the skills and knowledge to work in the same way with children.

THE FACILITATOR'S ROLE

To pursue this approach to learning the tutor, lecturer, or co-ordinator leading the course acts as a facilitator rather than as an instructor. Facilitation in this context means providing the setting and guidance to enable participants to come up with ideas themselves but also introducing points to be considered that may not have emerged. This role has some simple but basic aspects, such as timekeeping, maintaining momentum and managing the mechanics of the activities. It also has more complex aspects such as motivating, providing feedback that leads to further learning and managing the experiences flexibly to suit the needs of the participants.

THE MODULES AND FACILITATOR'S NOTES

The modular format means that a course programme or even a single session can be planned according to the requirements of the participants. The modules can be used in any sequence, although there is an obvious starting point in Module 1 for those unfamiliar with learning through enquiry and the modules dealing with ICT fit together. There is also a series of five modules relating to assessment with an obvious sequence within them.

HOW THE MODULES WORK

Each module begins with:

- a statement of its goals
- an overview of its content
- guidance as to timing
- a list of materials required.

There follow:

- suggestions for points to include when introducing to the module focus
- notes for each activity relating to procedures
- further possible points to make during discussion.

This guidance is offered as a way of using the material based on experience of running courses using it, but it is intended that facilitators will select and adapt as necessary to suit the particular group of participants. The workshop activities are set out at the end of each module and further reading is also suggested. The activities and associated resources are photocopiable.

Reference is made to the accompanying Study Book which also contains the workshop activities and resources. Although chiefly intended for individual teachers and trainee teachers who may not be able to join others in study groups, the Study Book also enables workshop participants to revisit material covered in a course and to go beyond the modules included in it (since the amount of material is far greater than is likely to be covered). Therefore, course leaders may decide to ask each participant to have a copy of the other book. Those who have the Study Book will not need photocopies of the activities and resources as these are the same. Please note, however, that the figure numbers may vary from those in the Study Book.

Module 1   **Learning science through enquiry**

Starting from children's ideas

MODULE GOALS

- To give participants direct experience of practical enquiry as a basis for reflection on what it involves.
- To provide a structure, or framework, for thinking about learning through enquiry and identifying the role of process skills in developing ideas.
- To recognise that children often have their own ideas about scientific phenomena prior to school science activities and the implications of this for teaching.
- To identify ways of accessing children's ideas so that they can be taken into account in teaching.

MODULE OVERVIEW

This module is about the nature of scientific enquiry and how ideas about scientific phenomena can be developed or changed through the use of enquiry, or process, skills. First-hand experience of enquiry is important for participants so that they can reflect on the processes that they have carried out and realise what is involved for children. Thus, Activity 1 sets up a situation in which a question is posed, asks participants to make a prediction and to test it in practice. To help reflection on what is involved, a framework for thinking about enquiry is introduced and applied to participants' own activity. The framework indicates the roles in the development of ideas of the enquiry skills of: raising questions, predicting, planning, gathering evidence by observing and measuring, interpreting evidence and drawing conclusions, and communicating and reflecting critically.

In Activity 2 participants apply this framework to one of two vignettes of children's activities. In these the children's own ideas that they bring to an activity clearly play an important part. In each case the teacher enables the children to test their own ideas first rather than just stating what is scientifically correct. This leads on to the consideration of the ideas that children often form from their own thinking about their experiences. Activity 3 gives some examples, all from research into children's scientific ideas, for discussion. These examples show how 'reasonable', in terms of the children's limited experience, the children's own ideas often are. Participants have the opportunity to discuss the implications of this for helping children to develop more scientific ways of looking at their experiences. The importance of knowing these ideas means that teachers need to have ways of accessing them. Activity 4 gives participants the opportunity to share ideas and discuss the appropriateness of different approaches for various ages groups. We leave the next stage, of how to develop children's ideas, for study in Module 2.

Timing

Total time: 2 hours 30 minutes

Introduction		10 mins
Activity 1	Group work	25 mins
	Feedback and discussion	20 mins
Activity 2	Group work	20 mins
	Feedback and discussion	15 mins
Activity 3	Group work	20 mins
	Feedback and discussion	15 mins
Activity 4	Group work	15 mins
	Feedback and discussion	10 mins

Materials required

For Activity 1

For each group of four:

- sources of green and red light (coloured bulbs or gelatines over torches);
- a ball (tennis ball size) on a stand;
- white screen, matt black screen, or matt black material that can be placed over the screen;
- a location where the ambient light can be minimised (curtains drawn or hung round a table with the equipment set up underneath);
- copies of Activity 1 for those who do not have the Study Book;
- an OHP of the enquiry framework (Figure 1.3).

Note: If there is only one set of equipment, groups can take turns to make the observations, but this limits their opportunities to 'play' with the equipment to test other predictions.

For Activity 2

- copies of Activity 2 and of the two vignettes for those who do not have the Study Book;
- copies of the blank enquiry framework for each pair of participants.

For Activities 3 and 4

- copies of the activities for those who do not have the Study Book.

INTRODUCTION

Points to make:

- This module is about the key features of learning through enquiry – the process skills and the way in which these are used in developing scientific ideas.
- We start with a practical enquiry in order to have a shared experience to talk about and to recognise what is involved in conducting an enquiry.

- Although we will be considering practical enquiry, not all enquiry is 'hands-on' so we will arrive at a meaning of enquiry that includes using evidence from secondary sources – books, CD-ROMs, the Internet, etc.

ACTIVITY 1

Arrange participants in groups of four. Keep the equipment out of the way so that the first part of the activity (a) is conducted by thought and discussion. Ask each group to write down their answers to (i), (ii) and (iii), but there is no need to collect them at this stage (12 minutes for all of this). Have the sets of equipment ready for part (b) and let the groups test their predictions in practice. They should then return to their tables to discuss what they found and whether this has changed their ideas about coloured light.

Feedback and discussion

There will generally be groups for whom the results were a surprise in some respects. There is often the expectation that the colour of the shadow of the lamp will be the same as the colour of the lamp, rather than the colour of the light from the other lamp.

Ask a group that found some difference between what they observed and what they predicted to report on what they predicted and their reasons. They probably now realise the limitations of their earlier ideas and understand why things were different in reality. If not, ask another group, who predicted correctly, to explain their reasoning. (This encourages participants to learn from each other, which is part of the message of this module.)

The third part, about the black screen, is likely to have produced some mixed results unless the black surface was really matt. (Any shininess would have reflected some light.) By definition, a truly black surface does not reflect any light, but absorbs all colours. So whatever the colour of light, it will still look black.

It may be necessary to remind participants who are unsure of the science here that the colour of a surface is the colour of light that it reflects (into your eye so that you can see it). In white light (composed of all the colours of the spectrum) a surface that looks red is reflecting just the red light and absorbs all the other colours, because of the pigment in the surface. When red light falls on a white surface (which reflects all the colours), it looks red because it can only reflect the light that is falling on it. If both red and green light fall on a white surface, both are reflected and together they make yellow. (When mixing light, red, green and blue are the primary colours and all other colours can be made by mixing them.)

Once the participants are satisfied about the science, turn to thinking about the processes that they went through in the activity. Ask them to recall what they did, after being given a problem. List on a whiteboard or flip chart – prediction, planning investigation, etc. Then show the OHP of the enquiry framework, in Figure 1.1. Using the framework identify the activities undertaken by participants in Activity 1 in terms of it:

- In this case the question was raised for participants (What will the colours be?)
- They used their pre-existing ideas to understand what was going on (ideas about coloured lights recalled and linked to new situation).
- The predictions were based on their ideas about coloured light.
- The test of the predictions was then planned (although in this case there was little detailed planning to do, as the set-up was given).
- Then the evidence was gathered (they made the observations).
- The results were interpreted in terms of the predictions (whether the expected colours were seen) and this also tested the hypotheses on which the predictions were based.
- By discussion and reflection the initial ideas were either changed (if not upheld) or strengthened (if they were upheld).

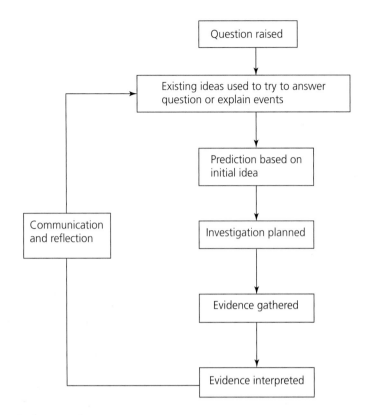

Figure 1.1 Enquiry framework

For cross-reference with Study Book see Figure 1.6

The next activity involves further use of the framework, so there is no need for more discussion after this 'modelling' of its application.

ACTIVITY 2

For this activity ask participants to work in pairs teaching the same age group (5–7 or 8–11). One vignette, about Emma, is more suitable for teachers of younger children and the one about Gavin for teachers of older juniors. Ask participants to read both but fill in the framework for one only. Distribute the blank framework copies and set a time limit of 20 minutes for the activity.

Feedback and discussion

Ask one pair to report on Emma and others to query or add as required. Then do the same for Gavin. The main points are not so much in the exact match to the framework of what the children did, but rather in seeing the learning as a cycle of events in which the children's ideas are tried out.

The important points to make during the discussion of the application of the framework are:

- There is a cycle of enquiry, which may be repeated in order to try different ideas (as in the case of Gavin, where the scientific idea of the moisture coming from the air had yet to be tested).
- The essential process/enquiry skills that are used in this enquiry are raising questions, predicting, planning, gathering evidence by observing and measuring, interpreting evidence and drawing conclusions and communicating and reflecting critically. While

these can be expressed in different ways – and various terms are sometimes used – they describe the important steps in the enquiry process.

- The ways the skills are used determine the outcome of the enquiry, for example, if the predictions are not tested fairly, then it may be that ideas that should be changed are confirmed. *Thus the development of ideas depends crucially on the use of enquiry skills in a scientific manner.* (The developmental progression in enquiry skills is discussed in Module 7.)

The vignettes also draw attention to the role of the ideas that children bring to the activity. Their predictions are based on these ideas. Research into children's ideas shows that they are firmly held. The implications of this will be taken up in discussion of the next activity.

First, however, bring together the points made about learning through enquiry by proposing as a definition:

> Learning through enquiry means building understanding by testing one's own and others' ideas through gathering evidence from direct experience, from books and other resources including computer-based ones, from the teacher, and from other informed adults. As a result, the idea tested may be found not to fit the evidence, in which case an alternative one has to be tried, or the idea may be found to fit, in which case it is extended in its application and becomes a little 'bigger'.

ACTIVITY 3

How important is it to take account of the pre-existing ideas that children bring to an activity (such as Emma's idea that seeds have to be small and pale in colour, or Gavin's assumption that metal can allow water to pass through it)? This activity looks at some examples of children's ideas that have been revealed by research. These are not idiosyncratic and non-typical, but are quite widely held by children of these ages.

Ask participants to work in the same pairs as for Activity 2 in the first instance. Each pair should complete the task (15 minutes). Then ask pairs to form groups of four by joining up with a pair of teachers of a different age group. They should look at any differences that they find in their responses.

Feedback and discussion

Take responses from one group of four about their combined answers and any differences they found between teachers of different age groups. Ask others for any points to add or challenge.

The aim of this activity is recognition that the children's ideas can seem reasonable in view of their limited experience and ways of thinking. For example:

- The everyday use of language can easily form misconceptions about the classification of living things – we generally refer to small garden plants as 'plants' but refer to trees and bushes by other names, although they are scientifically all plants.
- Children may well have seen rust seemingly emerging from the inside of metal, for example, when painted iron railings become rusted under the paint, which then flakes off to reveal the rust.
- The sensation of 'seeing' is of directing our eyes towards what is seen, so it may seem that the eye is active in 'doing the seeing' and needs to be switched on.

In all these cases, there is evidence of the children working things out from their observations, not just making up the ideas without reason. Research also shows that they make sense to the children and so they will hold on to these ideas if no other more reasonable explanation is available to them. Even when they are introduced to the 'correct' explanation, this often makes less sense to them than their own idea. So it is important to ensure that their idea is tested because, until it is shown to be less useful than an alternative one, they will still believe it. This argues for taking children's own ideas seriously and enabling them to see the evidence for themselves that requires a change in their view or suggests that an alternative explanation should be tried.

How can we encourage this change in ideas towards more scientific ones? First, as just suggested, by allowing children to test their ideas (but ensuring that they do this using enquiry skills in a way that gives a rigorous test). Then by encouraging them to discuss and reflect on their ideas in the light of evidence. Just by talking about their ideas children can begin to view things in a different way. But more important is the input from others, from the teacher, from their peers and sometimes from books or other sources. They are exposed to different views from their own and realise that there are different ways of explaining things. They may take an idea from someone else, think it through, and if it makes sense to them, make it their own. In this way they are constructing their understanding based, not only on evidence, but on others' thinking and views. This approach to learning is identified as social constructivism.

ACTIVITY 4

An outcome of the previous activities is the importance of the teacher taking children's own ideas seriously. This can only be done, however, if the teacher can find out what these ideas are. Some of the examples in Activity 3 provide some suggestions, but these were found in the context of research, where children can be given individual attention. This activity asks participants to share ideas about how to access children's ideas in the context of a normal classroom.

Teachers might best work in groups of three or four (teaching mixed aged groups) for this activity, pooling their experience and ideas and suggesting the suitability for different age groups.

Feedback and discussion

List the ideas given by one group and add to them from other groups. The final list is likely to include:

- questioning
- children discussing in groups, with the teacher listening
- drawing
- writing down predictions and explanations of particular situations
- annotating drawings
- concept maps
- concept cartoons.

Again, ask participants who suggest a particular approach to describe it to others who are not familiar with it.

If the point has not been made in the discussion, note that attention to children's ideas is not just something to be done at the start of a topic or an activity. It can be relevant at any time and the more it is part of the general teacher–pupil interaction, and not seen as a separate 'add on' to the lesson, the better. Responding to these ideas is a matter taken up in Module 2 and, as seen there, can be part of the same activity of gaining access to the ideas.

Activity 1

(a) Start by thinking about this problem.

In a darkened room there is a white screen with an opaque ball held between it and two light bulbs, one green and one red. Each light casts a shadow on the screen and there is a place where the shadows overlap.

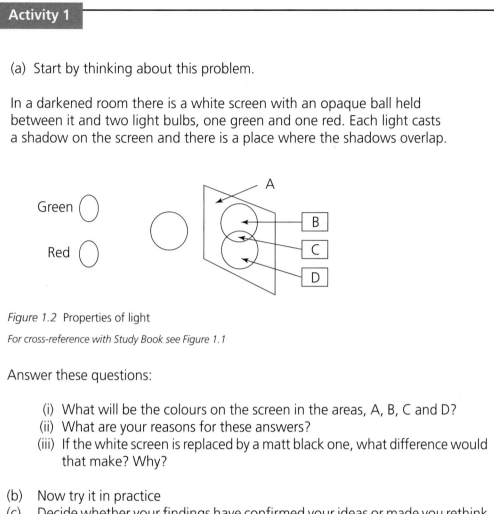

Figure 1.2 Properties of light

For cross-reference with Study Book see Figure 1.1

Answer these questions:

    (i) What will be the colours on the screen in the areas, A, B, C and D?
    (ii) What are your reasons for these answers?
    (iii) If the white screen is replaced by a matt black one, what difference would that make? Why?

(b)   Now try it in practice
(c)   Decide whether your findings have confirmed your ideas or made you rethink your ideas about light.

Activity 2

Choose either the account of Emma and the seeds, or Gavin and the Coke can, given in the box below. Analyse the activities in terms of the process skills in the enquiry model. Use the blank enquiry framework in Figure 1.3 to record your answers.

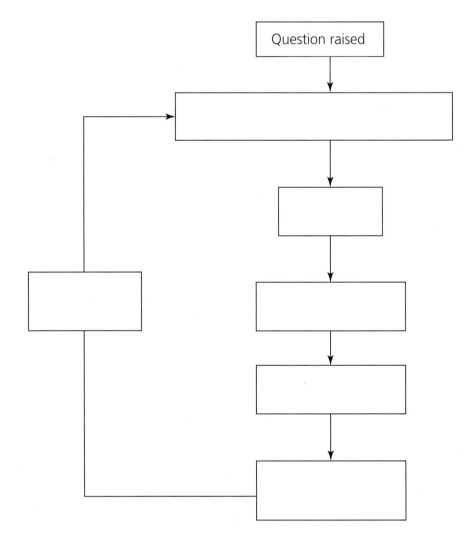

Figure 1.3 Blank enquiry framework

For cross-reference with Study Book see Figure 1.2

Emma and the seeds

The 6 and 7 year olds were collecting different kinds of seeds with a view to planting some of them in the classroom or the school garden. They included some mung bean seeds, broad bean and pea seeds, lupin and nasturtium and acorns. After the children had examined them, and added a few more from home, the teacher discussed with them whether they thought they would grow. Several children thought that the peas and beans would not grow, because 'we eat these; they are food'. She then asked them what they thought the other seeds would need to make them grow. All the children thought they needed soil and a few mentioned water. The teacher showed them some dry soil and asked them if they thought the seeds would grow in this. They then all agreed that the seeds need water. Emma was sure that they needed both soil and water – for food and drink. That was why people put them in the ground!

The teacher summarised this discussion: 'So we think that the seeds will grow if they have water and soil. What do you think will happen if they have only soil or only water?' Emma was sure they would not grow. So in a 'let's see' step the teacher guided them to think of what they could do to see if they were right. They decided to try some seeds with water only, some with soil only and some with both. The water-only ones were put on damp cotton wool. Each group of children tried all the seeds in the three different ways. They looked at their seeds daily and by the end of a week the mung beans were sprouting in the damp soil and on the damp cotton wool. In a few weeks the peas began to sprout also. The teacher discussed with Emma's group what they thought about the seeds growing without soil. At first Emma said that they were getting their food from the cotton wool. So they tried some other seeds without any cotton wool, just water. But before there was time for these seeds to sprout, the mung beans were growing up and the seed covers were pushed up with the leaves. Emma said that the seeds were 'empty' and the plant grew inside. The teacher suggested that the seed had the food for it to start growing and so all they needed was water. She asked Emma and her group to think about whether the food we eat as peas and beans is the food that the peas and beans have ready for them to grow.

Gavin and the Coke can

Like many children, 11-year-old Gavin tried to explain the wetness on the outside of a can of Coke just after it had been taken from the fridge in terms of water leaking through the metal from inside. He knew it was not Coke that was on the outside, because it was colourless and tasted like water, but he was quite prepared to explain this by saying that the metal only allowed the water in the drink to pass through. In order to work towards a more scientific explanation the teacher asked Gavin and his group to predict what would happen if an empty Coke can was cooled and then taken out of the fridge. They tried this and at first the observation of wetness forming was explained in terms of the can being still wet inside. So they were asked to find a way of getting a can quite dry inside. This they did by taking the top off, drying it thoroughly and filling it with dry cotton wool. She also asked them to think about the conditions in which the moisture formed and where else they had noticed surfaces misting over. So when they found the mist still forming on the can without water in it, they were already thinking about other reasons. One of them mentioned the bathroom mirror misting when they were too long in a hot shower and they thought it might be something to do with warm moist air meeting a colder surface. They planned further investigations to test out this idea.

Activity 3

Here are some examples of how children explain various phenomena that they observe:

(a) Asked whether a tree is a plant, a 10 year old replied that it isn't now that it is a tree, but it was a plant when it was little (Osborne and Freyberg, 1985, p. 7).

(b) An 8 year old explained the rust appearing on a nail: 'There is a liquid in the nail which leaks out of the nail. This forms big bumps as it leaks out. This liquid only comes out when it is wet. There must be some sort of signal to tell it to leak' (ASE Primary Science, 1998).

(c) A 10 year old drew the picture in Figure 1.4 of what he thought was inside a hen's egg when it was incubating.

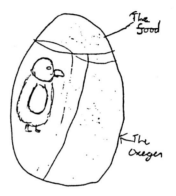

Figure 1.4 Child's idea of incubation

Source: SPACE Research Report (1992, p. 31)

For cross-reference with Study Book see Figure 1.3

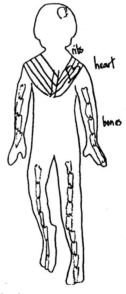

Figure 1.5 Child's idea of the human body

Source: SPACE Research Report (1992, p. 33)

For cross-reference with Study Book see Figure 1.4

Activity 3 *continued*

(d)   An 8 year old drew the picture in Figure 1.5 of what is inside her body.
(e)   When asked about why we can't see in the dark, a 9 year old explained: 'With no light your eyes cannot see anything. As soon as you turn the light on your eyes can see again. Your eyes sort of work like a light, when there's not light you can't see but when there is light you can see again' (quoted in Harlen, 2000, p. 51).

For each one discuss how the children might have arrived at these ideas as a result of early experiences, or applying ideas from other sources.
   What are the implications for helping children to change their ideas to the more scientific view? Fill in the grid in Figure 1.6.

	How the ideas might have been formed	Implications for developing scientific understanding
(a)		
(b)		
(c)		
(d)		
(e)		

Figure 1.6 Pro-forma: implications for developing scientific understanding

For cross-reference with Study Book see Figure 1.5

Activity 4

How can a teacher find out the ideas that children have already formed so that they can be taken into account in science activities? List as many different ways as possible and give your views on the age group for which each one is suitable.

REFERENCES

ASE Primary Science (1998) *Primary Science No. 56*, Hatfield: Association for Science Education.

Harlen, W. (2000) *Teaching, Learning and Assessing Science 5–12*, London: Paul Chapman Publishing.

Osborne, R.J. and Freyberg, P. (1985) *Learning in Science: The Implications of Children's Science*, London: Heinemann.

SPACE Project Research Report (1990) *Light*, Liverpool: Liverpool University Press.

SPACE Project Research Report (1992) *Processes of Life*, Liverpool: Liverpool University Press.

FURTHER READING

Harlen, W. (2001) *Primary Science: Taking the Plunge*, 2nd edn, Portsmouth, NH: Heinemann.

Harlen, W. and Jelly, S. (1997) 'Why this way of working?', *Developing Science in the Primary Classroom*, Chapter 4, Harlow: Longman.

Module 2 The teacher's role in promoting progress

MODULE GOALS

- For teachers to define enquiry skills and recognise them in practice.
- For teachers to recognise that development in understanding involves development both of skills and of ideas and concepts.
- To identify approaches to developing enquiry skills.
- To identify approaches to developing ideas.

MODULE OVERVIEW

This module provides practical activities and opportunities for planning teaching strategies. These are designed first of all to clarify understanding of the science process skills in action, as introduced in the enquiry framework in Module 1. Second, having recognised the importance of children's own ideas and considered ways of accessing them (Module 1), teachers reflect on their own practice and describe strategies for moving children's ideas forward.

There are four group activities:

- Activity 1 considers enquiry skills in practice.
- Activity 2 identifies strategies for developing skills.
- Activity 3 considers examples of children's ideas and how to deal with them.
- Activity 4 involves brainstorming to identify teaching strategies relating to the characteristics of children's ideas.

Timing

Total time approximately: 2 hours 45 minutes

Introduction		10 mins
Activity 1	Series of tasks (in pairs)	15 mins
	Group work	15 mins
	Feedback and discussion	15 mins
Activity 2	Group work	20 mins
	Feedback and discussion	20 mins
Activity 3	Group work	20 mins
	Feedback and discussion	20 mins
Activity 4	Group work	15 mins
	Feedback and discussion	15 mins

Materials required

- flip chart and pens;
- overhead projector.

For Activity 1

- two transparent containers, each containing a different minibeast;
- plastic bottles and dried peas;
- beaker with sea water;
- beaker with tap water;
- pendulum;
- copy of Activity 1 for those who do not have the Study Book;
- copy of Figure 2.4 and Figure 2.5 for each pair;
- OHT of Figure 2.1 and Figure 2.5.

For Activity 2

- copy of Activity 2 and Figure 2.6 for those who do not have the Study Book.

For Activity 3

- copy of Activity 3 for those who do not have the Study Book.

For Activity 4

- copy of Activity 4 and Figure 2.8 for those who do not have the Study Book.

INTRODUCTION

Points to make:

- A set of skills can be identified that is appropriate and useful for scientific investigation.

- Teaching strategies are important, both for encouraging the use of and for assessing competence in these skills.
- Children's ideas can be explored and developed, by the use of specific teaching strategies and interventions.

ACTIVITY 1

Enquiry skills in action. A series of tasks is offered; each task predominantly exemplifies one skill. Teachers, working in pairs, consider each of the five tasks and, using the grid (Figure 2.4) record which skill, in their view, is required. After 15 minutes, stop the pairs working on the tasks; ask pairs to join together and, in groups of four, to spend 15 minutes completing Figure 2.5.

Feedback and discussion

It is important to make the point that, although such tasks, individually, could be encountered or undertaken by primary children, it is not the intention here to suggest that such a series of tasks should be offered in the classroom. Rather, it is offered as a vehicle to focus on defining the characteristics of an appropriate set of enquiry skills.

Task 1 involves observing; task 2 focuses on predicting and some participants might attempt interpreting; task 3 begins with raising questions; task 4 requires a high order of planning skills and task 5 is about interpreting data that are presented as a graph (Figure 2.3). Some groups will have identified several skills in a task. For example, during task 3, it would be natural to move from raising questions to planning and to identify opportunities for measuring.

Some people might want to use different, or additional, words for the skills that they used. At this stage, accept contributions that use 'explaining', 'describing', 'predicting' or 'listening', for example. Gather the words used for each one and work towards an agreement as summarised in your version of Figure 2.1 (OHT).

None of the tasks explicitly requires the use of communicating or reflecting. An additional task could be included, to do this, depending on numbers and on time. However, a brief discussion about appropriate methods and media, for recording, would be useful. These will depend on the context and on the children's abilities. Paper and pencil methods might involve

---

Raising questions: Being inquisitive; asking questions that can be investigated; recognising questions that cannot; turning a question into an investigation; looking for answers

Predicting: Applying knowledge and experience to attempt a prediction; justifying or explaining a prediction; using hypotheses to make predictions, rather than just guessing

Planning: Making a plan that identifies variables; defining controls; deciding what to change, in an investigation; what to record; what to measure; selecting resources and equipment

Observing/Measuring: Using the senses; describing; noting similarities; noting differences; comparing; sequencing; sorting

Interpreting: Making conclusions from results; seeing patterns in data; using keys; generalising; inferring; using data; accepting alternative explanations

Communicating/Reflecting: following instructions; describing; reporting; using tables, graphs and charts; listening

---

Figure 2.1 Enquiry skills characteristics

For cross-reference with Study Book see Figure 2.7

pictures, a diary, notes, a table or a chart. For some investigations, an oral report, followed by a discussion can be useful particularly if several groups have done a similar investigation and their outcomes are to be compared.

ACTIVITY 2

Developing enquiry skills. Teachers, working in groups of three or four, produce plans for activities that will enhance children's skills and they identify strategies that they can deploy, to encourage the use of these skills. It might be useful for each group to select an age-group for which to plan.

Feedback and discussion

Investigations will derive from children's questions about growing conditions (temperature, water, light, soil type). Rate of successful germination of seeds from different sources can be compared and the experience of some children will lead to early predictions of outcome.

The teacher's role is first of all to encourage the children's questions and ideas for investigations to become practicable enquiries. The 'starting points' can all result in an investigation covering every step in the enquiry framework. It is, however, important to stress, as the teachers develop each 'starting point' that the focus, here, is the teaching strategies to employ rather than the content of the investigations.

Some investigations will require more input from the teacher than others and a balance between that input and opportunities for groups of children to share their own planning is desirable, in order that children retain some interest in and 'ownership' of their work.

There might be some concern expressed that it is in the nature of practical work involving growing plants, that there will be periods of apparent inactivity. Related activities, such as recording weather patterns or 'consumer' testing (on gardening gloves, for example) can be useful for these periods.

Examples of strategies that teachers have identified as useful include:

- *Raising questions*: if a topic is introduced with a 'brainstorm' or a mind-mapping exercise, try to harness the children's thinking by asking them what they would like to find out. Develop some of the ideas into investigable questions, such as: 'What happens if . . . ?', 'I wonder whether . . . ?', 'How can we . . . ?'
- *Predicting*: show interest in a child's ideas; give time for them to be expressed and invite others to endorse or contest an idea. This can help to foster an environment in which 'forming' an idea is accepted. Ask: 'What do you think might happen . . . ?', 'Why do you think . . . ?'
- *Planning*: if a fair conclusion is to be drawn from an investigation, encourage the children to ask: 'What shall I keep the same?', 'What do we need to change?', 'What should we record?', 'Which changes shall I measure (and when and how)?', as they develop their plans.
- *Observing/Measuring*: when they are making comparisons and looking for similarities and differences, ask the children: 'What else did you notice?' Encourage the (safe) use of more than one skill: 'What did you smell?', 'How did it feel?'
- *Interpreting*: encourage displays of the results of children's investigations, so that data (a table, chart or graph, for example) can form the basis of questions such as: 'What happened when . . . ?' or 'What would happen if . . . ?'
- *Communicating/Reflecting*: arrange for children to report the outcomes of their investigations to different audiences; encourage the use of a variety of media for recording; require children to listen to the reports of others.

ACTIVITY 3

Respecting children's ideas. Teachers work in groups of three or four, for 20 minutes, to decide on tactics or strategies, rather than on outcomes in terms of what children 'should know'. After 15 minutes, invite the groups to think about how such ideas might arise.

Feedback and discussion

Invite responses to each example from each group in turn.

Evaporation

Sometimes evidence for children's ideas is written. This gives the opportunity to talk to the individual or for a group or class discussion, about the ideas. An individual child might attempt to explain whether clouds are involved in the evaporation of water from a saucer in the classroom. A discussion of the phenomenon of evaporation with a group might elicit different ideas: 'The water just soaks in. It doesn't go up, it goes down.'

Growing

In an atmosphere of mutual respect, where ideas can be openly shared, the opportunity can arise to turn ideas into investigable questions. If the growing medium is 'consumed' by the plant, presumably there is a measurable change and children could devise an appropriate investigation. As before, trying to apply the idea to a different context would lead to a discussion about whether soil in the garden is being used up – and replaced?

Light

Ideas based on intuition could be challenged by an alternative suggestion: 'Do you think the light could be coming from the candle?' However, discussion of alternative ideas will not change a child's understanding if there is no apparent (to the child) reason to do so. After all, if a child is frequently told to 'look closely' in order to 'see everything', the words convey a suggestion that seeing is 'active' and that the means to see (light) must come from us.

Forces

Encouraging consistent use of language (even if it is not, at first, the usual scientific termi-nology) can help in interpreting different phenomena. A lot of experience with 'pushing' and 'pulling' and how things move will help to explain some aspects of forces and movement. However, in this example, the intuitive interpretation of the rolling ball is that there must be something (the 'force pushing' . . .) to keep it moving. In fact the child has identified momentum – but is unlikely to be helped by being told that!

The four examples were elicited from children talking, writing and drawing. After considering the responses to each of the ideas turn the focus towards possible reasons for or origins of such ideas. For example:

- with only *limited experience*, a child who thinks that 'light things always float' can be encouraged to explore floating and sinking further;
- a *perception* that there is less water than there was ice or snow, before melting, is based only on looking;
- with a *restricted focus* on possible variables, during an investigation, a child might conclude that 'the smallest ball bounces best';
- a lack of rigour can result in an idea based on *faulty reasoning*: water might pass through soil in less time than it takes to pass through stones, in a funnel, but the effect of clay binding the stones might have been overlooked;

- the influence of *context* – for example, indoors/outdoors – can affect the nature of an idea;
- the *common use of words* can cause ideas to be expressed in misleading ways: 'No animals allowed . . .' or 'The clouds will melt away . . .'.

The next activity considers appropriate strategies for dealing with ideas that apparently have different bases.

ACTIVITY 4

General strategies for developing children's ideas. Responses to specific ideas were considered in Activity 3 and the possible bases for them have been identified. In this activity, teachers work in groups of three or four to describe general strategies to use, to help to develop children's ideas, according to the likely bases of those ideas. Give each group a copy of Figure 2.2 and allow 15 minutes before drawing the suggestions together.

Basis of children's ideas	Response
Derived from limited experience	Provide wider experience to challenge ideas: plants growing without soil; wood that doesn't float; hearing sound through water and solid material; light and heavy items falling through air at the same rate
Based on limited perceptions	Review the investigation; focus on the process of change, not just on the starting and ending conditions, leading to a different interpretation of the perception
Focused on one feature, ignoring others	Ask them to go on thinking: 'Anything else?' 'Would it be enough just to give the plant water?'
A consequence of faulty reasoning	Help children to test their ideas more rigorously (fairly) and to use all the evidence in drawing a conclusion: 'Was each one measured for the same length of time, with the same amount of water?'
Tied to a particular context	Encourage them to apply the idea in a different but related context to see if it still 'works': 'Can the idea that water condenses from the air explain the moisture on cold cans taken out of the fridge?'
Based on misunderstandings and everyday use of words	Ask them for examples of what they mean and introduce scientific terms alongside the ones children use, for example 'see-through' or 'transparent'; 'melting' or 'dissolving'

Figure 2.2 Summary of appropriate outcomes

Source: Based on Harlen (2001, p. 61)

For cross-reference with Study Book see Figure 2.8

Feedback and discussion

Where there are examples specific to the conceptual basis of an idea, try to tease out both the possible origin of the idea and the nature of, or reason for, the teaching strategy/intervention suggested.

Activity 1

Task 1 Minibeasts

In each container there is a different animal. Note two similarities and two differences between them.

Task 2 Pea in a bottle

Hold a plastic bottle horizontally and put a pea inside the neck of the bottle. Hold the bottle level with your mouth and blow a short, sharp breath into the bottle. The result might surprise you, so repeat this experiment several times to be sure about what happens. Try to describe a reason that explains what you have seen happening. Devise tests for your explanation.

Task 3 Water

One beaker contains sea water; the other tap water. What are the differences between them? Make a list of questions you might investigate.

Task 4 Pendulum

Plan an investigation to find out what affects the time taken for one swing of the pendulum.

Task 5 Pulse rate

Figure 2.3 shows a child's pulse rate during three different activities. The activities were writing, walking and skipping. Explain the shape of each line on the graph and decide which line represents which activity.

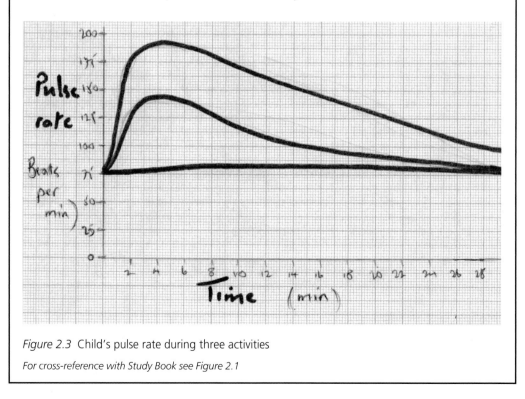

Figure 2.3 Child's pulse rate during three activities

For cross-reference with Study Book see Figure 2.1

Activity 1 *continued*

Use the grid in Figure 2.4 to record the main skill required, for each task. Then look at Figure 2.5 to identify the main characteristics of each of these skills. One example is given for each skill.

	Raising questions	Predicting	Planning	Observing/ Measuring	Interpreting	Communicating/ Reflecting
Task 1						
Task 2						
Task 3						
Task 4						
Task 5						

Figure 2.4 Skills required in the five tasks

For cross-reference with Study Book see Figure 2.2

Raising questions: Asking a question that can be investigated

Predicting: Using knowledge rather than guessing

Planning: Identifying variables

Observing/Measuring: Noting similarities

Interpreting: Using data

Communicating/Reflecting: Using graphs

Figure 2.5 Enquiry skills characteristics

For cross-reference with Study Book see Figure 2.3

Activity 2

Children were working on a 'Gardening' topic. In a discussion at the start of their work, children described their gardening experiences. Several reported success with projects growing flowers or vegetables. A few thought that 'gardening' was always about weeding. Some said that it is always too wet or windy to do much in the garden and most agreed that when the weather is sunny, it's usually too hot to bother gardening.

The class visited a market garden and another day they spent some time in a local park, studying trees. The idea of growing their own plants began to appeal to them and an area of the school grounds was designated as theirs, to cultivate.

Some of the children who had gardened before volunteered to be an 'Expert Gardener' panel. The rest of the class asked the panel questions and shared ideas about gardening and growing things. The teacher took notes. Ideas were shared, views were expressed, questions were raised and activities were suggested. The teacher summarised these as 'starting points' for their topic work:

- Buy some flower seeds to germinate.
- Buy some vegetable seeds to germinate.
- Collect some fruit and/or vegetable seeds (tomato, cucumber, lemon, avocado) to germinate.
- Experiment with a 'cloche' (old lemonade bottle).
- Collect and compare leaves from trees.
- Identify trees.
- Test different gardening gloves.
- Record weather conditions.
- Grow the tallest sunflower.
- Compare commercial composts.

For each starting point:

- Outline a possible investigation.
- Identify the enquiry skill(s) being used.
- Describe what the children could actually do and how your intervention or encouragement would help to develop the skill(s).

Use Figure 2.6 to collate examples of teaching strategies that are useful for developing each skill.

Activity 2 *continued*

SKILL	STRATEGY
Raising questions	
Predicting	
Planning	
Observing/Measuring	
Interpreting	
Communicating/Reflecting	

Figure 2.6 Examples of teaching strategies

For cross-reference with Study Book see Figure 2.4

Activity 3

Read these examples of children's ideas. Describe how you would respond to each idea and why. When you have considered each idea, compile a list of possible reasons for or origins of children's ideas.

Evaporation

One child considered that clouds have an 'active' role in the process of evaporation:

> When the water evaporates, it goes on a cloud and then the cloud goes in any place and later it will go out as rain. It will keep going until it is all gone and then it will go to another place with water and do the same. The cloud is like a magnet so the water goes through the cracks and goes up, that is what I think.
>
> (SPACE Research Report, 1990a, p. 30)

Growing

Children collected some seeds to germinate. They put them in pots. The teacher asked the children what the seeds would need, to grow well. Warmth, light and food were suggested. One child recorded: 'The seed will grow in the pot. The mud in the pot will get used up because that's where the food for the seed comes from. When it gets bigger we'll give it some plant food.'

Light

A 10 year old drew a picture to show how she sees the light from a candle.

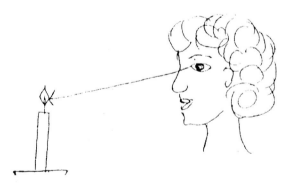

Figure 2.7 Child's idea of seeing light from a candle

Source: SPACE Research Report (1990b, p. 24)

For cross-reference with Study Book see Figure 2.5

Forces

Some children, learning about forces and their effects, concluded that: 'The ball keeps rolling because there is a force pushing it. When it stops rolling there is no force on the ball' (adapted from Gunstone and Watts, 1985).

Activity 4

Figure 2.8 summarises the possible bases for the origin of children's ideas. For each one, define or exemplify teaching strategies to use, in response to children's ideas.

Basis of children's ideas	Response
Derived from limited experience	
Based on limited perceptions	
Focused on one feature, ignoring others	
A consequence of faulty reasoning	
Tied to a particular context	
Based on misunderstandings and everyday use of words	

Figure 2.8 Basis of children's ideas

Source: Harlen (2001, p. 61)

For cross-reference with Study Book see Figure 2.6

REFERENCES

Driver, R., Guesne, E. and Tiberghien, A. (eds) *Children's Ideas in Science*, Milton Keynes: Open University Press.

Gunstone, R. and Watts, M. (1985) 'Force and motion', in R. Driver, E. Guesne and A. Tiberghien (eds) *Children's Ideas in Science*, Milton Keynes: Open University Press.

Harlen, W. (2001) *Primary Science: Taking the Plunge*, Portsmouth, NH: Heinemann.

SPACE Research Report (1990a) *Evaporation and Condensation*, Liverpool: Liverpool University Press.

SPACE Research Report (1990b) *Light*, Liverpool: Liverpool University Press.

Module 3   Teachers' questions and responses to children's questions

MODULE GOALS

- For participants to identify the type and wording of questions that invite children to express their ideas.
- For participants to identify the questions that encourage children to use and develop enquiry skills.
- To consider the importance of responding to children's questions of all kinds and how categorising their questions can help.
- To identify approaches for handling children's questions, particularly the ones requiring complex answers.

MODULE OVERVIEW

Questions occupy a large part of teachers' verbal interaction with children. In this module we look first at teachers' questions that have a role in learning through enquiry. These are questions that elicit children's ideas and those that encourage children to engage in enquiry, using and developing the mental skills that are needed. Such questions include ones that encourage children to ask questions. Questions are important in maintaining the curiosity that motivates learning and also because their questions indicate to teachers where children can and cannot make sense of something. But primary teachers are often concerned about their own capacity to deal with children's questions in science, so the module also considers how teachers can 'handle' rather than necessarily 'answer' the different kinds of questions that children ask.

There are four group activities:

- In Activity 1 participants are asked to observe a particular event that is demonstrated and then to consider what questions they would ask of children to find out the ideas they have about what is happening and why. These questions are written down by participants and analysed by the facilitator during the second activity. So feedback on Activity 1 comes after the second activity.
- Activity 2 concerns questions for encouraging the use and development of enquiry skills. With a particular investigation in mind, participants work out questions such that children have to use enquiry skills to answer them.
- In Activity 3 the focus turns to the questions that children ask. A categorisation of children's questions is offered and applied to some questions that were asked by children who were looking at some tadpoles in a classroom aquarium. As well as categorising, participants begin to think about how to handle the questions.

- Activity 4 looks at the type of the question that teachers often find most difficult to handle – ones that require a complex scientific answer that the teacher may not know and that the children would, in any case, be unlikely to understand. An approach is offered that enables the children to investigate aspects of the question and, while not giving a full answer, responds to the child's interest and sustains curiosity.

Timing

Total time: 2 hours 20 minutes

Introduction		10 mins
Activity 1	Group work	5 mins
	Feedback and discussion	
	(after Activity 2)	15 mins
Activity 2	Group work	30 mins
	Feedback and discussion	15 mins
Activity 3	Group work	15 mins
	Feedback and discussion	15 mins
Activity 4	Group work	25 mins
	Feedback and discussion	10 mins

Materials required

For Activity 1

- copies of Activity 1 for those not having the Study Book;
- small slips of paper (e.g. 5 × 10 cm): two for each participant;
- equipment for a demonstration of an intriguing phenomenon. The exact nature is not critical, but it should be quick to carry out. Examples:

  - a Newton's cradle (six large metal balls suspended by two strings from a bar). Pull one ball aside and let it fall back onto the others. Then pull two balls aside and repeat.
  - a Cartesian diver (a 2-litre plastic drinks bottle almost filled with water, with a dropper floating in the water. Weight the dropper with plasticine so that it floats upright. Adjust the amount of plasticine and of water in the glass part of the dropper so that it sinks when the sides of the bottle are squeezed with the cap screwed firmly on.). Squeeze the bottle so that the diver sinks; when the sides are released it rises again.

For Activity 2

- copies of Activity 2, including the scenario, for participants not having the Study Book.

For Activity 3

- copies of the 'categories of children's questions' in Figure 3.1 and of Activity 3 for participants who do not have the Study Book.
- an OHP transparency of the questions (Figure 3.2) would be useful for capturing answers during feedback.

For Activity 4

- copies of the extract from Jelly (2001) and of Activity 4 for those not having the Study Book.

INTRODUCTION

Points to make in introducing the module:

- Questions make up a large part of the teacher's verbal interaction with children. Therefore they are an important aspect of the teacher's role.
- There are many different kinds of questions and they serve a variety of purposes, e.g. to gain children's attention, to monitor, to control, to check on understanding of instructions, to probe conceptual understanding, to develop children's thinking.
- Here we are concerned with questions that help understanding in science but there are still many different kinds. Various ways of categorising questions for helping science have been proposed. For example, Sheila Jelly (in *Primary Science: Taking the Plunge*, 2001) divided teachers' questions into 'productive' and 'unproductive' (of scientific activity), while Jos Elstgeest in the same book distinguished between different kinds of 'productive' questions. He identified 'attention-focusing questions', 'measuring and counting questions', 'comparison questions', 'action questions' and 'problem-posing questions'. He pointed out that teachers not only need to know the difference between these but also when particular kinds of questions are appropriate.
- Therefore it is important to think about the purpose of a question and to ensure that the words used enable it to serve that purpose.
- In this module we are considering just two main purposes: questions to elicit children's ideas and questions to encourage the use of enquiry skills.
- After that we turn to the teacher's role in answering questions that children pose. Just as with teachers' questions, children ask questions of different kinds and for different reasons.
- It is important to be able to deal with children's questions, for if their questions are ignored or they receive unsatisfying answers, there is a danger of questioning being discouraged and a crucial motivation for learning stifled.

ACTIVITY 1

Put the demonstration (e.g. Newton's cradle or Cartesian diver, or similar) where it can be seen by everyone. It is a short event and so participants can group round if necessary. Ask them to imagine that they are showing this to children and to think about questions they would ask the children to find out what ideas the children are using to explain what happens. Give each participant two slips of paper to write down their individual questions, one on each slip. Allow 5 minutes and then collect the slips in a box. Mix them up so that you will not be able to tell who wrote each one.

Proceed to Activity 2. Use the time during group work on Activity 2 to look at the questions and put them into groups. If possible, pin them onto a board in groups. If not, just lay them out on a table. Make the groups as far as possible like these:

- questions which are person-centred (i.e. they ask 'What do you think . . . ?');
- questions which are subject-centred (i.e. ask 'What is happening?', 'Why does the diver go down?');
- questions which are asking for processes not explanations ('What did you notice?', 'What do you think will happen if . . . ?');
- questions which are closed, requiring perhaps single word answers ('Will the diver go down more quickly or more slowly if you press harder?', 'Did you expect that to happen?').

Feedback and discussion

In the feedback on Activity 1 (which will come after the feedback on Activity 2), don't describe your groups, but read out a few questions from each. Ask participants to identify what is similar about the questions in each group. Then add labels to the groups: 'person-centred', 'subject-centred', 'process-linked' and 'closed' if you have all of these. It may be necessary to create another group or a 'miscellaneous' group.

Then take the 'person-centred' group and read out some more so that participants can identify the characteristics of the questions:

- they demonstrate interest in the children's ideas (the important emphasis on 'what *you* think');
- they don't ask for a 'right' answer;
- they can be answered by all children even if they realise they don't know the reason, but they have their own ideas.

By contrast, the subject-centred ones indicate that there is a 'right' answer and children who do not know it will not be able to provide an answer to the question (and the teacher loses the opportunity to know what the children are thinking).

The 'process' questions will not need to be discussed further, since they will have been dealt with in Activity 2.

Then consider all the questions in terms of whether they are 'open' or 'closed'. It is probably the case that most of the person-centred questions are open and more of the subject-centred ones are closed. Discuss the reasons for preferring 'open' questions.

Finally, in the discussion of Activity 1, make the point that it is the open, person-centred questions that invite children to give their ideas. Thus these are very important for 'starting from children's ideas'. Participants may like to spend a minute or two rephrasing their own questions (they will remember what they wrote).

ACTIVITY 2

To develop understanding in science, children need to use and develop both their ideas and their enquiry skills (see Module 1). This activity concerns teachers' questions designed to require children to use enquiry skills. Questions have to be matched to the skills that are appropriate at a particular time.

Before the group work begins, it may be helpful to 'model' the approach in terms of a different scenario. Describe an activity where children are exploring a collection of dry seeds before planting them. The children then plant them in various conditions, which the teacher wants them to decide for themselves. They predict what will happen in different situations. As the seeds germinate and the plants grow, the children observe, measure and discuss the growth. They look at the results and see whether these are what they expected.

What questions might the teacher ask

- To encourage children to raise questions?
- *What would you like to know about these seeds?*
- To encourage them to make predictions?
  What do you think will happen to these seeds if you give them more water than those?
- To encourage planning?
  What will you need to do to see if your idea about the temperature making the seeds grow more quickly is right?
- To encourage data collection when the plants have grown?
  How many of the seeds of each kind are growing?
  How much do they grow in a week?
- To encourage interpretation?

Was there any connection between the size of the seed and how big the plant is?
How does this compare with what you thought would happen?
- To encourage communication and reflection?
What is the best way to show the others what you found?
How could you improve your investigation to be more sure of the result?

Then ask the participants to work in groups of three to think up two or three questions for each enquiry skill relevant to the given scenario.

Feedback and discussion

Briefly ask for one example of 'raising questions' from each group and check that these do invite children's questions. If there is a question that relates to another enquiry skill, ask the group to say what kind of response they would expect from the child. This should reveal that a different skill is required. Continue for each enquiry skill.

(This will then be followed by the feedback on Activity 1.)

Draw these activities together by making these points:

- Teachers' questions can be used to advance children's thinking.
- Changing the wording of a question is a simple (but not always easy) way of encouraging learning through enquiry.
- Patterns of questioning are difficult to change and this requires practice.
- Plan questions carefully as part of lesson preparation.
- Note also that it is not just the framing of the question that is important, but the teacher's reaction to the children's answer. They must not be made to feel that their answers are 'silly' or not valued – or they will cease to respond, or will conceal their true thinking.
- The responses of all children are equally relevant, so the teacher has to create a classroom ethos in which all ideas are respected and can be challenged without children feeling discouraged.

ACTIVITY 3

One of the consequences of encouraging children to ask questions and creating an atmosphere in which they feel free to do so is that the teacher has to be able to deal with the questions that are asked. Many primary teachers feel that their own knowledge of science means that they cannot answer children's questions and so, consciously or unconsciously, work in a way that discourages children from questioning. There are two points that should counter these concerns:

1 It is often not the best thing to attempt a straightforward answer to a child's question. This is because if they don't understand the answers they may be put off from asking questions. Also, to give answers to questions when children could find the answers for themselves prevents them from 'learning how to learn'.
2 By studying children's questions and finding how to handle different types of question, we can make the best use of their questions to help their learning.

This activity suggests a categorisation of children's questions for trial and discussion. Go through the categories (a) to (e) and the examples given. Take time to discuss them and invite participants to suggest others that may not be included. There may not be suggestions at this point, as participants will need time to think through the kinds of questions that have baffled them in the past.

Participants then work in groups of three on the activity of categorising the ten given questions. Suggest they finish categorising before starting on suggesting how to handle the questions.

Question	Category	How to handle
Why are they called tadpoles?		
Are they fish?		
What do they eat?		
Can they see me?		
Will they turn into frogs?		
What do they feel like?		
Why does the surface of the water look shiny when you look from underneath?		
How old are they?		
Why are they so wriggly?		
Why do some creatures turn into something else, like caterpillars turn into butterflies?	.	

Figure 3.1 Pro-forma: questions on tadpoles

Prepare an OHP transparency or a chart of this kind for collecting responses, as shown in Figure 3.1.

Feedback and discussion

Ask one group to give their categories and write them into Figure 3.1. Ask others for differences in categories and resolve these by asking the participants for their reasoning and their interpretation of the question. Some questions may well seem to fall into more than one category, for example, question 5 could be (b) or (d). In practice, this could be clarified in discussion with the child. Children don't always choose their wording precisely and it is helpful to try to find out what kind of answer they are looking for.

Then gather ideas for how to handle the questions. Note these briefly in terms of the main intention (e.g. 'refer child to information source' or 'ask child how they could find out' or 'plan investigation'). (See the Study Book for some examples.) There may be some patterns emerging linking the type of question to the type of response; this is a matter taken further in Activity 4.

Ask if participants want to modify the categories or add others. (But beware of adding more than one, since too many categories are not useful – it is better, in fact, to collapse rather than add categories.) Then move on to Activity 4.

ACTIVITY 4

Some of the questions that children ask can be immediately investigated by the children. These are the questions to be encouraged because they enable children to experience learning through their own activity. But many questions require some discussion before they become investigable by the children. Some of the important questions for the children's learning, and the most difficult to handle for the teacher, are the questions that ask for scientific explanations. Often, but not always, these are 'why' questions. They are the focus of this activity.

We start by considering an idea from Sheila Jelly (2001) for turning these 'difficult' but important questions into ones that children can investigate for themselves. This approach takes a 'big' question and turns it into some smaller ones that children can investigate for themselves. Often this changes a 'why' question into a series of 'what will happen if . . . ?' questions.

Ask participants to read the extract from the chapter by Sheila Jelly in the Study Book, then work in pairs or groups of three on Activity 4.

Feedback and discussion

It is possible that participants feel that the approach short-changes the children, since it does not answer the initial question. However, it does take the child's question seriously and leads to some worthwhile investigation. Indeed, some of these difficult questions are very close to the 'comments expressed as questions category'. A young child who asks question 7, for instance, might easily have meant 'look at how shiny the surface looks from underneath!' However, if the child persists in asking 'Why does it look shiny?' then a 'Yes, that's inter-esting' reply will not be sufficient. The phenomenon could then be investigated, through looking at the surface from various angles. They could hold an object above the water and see whether they can see it from underneath when it is moved to various places. The investigation could be extended to a thick block or sheet of glass, when surfaces can look like mirrors from some angles. (The phenomenon is the result of the bending of light at the surface between water (or glass) and air. Light coming from an object close to the surface inside the water or glass cannot escape and is reflected. An eye placed below the surface but close to it will see this reflected light, not light coming through the surface. If participants find this difficult, then this is the reason for not attempting to explain it directly to children!)

Finally, turn to the second part of the activity and review the approaches to different kinds of questions in the light of this way of handling type (c). The points to bring together are:

- Identifying the type of question is a quick way of recognising how to deal with it.
- Questions that are comments ('Why are they so wriggly?' could be in this category) can be handled by sharing the observation 'Yes, they seem always to be moving don't they?'
- Questions that require factual answers only ('How old are they?') can be answered directly if the teacher knows the answer, or if not children can be directed to a source of information. For example, 'I don't know how old these particular ones are, but you can find out how old tadpoles of different sizes are from a book (or the Internet)'.
- Questions requiring complex answers can be handled by 'turning'.

- Questions that lead to enquiry ('What do they eat?') can be answered by the children's own actions (they can plan an investigation of giving them different kinds of food in a controlled way – and without polluting their water).
- Philosophical questions (quite rare) have to be answered by saying that no-one knows the answer; people have different ideas. (For older children you can add that we cannot answer it by scientific investigation in the same way that we can find out what happens when we do something.)

Activity 1

Watch the demonstration. Suppose you are showing this to children and want to find out the children's ideas on how it works. What questions would you ask the children?

Write down two questions on separate slips of paper (don't put your name on them). Work out and put down the exact words that you would use, not just indications of the questions.

Activity 2

Consider this scenario:

> During a period of cold weather with snow and ice on the roads, children ask about why there is salt on the road. So at a convenient time the teacher provides the equipment for them to investigate the melting of ice in fresh water and in salt water. The teacher wants them to make predictions, then test these with fair tests, make relevant measurements, interpret what they find and then see if this affects their ideas about the difference the salt makes.

During the various stages of the investigation, what questions would the teacher ask in order to encourage children to use and develop their enquiry skills? Working in pairs, write down some questions for each of the skills, using the wording you think is most effective. Complete Figure 3.2.

Enquiry skill	Teacher's questions
Raising questions	
Predicting	
Planning an investigation	
Gathering evidence by observing and measuring	
Interpreting evidence	
Communicating and reflecting	

Figure 3.2 Pro-forma: developing enquiry skills

For cross-reference with Study Book see Figure 3.1

Categorisation of children's questions

Types of question (illustrated by questions asked when a bird's nest was brought into a classroom)

(a) Questions that are really comments expressed as questions ('Why are birds so clever that they can weave nests with their beaks?').
(b) Questions requiring simple factual answers ('Where was the bird's nest found?').
(c) Questions requiring more complex answers ('Why do some birds nest in trees and some on the ground?').
(d) Questions that lead to enquiry by the child ('What is the nest made of?').
(e) Philosophical questions ('Why are birds made so that they can fly and not other animals?').

Activity 3

Here are some questions asked by children during observation of tadpoles in an aquarium:

1 Why are they called tadpoles?
2 Are they fish?
3 What do they eat?
4 Can they see me?
5 Will they turn into frogs?
6 What do they feel like?
7 Why does the surface of the water look shiny when you look from underneath?
8 How old are they?
9 Why are they so wriggly?
10 Why do some things turn into something else, like caterpillars turning into butterflies?

Try to categorise the questions into the categories (a) to (e) or some other category that you suggest (see Figure 3.3). Then consider what you as a teacher would do, to enable the children to have an answer to each question.

Question	Category	How to handle the question
1		
2		
3		
4		
5		
6		
7		
8		
9		
10		

Figure 3.3 Handling questions

For cross-reference with Study Book see Figure 3.2

Resource for Activity 4

'Turning' questions into investigable ones

While encouraging children to ask questions of all kinds is important to children's learning, in science it is particularly valuable to help children to ask questions that they can answer through enquiry. Some questions of this kind (category (d)) are ones that they can straight-away answer for themselves by their own actions. More difficult to handle are the ones that require complex answers.

In a chapter on questioning in *Primary Science: Taking the Plunge* Sheila Jelly (2001) suggests a way of 'turning questions' of a complex kind into ones that are more easily investigated by children:

> Essentially it is a strategy for handling complex questions and in particular those of the 'why' kind that are the most frequent of all spontaneous questions. They are difficult questions because they carry an apparent request for a full explanation which may not be known to the teacher and, in any case, is likely to be conceptually beyond a child's understanding.
>
> The strategy recommended is one that turns the question to practical action with a 'let's see what we can do to understand more' approach. The teaching skill involved is the ability to 'turn' the question. Consider, for example, a situation in which children are exploring the properties of fabrics. They have dropped water on different types and become fascinated by the fact that water stays 'like a little ball' on felt. They tilt the felt, rolling the ball around, and someone asks 'Why is it like a ball?'. How might the question be turned by applying the 'doing more to understand' approach? We need to analyse the situation quickly and use what I call a 'variables scan'. The explanation must relate to something 'going on' between the water and the felt surface so causing the ball. That being so, ideas for children's activities will come if we consider ways in which the situation could be varied to better understand the making of the ball. We could explore surfaces keeping the drop the same, and explore drops keeping the surface the same. These thoughts can prompt others that bring ideas nearer to what children might do. For example:

> 1 Focusing on the surface, keeping the drop the same:
> What is special about the felt that helps make the ball? Which fabrics are good 'ball-makers'?
> Which are poor?
> What have the good ball-making fabrics in common? What surfaces are good ball-makers?
> What properties do these share with the good ball-making fabrics?
> Can we turn the felt into a poor ball-maker?

> 2 Focusing on the water drop, keeping the surface the same:
> Are all fluids good ball-makers?
> Can we turn the water into a poor ball-maker?

Notice how the 'variables scan' results in the development of productive questions that can be explored by the children. The original question has been turned to practical activity and children exploring along these lines will certainly enlarge their understanding of what is involved in the phenomenon. They will not arrive at a detailed explanation but may be led towards simple generalization of their experience, such as 'A ball will form when . . .' or 'It will not form when . . .'.

Activity 4

Try the variables scan approach to question 7 in the list considered in Activity 3. Suggest other general approaches to the different kinds of questions that teachers can take to ensure that children find answers to their questions.

REFERENCES

Elstgeest, J. (2001) 'The right question at the right time', in W. Harlen, *Primary Science: Taking the Plunge*, 2nd edn, Portsmouth, NH: Heinemann.

Jelly, S. J. (2001) 'Helping children raise questions – and answering them', in W. Harlen, *Primary Science: Taking the Plunge*, 2nd edn, Portsmouth, NH: Heinemann.

Module 4 Managing practical work in the classroom

MODULE GOALS

- To consider how teachers manage practical work in the classroom in order to provide opportunities for children to investigate and learn science concepts.
- To reflect on how teaching is organised and how adult help is used.
- To consider how to encourage children to identify and collect the equipment which they need for their investigations.

MODULE OVERVIEW

This module provides opportunities for teachers to comment on features of good practice and to discuss alternative methods of organisation. It deals with the following:

- evaluating good management;
- classroom organisation and planning;
- storing and using equipment.

There are four group activities:

- Activity 1 uses video material to evaluate good practice when children are engaged in practical work.
- Activity 2 is focused on the medium-term plans of a teacher and participants are asked to suggest how some of the activities might be organised.
- Activity 3 deals with the organisation of practical work for very young children.
- Activity 4 addresses the storage and accessibility of resources.

Timing

Total time: 2 hours 55 minutes

Introduction		10 mins
Activity 1	Video	20 mins
	Group work	20 mins
	Feedback and discussion	20 mins
Activity 2	Group work	20 mins
	Feedback and discussion	20 mins
Activity 3	Group work	15 mins
	Feedback and discussion	15 mins
Activity 4	Group work	15 mins
	Feedback and discussion	20 mins

Materials required

General

- flip charts and pens;
- copies of the activities for those who do not have the Study Book;
- copies of the observational schedule (Figure 4.4) and the pro-forma (Figure 4.6);
- copies of the medium-term plans (Figure 4.4) and the completed pro-forma (Figure 4.2). If people do not have the Study Book you will also need some copies of the resource list (Figure 4.3).

For Activity 1

A video which shows a teacher managing a practical science session. There are many videos available which would suit your purpose. Many local education authorities produce these and there is one available from the SCIcentre www.le.ac.uk/se/centres/sci/scicentre *Classroom Organisation for Primary Science*. This looks at several classroom situations. Alternatively, you could video a short sequence in a local primary school.

For Activity 4

It would be useful to have a range of catalogues provided by educational suppliers so that participants can be aware of the latest equipment which is available. You may consider that this activity would be more appropriate for science subject leaders.

INTRODUCTION

Points to make in giving an overview when discussing module goals:

- There are many ways of organising practical work in the classroom. What is appropriate for one classroom may not be suitable for another group of children in another classroom.
- Teachers will keep the learning objectives in mind when deciding how to manage a practical teaching session.
- Although the development of independence and the ability to plan for themselves are very important, there may be times when a teacher wants to provide a demonstration

or a set of instructions. In the module there will be opportunities to consider how and why this type of practical science is occasionally used.

- The management of resources, including human resources, has a direct influence on the opportunities for learning.

ACTIVITY 1

Ask participants to study the features of good practice as identified in the observational schedule (Figure 4.4). They may like to add any other aspects of good management which they think might be missing from the list. Ask them to focus specifically on how the various parts of the practical lesson give children the opportunity to develop skills but also to learn scientific ideas. Watch the video and suggest that they write only brief notes about what they see so that they are not distracted from the subject matter. If the video is short (i.e. about 10 minutes) then you might find it useful to watch it twice so that more detailed notes can be made during the second viewing.

Feedback and discussion

- Encourage feedback about the structure of the session.
- Was the introduction lively? Did it enthuse the children?
- Was there sufficient time for the children to express their ideas about the science which they were studying?
- How was the practical work organised?
- If the children were working in their own groups without close adult supervision, then how did the teacher monitor what was going on?

The questions on the observational schedule should enable you to structure the discussion. There may be some participants who question the viability of children planning for themselves and deciding what results they should collect. The sceptics refer to a lack of focus and mention the fact that some children collect measurements or observations which are not relevant to the scientific concepts which are being studied and do not help them to draw conclusions. A good teacher will avoid these pitfalls and help children to make the appropriate decisions. Draw out ideas about how the teacher did this.

Good management includes time for thinking as well as carrying out the practical work and decision-making is an important skill which should be encouraged. This decision-making could be demonstrated in the way in which children choose their own resources; perhaps from a selection provided by the teacher. Consider how the teacher encouraged the thinking and provided the children with the opportunity to evaluate their own learning (see Module 9).

ACTIVITY 2

Discuss the points raised in the section on organising lessons. You will probably want to discuss the different types of practical work; the situations when we want children to investigate for themselves, those situations where a demonstration is relevant and the *illustrative* type of science (NCC, 1993). Consider too that there are times when skill development, such as when the children are learning to use a particular piece of equipment, is the teacher's objective.

Give participants copies of the task and the trainee's medium-term plan. Ask people to work in groups of three or four and to consider at least one if not two of the 'stages'. In some classes one stage may be covered in one lesson of 90 minutes and in other classes the teachers might decide to spread the work over a longer period.

This is not the place to discuss the format of the planning, instead focus attention on the activities which the teacher has planned. Ask that the factors such as how the lesson would

Figure 4.1 Claire is squeezing the flubber and trying to find out how far it will stretch

be introduced, how the teacher collects ideas, how the children might be encouraged to plan for themselves are considered by the groups. The medium-term plans do not suggest a structure for the lessons. You will be asking the participants to do this.

Feedback and discussion

As the groups describe how they would plan and organise the lessons, you will want them to refer to the learning objectives and to justify their organisation with reference to these objectives. For instance, when discussing the work planned for stage 1, some people might suggest that the introduction to the topic of transport is not actually science-based and that this discussion and the sorting activity might take place in a session before the investigation into how the autogyros fall. Perhaps then the focus could be more clearly placed on the skill of observation and the ideas about why the autogyros spin and fall in a different way from flat pieces of paper. On the other hand, perhaps the teacher planned to work with small groups who were investigating autogyros while other children were doing the sorting activity. Discuss group size and the composition of the groups. Harlen (2000, p. 88) suggests that 'research points clearly in the direction of mixed ability groupings'.

There will be a consideration of timings and the importance of finding time for children to listen to the ideas of others. As Harlen (ibid., p. 83) suggests: 'This may mean less time for doing, but increased learning from what is done.' Consider the teacher's role when working with small groups and with the whole class and discuss the way in which the vocabulary is introduced and used.

ACTIVITY 3

When teachers are thinking about how to organise provision for the youngest children aged between 3 and 5 they will concentrate less on providing for whole-class lessons and more on providing materials and situations where children can interact with and explore materials which are provided (see Module 5). There will be times when a focused task is planned for a small group and times when the whole class comes together for short periods. Continuous provision is provided by having role play areas, malleable materials, the water tray and the sand tray available every day. What is changed is the materials which are in these areas. So, for instance, the water tray may have in it objects with holes in such as sieves and colanders for one week and materials which may float or sink available for another week. In some early years classes the materials for exploring in the water tray may be stored on open shelves and be freely available all of the time.

The focused tasks for science-based learning are usually planned each week and children are encouraged to spend time with an adult on one of these tasks. In most schools children choose for themselves whether or not they take part in the focused activity, but in others, the children are all asked to join in at some time during the week.

Give out the copies of the task and the blank pro-forma (Figure 4.6) and ask for it to be completed. It might be useful to have at least one member of each group who is familiar with the organisation and management of early years classes.

Feedback and discussion

It is the discussion about the management which will be most fruitful for this activity. There is no right or wrong way to organise the practical work. It is a matter of having a balance between work with the teacher and play activities which children initiate for themselves. Perhaps the pro-forma will be filled in a similar way to Figure 4.2.

You might want to consider the teacher's role in the organisation of these activities and to think about the learning opportunities. Note how, what has been suggested in the completed pro-forma is that the teacher spends a short time with the whole class so that he or she can introduce the sliding and rolling activity. Children will be introduced to the vocabulary and have the opportunity to suggest ideas about why some objects roll and some slide and later they will have the opportunity to play with the resources on the grassy slope. Perhaps some participants might suggest that this should be a focused activity so that the teacher has the opportunity to talk to children in a non-threatening situation. Some very young children are often reluctant to express their ideas if they are placed in a large group.

Some of the activities use the same materials as those which have been planned by the teacher of the class of 6 year olds (Activity 2). It might be appropriate here to consider that the children referred to in Activity 2 are two years older than those in the early years class. The concepts which they will meet are similar but the organisation of the work will be different. The teacher of the older children approaches the sliding and rolling activity in a

Child-initiated enquiry Continuous provision	Focused task with an adult	Whole-class activity	Advantages and disadvantages of this type of organisation
Flubber- exploring the properties of the material			Advantages: children have the time to explore on their own. Disadvantages: teachers are not always present to guide the enquiry and to develop vocabulary.
Play-dough – exploring, making shapes, cutting and making marks on the dough			As above
	Investigating a range of materials and sorting into those which can be stretched		Advantages: teachers can guide the enquiry, and question children as appropriate. Disadvantages: all children might not have chance to take part.
Water play – having containers with holes available			Advantages: children have the time to explore on their own. Disadvantages: teachers are not always present to guide the enquiry and to develop vocabulary.
		Introduction to the sliding and rolling activity. Teacher and children all together on carpet. Classify those objects which roll and those which slide down a slope. Discuss the terms sliding and rolling. Ask for children's ideas about why some objects slide and some roll. Think about the materials from which the objects are made as well as their shape.	Advantages: teacher has the opportunity to direct specific question at individuals. Teacher can guide the enquiry. Disadvantages: the management might be difficult with so many young children involved.
Follow-up activity to the whole-class exploration of sliding and rolling. Children to have objects available out of doors near to the grassy slope. Also to have a small ramp out of doors near to the			Advantages: children have the time to explore on their own. Disadvantages: teachers are not always present to guide the enquiry and to develop vocabulary.

continued

Child-initiated enquiry Continuous provision	Focused task with an adult	Whole-class activity	Advantages and disadvantages of this type of organisation
objects so that comparisons can be made about the way in which the objects roll and slide down the two different slopes.			
	Ice cubes on a very large tray. Children to observe as the blocks slide across the tray. Draw out observations about the way in which the cubes slide as the tray becomes very wet.		

Figure 4.2 Examples of early years planning

For cross-reference with Study Book see Figure 4.4

way which encourages them to think about planning to find out the answer to questions which they have asked, whereas the focus with the younger children is on learning through play.

ACTIVITY 4

As science is essentially a practical subject, there is a need for resources and a need to consider what resources should be purchased and collected. Schools have also to consider how to store the resources. The larger pieces of equipment such as microscopes and model skeletons will have to be purchased and shared and, on the other hand, the resources such as fabrics, yoghurt pots, pieces of wood and plastic can be collected by the children and teachers.

This activity will enable participants to share their knowledge of a range of resources. Some local education authorities provide lists of equipment which are suitable for the implementation of the primary science curriculum and many of the published schemes provide resource lists. There is also a useful book, published by the Association for Science Education, *The Primary Equipment Handbook* (Feasey, 1999) which considers what schools should purchase and collect.

Give out copies of the task and allocate catalogues and resource lists.

Feedback and discussion

Begin by addressing the idea that children should be independent and choose and collect their own resources. Some might say that this is manageable only if each class has an unlimited supply of equipment but others might argue that if the teacher collected the larger and more expensive pieces of equipment from a central store and showed the children what was available, then there would be some element of choice. Children will realise what is stored in their classroom as these are usually kept in boxes on open shelves. Labels will help the older children to identify the location of resources and younger children can have pictures on their resource boxes. Children in nursery classes are very capable of finding what they want, but unfortunately in some classrooms the older children are discouraged from moving about. There will probably be a discussion about this issue and about the ethos

balances	string	polythene bags
timers	scissors	rubber bands
magnifiers	tape measures	measuring scoops or
funnels	play-dough	spoons
measuring cylinders and	plasticine	water containers
beakers	paper clips	bowls for mixing
yoghurt pots	paper towels	masses
for younger children	bubble blowers	magnifying collecting
balances	candles	boxes or containers
balloons	colour filters	jelly mould
balls	cellophane	cooking equipment
mirrors	fabrics	microscope
musical instruments	cotton reels	mechanical toys
camera	batteries	wires
building blocks	fans	cells
construction kits	plastic pipettes	bulbs
garden tools	feathers	buzzers
plastic tubing	articles for the water tray	motors
straws	including water wheels and	pooters
tuning forks	watering cans	bowls
wind gauge	large paint brushes	sand
woodworking tools	food colouring	rocks
prisms	magnifiers	stethoscope
ramps		shells
wooden articles		sieves
plastic articles		squeezy bottles
aluminium foil		plastic syringes
collection of seeds		

Figure 4.3 Resources often kept in classrooms

For cross-reference with Study Book see Figure 4.5

of the classroom. Those teachers who encourage children to be enthusiastic about their investigations will probably find that children do not take very long in deciding what to use and assembling the resources, as they are so anxious to begin the practical work.

If resources for scientific enquiry are to be used regularly by every class in the school, then it makes sense to have a supply of these in each classroom. Fortunately these are not very expensive and last for many years. Perhaps some of the items in Figure 4.3 might be suggested.

In most schools the classrooms where the very young children are taught have their own supplies of both consumable materials such as paint, paper and cooking ingredients as well as the more durable items as these are needed regularly.

The lists in Figure 4.3 are not exhaustive nor are they meant to be definitive. You will have other suggestions which can be added to the list. The catalogues will describe many items which are useful but not essential and perhaps there will be some sharing of ideas about the effectiveness of these items.

There are many systems for sharing equipment. Some schools have boxes in which they place the materials and equipment needed for each topic but this system has its drawbacks as some expensive items are needed for more than one topic. Many schools have a science store room where equipment is housed on open shelves and is clearly labelled. A loan book is provided and teachers record what they have taken. This system works as long as two classes do not need all the electrical equipment at the same time and if teachers are punctilious about returning equipment when they have used it. You might want to point out that attention needs to be paid to the curriculum planning cycle to make sure that resources can be allocated efficiently.

When considering the items needed for the particular topics you might want to have some copies of schemes of work available, particularly if you are working with trainee teachers. By considering what has to be taught it will be possible to identify the resources which are needed.

MANAGING ACTIVITIES

There is no single way to organise science in the primary classroom. How the teacher manages the activities will depend on:

- the nature of the task and the subject matter which is being studied;
- the resources available;
- the age of the children;
- the ancillary help which is available.

Evaluating classroom management

Although many schools use government or local schemes of work in order to plan their teaching, the way in which the lessons are organised depends on the space available, the learning styles of the children as well as the preferred teaching style of the teacher. What is important is that the children develop the appropriate attitudes to science and that they make progress in their scientific skills and their understanding of concepts. Practical work is enjoyable and children are usually highly motivated when they handle materials and equipment but there is no doubt that it makes many demands on teachers. It is much easier to begin a lesson by giving the children information, to go on to do a demonstration and then to ask the children to write an account of what has been done and what they have learned. Some children might learn by this method but they would not be experiencing scientific enquiry at first hand and understanding what this means.

In order to plan for practical work for a class of thirty children, the teacher has not only to collect equipment and resources together but also has to deal with the excitement which is often generated by practical investigation. However, the effort is worthwhile if children develop a sense of wonder as they begin to learn science ideas and begin to be able to plan investigations for themselves. It is surprising how quickly children begin to be independent and become able to collect and tidy away their own resources.

Activity 1

Consider the features of good practice in primary science teaching which are listed on the observational schedule (Figure 4.4) and then watch a video sequence of a teacher in the classroom. Naturally, what you observe about the teaching strategies will depend on the nature of the lesson which you are watching, but note the evidence that shows how the teacher is developing good practice. The purpose of this activity is not to be judgemental about a particular teacher but to emphasise the positive aspects of good management (see also Module 16).

Features of good teaching	Comments and examples
Were lesson objectives shared?	
How did the teacher introduce the activity? Was there reference to children's earlier work? Is the work related to children's own experiences?	
Were the children engaged in scientific enquiry? Were they raising questions, predicting, planning, gathering evidence by observing and measuring, interpreting evidence and drawing conclusions? Were they communicating and reflecting critically?	
Did you notice how the teacher helped the children in the development of science skills?	
Were there opportunities for children to express their ideas? Were children involved in planning their own investigations?	

Features of good teaching	Comments and examples
Were all resources ready and well prepared? Were the resources suitable for the task?	
Was there any evidence of the teacher handling any misconceptions?	
Did the teacher find time to talk to all the groups? Is this necessary? Were any support staff used? Did they seem to be adequately prepared?	
Did any of the children say or do anything which would help the teacher to assess their understanding?	
Did the children enjoy their lesson? Did the teacher show enthusiasm?	

Figure 4.4 Observational schedule

For cross-reference with Study Book see Figure 4.1

Organising lessons

If we consider that children have their own ideas about science and that we have to build on their ideas when we organise practical work (see Module 1), then we have to consider how to organise the teaching so that there are opportunities for children to express these ideas. We have to be prepared to help them to modify their ideas if there is evidence of misconceptions. We also have to be aware of the fact that, in order to develop the skills of science, then we have to give children practice in planning their own practical investigations based on questions which they have raised. Teachers are clear about the learning outcomes of their lessons and they plan to manage the practical work in a way which best suits their purpose.

Activity 2

Look at the medium-term plan for a class of 6 year olds in Figure 4.5. These were prepared by a trainee teacher. The learning outcomes are identified as are the activities which the teacher wants to carry out. Think about how you would manage the practical work. Select a 'stage' and consider the following questions:

- Would the experiences take place over one or two weeks?
- Would you have all of the children doing the same thing at the same time?
- Would you have some children carrying out an activity while others were engaged on unrelated tasks?
- What would the teacher do? Would he or she be with one group in order to find out their ideas and help them to develop skills or would he or she circulate and talk to as many children as possible? Would there be times when he or she would want to do a demonstration or even have all the children carrying out an investigation which he or she has planned?
- Would the children move around from one activity to another?
- How would you introduce and end the lessons?

Science class 1E 4 lessons 1hr 30 mins each week		
Learning objectives	Learning experiences	Resources and cross-curricular links
Stage 1 • Children will understand the meaning of the word 'transport' • Children understand that there are many forms of transport • Modes of transport can be classified • To observe carefully and to describe what they notice	Introduce topic by asking children: (a) How do they get to school? Is it by bus, car, or do they walk? Do they come in a train, an aeroplane or a boat? (b) When do they go in trains, boats, cars, aeroplanes, etc.? (c) Show pictures of helicopters/gliders/aeroplanes/hot air balloons – do they move through air, sea or along the land? (d) Children to use storyboard to classify pictures of transport (Low Attainers) (e) or sorting circles (Middle Attainers), then draw large pictures or fill in sheet with drawings (Higher Attainers) to show which modes of transport travel through air, sea or land. Make autogyros or parachutes (or perhaps land yachts or boats) and describe how they fall and move.	• Pictures of helicopters, gliders, etc. for sorting on storyboard • Smaller pictures for sorting circles • Frame for children to use for classification • Materials for making autogyros Cross-curricular links English – speaking and listening Mathematics – sorting into sets *Vocabulary* Helicopter, glider, hot air balloon, car, aeroplane, train, tractor, lorry, boat, ship, raft
Stage 2 Children will understand that: • There are many sorts of movement which can be described in many ways • Children will observe and describe different ways of moving	A *Children in circle on carpet* Link to last week's lesson on transport • How does a bus move? – on wheels • How does a car move?– on wheels • How does a train move? – on wheels	• Pendulum to show swinging • Ball • Block and board to show sliding • Empty Coke bottle • Spinning top • Autogyros • Bubbles (floating in the air?)

Activity 2 *continued*

Science class 1E 4 lessons 1hr 30 mins each week		
Learning objectives	Learning experiences	Resources and cross-curricular links
• Children will recognise hazards in some moving objects • Children to suggest ideas about why the plasticine man gets squashed	• Show a toy car – child to move it – the wheels *rolled*. • Show a wheel – child to move it. How did it move? (it rolled) – similar activity in circle with a ball, block *slid* across a board, child opening a bottle of Coke/water, etc. to classify movement into swing, twist, roll, jump, hop, etc. (Use children to show hop/jump/swerve, etc.) • Use toy cars to demonstrate moving slowly/quickly. Compare speeds – bringing in vocabulary fast/slow/faster/slower – go further. • Make a model person using soft home-made dough – demonstrate how he becomes *squashed* if he is in a toy car which is rolled down a slope and *STOPPED*. Moving objects can hurt us if we stop them. Link to road safety. Group work • Children to make a soft model (for in a car) and show how he becomes squashed if stopped at bottom of a ramp. • Children to sort objects by criteria of how they move	• Toy car/ramp • Home-made play-dough Cross-curricular links Music – 'Wheels on the bus' song PE – rolling, jumping, twisting, etc. Maths language – slow, slower, fast, faster, etc.
As for lesson A	B *Alternative lesson* (or perhaps additional children) • Visit to playground. Children to notice how swings/roundabouts, etc. move. • Return to classroom and draw pictures and annotate to show *how* they move, e.g. swing/slide/turn/spin, etc. • How do *they* move when they are on the rides? • What happens to 'dough man' when his car is moving fast down the real slide and then stopped? • Take two scooters. Can children scoot slowly and quickly?	• Parent helpers? • Letter to parents about the visit to playground • Dough man • Toy cars Cross-curricular links PSE • Walking to playground safely • Care and consideration for other playground users
Stage 3 Children should understand that pushes or pulls can make things speed up or slow down.	Watch video (*Think about Science – Push and Pull*) • Ask child to move a toy car or a box containing bricks. Has it been pushed or pulled? • Experiment with other articles – children to *move* them and identify *pushes* or *pulls*. *Tell* child that a *force* is a push or pull.	• Video – *Think about Science* – push and pull • Toy cars • Large box with toy bricks • String • Play-dough/flubber • Picture for labelling • Pictures for classifying

Activity 2 *continued*

Science class 1E 4 lessons 1hr 30 mins each week		
Learning objectives	Learning experiences	Resources and cross-curricular links
Vocabulary Move, push, pull, stretch, squash	• Can child make the toy car move by pulling? How could we do this? Children to think of a solution. • Show how a *big* push can make things move quickly, a *small* push slowly. • Show how a push against a moving ball can slow it down or stop it. Children in circle on carpet – 2 children demonstrate this. • Child to show how play-dough can be changed by pulling (use stretchy flubber to show this). Group work • Identify pushes and pulls on a picture (labelling) (HA) (MA). • Use storyboard to classify pushes and pulls. • Table with soft play-dough and flubber. Children to make shapes and change by pushing and pulling. • Children to go on forces safari and label with Post-it notes how doors/ cupboards, etc. are made to move (push or pull).	

Stage 4
Children should learn to:
• suggest a question to test
• predict what will happen
• try it out
• make measurements
• discuss results
	• Children to explore with toy cars on ramps. Notice how they move. Describe movement.
	• Show how to change:
	  • height of ramp
	  • surface on ramp
	  • different sorts of vehicles (types of tyres – e.g. home-made vehicle and wrap elastic bands onto wheels)
	• With children, decide on questions they might ask starting with 'What happens if . . . ?'
	
	• Children to devise own test (in groups) – guide if appropriate.
	• Discuss fair test and adapt.
	• Carry out test. Think about how to record the results.
	• Tell others about their investigations.
	• Group to use ICT to record results.
		• Wood for ramps
		• Bricks – wooden or real
		• Box
		• Pull along toys
		• Push toys
		
		Cross-curricular links
		Maths – measuring either distance travelled or time taken for vehicles to move down ramp

Figure 4.5 Example of a trainee teacher's planning

For cross-reference with Study Book see Figure 4.2

Activity 3 Managing practical work with very young children

When you are planning the work for very young children between the ages of 3 and 5 it will usually be practical. Young children learn best by active involvement with materials. What the teacher has to do is to find a balance between work which the children can plan for themselves, using resources provided by the teacher and those which will need more teacher direction and interaction.

Here are some activities which the teacher of a class of 25 3 and 4 year olds has planned. It is expected that the work will take place over a period of two weeks (see Module 5). The outdoor area is partially covered and there is a grassy slope.

- investigating stretchy and non-stretchy materials – play-dough, flubber, elastic bands, foam rubber, wooden rulers, paper, plastic materials, fabrics, both stretchy and non-stretchy;
- water play involving containers with holes;
- sliding and rolling – wooden blocks, ice-cubes on a large tray, balls, cylinders, foam blocks in a variety of shapes, vehicles with wheels.

Think about how this work might be managed. Some of it might be part of the continuous provision which teachers provide every day in classrooms where there are young children. Some might take place with the whole class and some may be planned for when children are working in small groups with an adult.

Complete the pro-forma in Figure 4.6 which might help you to structure your ideas.

Child-initiated enquiry Continuous provision	Focused task with an adult	Whole-class activity	Advantages and disadvantages of this type of organisation

Figure 4.6 Pro-forma for planning

For cross-reference with Study Book see Figure 4.3

Activity 4 Managing resources

If we are to help children to become independent and to design their own investigations, they will have to have access to a range of resources which will help them to carry out their enquiries. There will be equipment which is housed in individual classrooms and will be used frequently and there will be some more expensive or bulky items which have to be shared between classes. Children will be encouraged to decide what equipment they need in order to carry out a task and to collect and tidy away their own equipment. However, if they are to do this, then they will need easy access to the resources.

It is frustrating for teachers who want their children to use force meters to find that they are being used by another class or that they have not been returned to a central store. If we are to manage the practical work effectively, then we need to have a suitable system for storing and collecting resources. The science subject leader is usually the person who is responsible for setting up an effective system and individual teachers are responsible for managing the resources which are stored in the classroom.

- How can the teacher encourage children to identify and collect their own equipment? How can this be encouraged with the younger children?
- List the resources for scientific enquiry which you think should be stored in individual classrooms. Consider how these would be stored to provide easy access. Describe a system for 'borrowing' from a central store.
- Choose one of the areas of science from the list below and suggest what pieces of equipment are (a) essential and (b) desirable in order to teach effectively and give the children the opportunity to pursue enquiry in small groups.

  - forces
  - investigating living things
  - light and shadows
  - sound
  - materials
  - earth and space

REFERENCES

Feasey, R. (1998) *The Primary Equipment Handbook*, Hatfield: Association for Science Education.
Harlen, W. (2000) *The Teaching of Science in Primary Schools*, London: David Fulton.
NCC (1993) *Teaching Science*, London: National Curriculum Council.

FURTHER READING

Coates, D., Jarvis, T., McKeon, F. and Vause, J. (1998) *Mentoring in Primary Science*, Leicester: SCIcentre, School of Education, Leicester.

Module 5

Science in the early years

The foundation stage

MODULE GOALS

- To consider how a curriculum for early years children based on experiential learning can develop science skills and ideas.
- To consider the teacher's role in planning for play.
- To consider positive adult interactions with children.

MODULE OVERVIEW

This module provides opportunities to consider what it means for young children to behave in a scientific way and the adult role in planning and providing resources. It deals with:

- identification of skills;
- how to develop thinking skills such as problem solving in a science-based context;
- providing opportunities for developing science ideas in a role play context;
- teacher-initiated play;
- the interactions between adults and children.

There are five group activities:

- Activity 1 relates to the relationship with the generally recognised scientific skills and early years children. A scenario is described and participants are asked to identify the skills used by the children.
- Activity 2 encourages participants to handle a variety of materials which are commonly used in early years settings. They then consider how thinking skills might be developed through the use of these materials.
- Activity 3 relates to the planning of a role play area and the identification of potential learning.
- Activity 4 considers a scenario where a teacher has planned for teacher-initiated play. Using this as a model, participants are asked to plan similar experiences using different contexts.
- Activity 5 considers the interaction between child and adult.

Timing

Total time: approximately 3 hours

Introduction		5 mins
Activity 1	Group work	15 mins
	Feedback and discussion	15 mins
Activity 2	Group work	25 mins
	Feedback and discussion	20 mins
Activity 3	Group work	20 mins
	Feedback and discussion	20 mins
Activity 4	Introduction	5 mins
	Group work	15 mins
	Feedback and discussion	15 mins
Activity 5	Group work	10 mins
	Feedback and discussion	15 mins

Materials required

- flip chart or overhead projector;
- copies of the module activities for each participant if they do not have the Study Book;
- resources for the practical exploration in Activity 2:

  - cornflour (cornstarch), water, jugs, deep trays for mixing, food colouring. Mix the cornflour with water until it has the consistency of thick pouring cream.
  - plastic tank with a 5cm layer of gravel on top of which is placed an 8cm layer of soil, some large stones, magnifiers, snails, food for snails, peppermint essence, sliced onions, cotton wool (for observing how snails react to strong smells), a torch (for observing the snails' reactions to light).
  - white paint, red paint, black paint, flour, water, mixing palettes, shallow dishes, large sheets of paper, sheets of plastic or plastic plates, straws, brushes;
  - a collection of balls and skittles of different weights and sizes;
  - a washing-up bowl containing worms and soil, torch, peppermint essence and a water spray to keep the worms moist. (Be aware of the Health and Safety Guidelines when including living creatures in activities.)

INTRODUCTION

Points to make:

- State the aims of the module.
- If the participants are experienced teachers, then there should be some explanation about the fact that the actual resources used will be very familiar. The teachers will bring their experience of how young children learn to the discussion.
- The aim of the activities is to provide opportunities for reflection about how the *existing* curriculum can develop science skills and ideas and the role of the teacher in this process.

ACTIVITY 1

Before giving out the details of the activity, you might ask the participants to list the skills which they think are used by scientists. Compare these with those suggested in the text.

Allow time for the reading of the scenario and for the group to list the skills which they think have been used.

Feedback and discussion

Teachers will probably consider that the children have observed, predicted and communicated their ideas about the sounds. Perhaps someone might consider that the child who suggested that 'there was no room for the sand to move' was interpreting evidence. Although children did not articulate any questions on this occasion, there could have been evidence of questions in the mind as the children experimented with the different materials. Consider the teacher's role in the scenario and make particular reference to the fact that he or she played alongside the children.

ACTIVITY 2

Refer the participants to examples of their own scientific enquiry when they asked a question and carried out a controlled test in order to find out the answer. They may have undertaken this type of scientific enquiry with slightly older children. In order to carry out scientific enquiry children need to be able to think about problems. They need to be able to make decisions for themselves about how to carry out investigations. Few 3 year olds are able to do this but educators are anxious to develop skills which encourage *thinking*. Refer to Drummond's (1995) research.

It might be useful to allow a few minutes for the participants to consider Figure 5.1. Discuss the fact that at this stage of development the teacher will probably set the problems but that when children do suggest problems to investigate then they are praised. Give out the pro-forma (Figure 5.2) which the participants will complete.

Divide the teachers into groups of three or four and allocate one of the resources to each group. It is not necessary to use all the resources but the feedback will be richer if you can include at least three of the contexts.

Encourage the participants to handle the materials and to think of questions and problems which can be tested out by the use of the resources. Ask people to note their observations as they explore and play with the materials. For instance, what do they notice about how paint behaves when it is mixed with flour? Does it drip as easily from a straw as the more liquid paint? What happens to the paint as it is splattered onto paper?

You will probably want to move around the groups in order to suggest what might be done with the materials.

Allow about 10 minutes for the exploration and then refer people to the pro-forma (Figure 5.2). The completion of this should channel thoughts towards anticipated learning and the teacher's role.

Feedback and discussion

The materials which are being considered will be familiar to teachers of young children. As the materials are being explored, you will no doubt use your own experience to help the less experienced participants to suggest ways in which they can encourage children to develop observational skills. Stress the importance of working alongside the children and helping them to notice not just features such as colour and texture but also, where appropriate, similarities and differences.

Ask one person to feedback from each group. Focus this discussion particularly on the development of skills and ideas and the way in which children might demonstrate proficiency in the skills and the understanding of ideas. Pay particular attention to the *problems* suggested. Are the contexts familiar to the children? Would they be able to solve them with the materials which are available in the classroom?

Discuss the decisions which children might make. Encourage people from other groups to add to what is suggested by each spokesperson.

Activities 3 and 4 are related to learning through play. As an introduction refer to the section in the module on learning through play. If participants do not have the Study Book, then they will need a copy of the discussion. Refer to both child-initiated and teacher-initiated play. Allow time for participants to read this section before considering the example given in Figure 5.3 and Activity 3.

There may be some people who are concerned about the use of hammers and nails, which is suggested on the handwritten plan for the role play area (Figure 5.3). Obviously this will be a matter for the school and the teachers who plan the curriculum; however, there are many examples of children as young as 3 or 4 using hammers and nails safely and effectively. Supervision will, of course, be essential.

ACTIVITY 3

Give each of the groups of teachers a different context and allow them time to produce a plan similar to Figure 5.3.

Feedback and discussion

During the feedback there will be an opportunity for course participants to share information about resources which they have used successfully. If the participants are trainee teachers, then the course leader will be able to tell them about available resources.

You might like to consider the teacher's role when the children are engaged in independent role play. There may be an opportunity to consider the views of writers such as Ishiggaki and Lin (1999) and Hendy (1995) who advocate playing with the children so that pupils and learners can adopt the same status: that of learners together.

ACTIVITY 4

You will probably want to begin by differentiating between child-initiated play and teacher-initiated play. Allow time for the participants to read the scenario and then allocate one of the contexts to each group. Give each group a large sheet of paper from a flip chart to facilitate the feedback.

Feedback and discussion

Again this will be an opportunity to share ideas. The focus here is on getting the children started so that they can explore for themselves. This type of experience should not be confused with a focused task which will be much more tightly structured by the teacher. The groups should state the learning goals for each of the experiences as they describe them. It will be important here to identify both the science ideas and the skills which could be developed. Make reference again to the teacher's role and discuss the point at which the teacher should leave the group to their own explorations.

ACTIVITY 5

Feedback and discussion

The emphasis here is on the importance of engaging in a *conversation* with the child rather than bombarding the child with questions. While a carefully timed question can encourage the child to think, it should be in the context of a dialogue in which the child is a valued partner. Point out that sometimes it is more important for a teacher to show by his or her actions that he or she is enjoying the experiences as much as the children. For instance, a teacher who is playing with play-dough might say, 'Oh look ! I can make a very long snake with my dough.' The teacher will sometimes refer to his or her own observations rather than questioning the children about what they notice. This may be less threatening than a questioning approach and could encourage the children to talk. The teacher should be aware of the opportunities for science learning in spontaneous situations like those described but realise that the confidence of the child and the opportunity to explore are important at this early stage in a child's education.

PLANNING SCIENCE IN EARLY YEARS CLASSROOMS

This module considers how teachers plan for science in early years classrooms. The activities involve course participants in examining the appropriate skills and concepts, which enable children to learn effectively through an experiential curriculum.

Becoming scientific

When teachers in kindergartens and nurseries plan a developmental curriculum for science they first need to define the skills which they are hoping to develop. These skills cannot always be separated (Harlen, 2000, p. 31) but it is useful to think about each of them in order that appropriate experiences and resources can be provided. It is generally accepted that scientific enquiry involves:

- observing
- asking questions
- predicting
- planning investigations
- interpreting evidence
- hypothesising
- communicating findings.

These skills are used by scientists who might be 8 or 80 years old but are they used by 3 and 4 year olds and are they appropriate skills for these young children?

Activity 1

Read the vignette and consider the questions that follow.

Consider the following situation where a teacher is working with a small group of 4 year olds:

> The teacher has a closed box by the side of her chair. She reaches into the box and pulls out a tin. She has made a tinfoil lid for the tin and secured it with an elastic band. She passes the tin around the group and asks the children to shake it. She asks if they think there is anything in the tin. There is no sound as the children shake the tin. Most children say that there is nothing in the tin. The teacher takes off the lid and shows the children that inside the tin is some cotton wool. She gets out another tin and again allows the children to shake it in turn. This time they do hear a sound as she has placed some marbles in the tin. She tries a few more tins which contain small pieces of wood, some plasticine and some sand. The children describe the sounds which they hear. They talk about soft sounds, tinny sounds, 'lumpy' sounds and swishy sounds. She then brings out a tin which is full of sand. The children can tell that the tin is heavy and they immediately say that there is something in the tin. However, they can hear no sound. One child suggests that there is no room for the 'stuff' to move.
>
> The teacher presents the children with a collection of materials which include dried peas, sand, lentils, and the tops from old plastic pens. She also gives them a collection of containers with lids. The containers are tubular containers made of both metal and cardboard. She invites the children to make some shakers for themselves by putting the materials inside the containers. They play with these for a few minutes and talk about the sorts of sound which they hear. The teacher joins in the play. She then asks them to predict whether paper tissues, nails and a small plastic spoon would make a sound if they were put into the containers. They make their predictions and then test out their ideas. To finish off the activity she puts on a music tape and the children shake one of their chosen shakers in time to the music. She joins in with the play and shakes her own container. At group time later in the morning the children talk about what they have done and together they demonstrate their shakers in time to the music.

Have any of the skills of scientific enquiry been used by the children? Consider each of the skills in turn and note down any evidence which may indicate that children have been using the skills. The evidence may be indicated by children's dialogue or actions.

Encouraging thinking

Teachers of very young children provide an experiential curriculum and are often provided with guidelines which suggest that the children should be encouraged to develop the skills of:

- observation
- prediction
- problem solving
- decision-making
- communication.

Activity 1 *continued*

While these skills may seem, at first glance, to be different from those skills which form the basis of scientific enquiry, if you examine closely what children actually do when they are learning science, you will find that many of the features of their thinking could be said to be developing the skills listed above.

Teachers are also anxious to develop independence in children and the ability to collaborate with other children and these too can be developed as children investigate the materials, plants and animals which make up their world.

Drummond (1995) reported on research which showed that, where activities made demands on children's powers to think for themselves and to solve problems, then the quality of the learning was high and the children were enthusiastic. Children can use their reasoning powers at a very early age and we have a responsibility as educators to provide opportunities for children to do this.

The recognition of opportunities for problem solving is usually done by the teacher at the planning stage, but, as children become more practised in thinking about problems identified by the teacher, they will perhaps move towards questioning for themselves. The solving of the problems is not always the main objective for the children; talking about the problem and trying out ways to solve the problem with adults are often seen as more important (Hartley, 2000). After children have worked with adults on exploration and problem solving over many months, they will perhaps be ready to move towards a more structured form of enquiry, where they begin to consider whether or not their tests are fair.

Activity 2

Use Figure 5.1 as a model and consider the anticipated skill development and concept development when providing one of the following learning contexts. Complete the pro-forma (Figure 5.2) to show how you would help children to develop skills, what the evidence of learning might be and the science concepts which could be developed. Do this in relation to the resource which you have chosen. You should handle some of the materials yourself before you consider the potential for learning. By exploring at your own level you will be able to consider what children might observe, what problems might be posed and what scientific concepts could be addressed:

Resources and contexts
Soap flakes, bowls, water, variety of whisks.
Each child to have his own large bowl. After whisking the mixture until it is thick, it is tipped onto a plastic table so that children can handle it more easily.

	How to help children to develop the skills	Evidence of skill development	Science concepts which may be developed
Observation	Observe alongside the children. Show delight in certain features and point these out (e.g. dip hands in the mixture and then clap hands together)	Do children observe . . . ? • flakes floating before they are whisked; • that the more we whisk the more frothy the mixture becomes; • that the addition of more flakes changes the mixture ; • the smell of the mixture.	Change in materials when they are added to water Change as air is whisked into the mixture Some small flakes float on top of the water
Prediction	Ask questions as appropriate to elicit a response.	Do children predict what will happen? When . . . ? • we add more flakes • we add more water • we squash the foam • we leave the foam for a long time • we sprinkle glitter dust onto the mixture	
Problem solving	Identify problems and encourage children to think about how to solve them, e.g. Can you make the mixture flat instead of frothy? Would washing-up liquid and water make the same sort of mixture if they are whisked together? Which is the best whisk for . . . ? Give children time to express their ideas.	Do children show by their words and actions that they are trying to solve the problems?	Change when air is squashed out of the mixture

Activity 2 *continued*

	How to help children to develop the skills	Evidence of skill development	Science concepts which may be developed
Decision-making		Do children choose own whisks? Do they talk about or show that they can test out the different mixtures and whisks? Do they decide how many flakes to add to the water?	
Communi-cation		Do children talk to the adult or other children as they work? Are they able to describe sequences of events to other children at group time? Are they able to sequence a series of photographs showing the stages of the activity?	

Figure 5.1 Whisking soap flakes: identifying and developing learning

For cross-reference with Study Book see Figure 5.1

Resources and contexts			
	How to help children to develop the skills	Evidence of skill development	Science concepts which may be developed
Observation			
Prediction			
Problem solving			
Decision-making			
Communication			

Figure 5.2 Pro-forma: identifying and developing learning

For cross-reference with Study Book see Figure 5.2

Activity 2 *continued*

- making and using cornflour slime (sometimes called Gloop or Ooblick);
- a plastic tank which has been converted into a temporary habitat for snails;
- white paint, red paint, black paint, flour, water, mixing palettes, spoons, brushes, straws and paper;
- a collection of balls and skittles of various weights and sizes;
- a washing-up bowl containing soil and worms (be aware of Health and Safety Guidelines when including living creatures in activities);
- some peppermint essence or other strong smelling foods.

Learning through play

A curriculum for the early years will have been planned to include a wide variety of opportunities for play. However, it is not enough merely to provide the environment and resources. Practitioners will need to consider the learning outcomes and the needs of a particular group of children before they plan the environment. The needs of a child who has just turned 3 will probably not be the same as for a child who is almost 5. Some children in early years settings will be able to make decisions for themselves and to articulate ideas, while others will be at the stage where they play without speaking to other children and adults.

Some play is adult-initiated and some is child-initiated. A well-planned curriculum will include both types of play. Through interaction with materials and the exploration of these materials, children may learn scientific concepts and develop scientific skills. Curriculum developers often list these skills and concepts and suggest that practitioners plan to include opportunities for children to develop ideas and practise the skills. An examination of these guidelines shows that they might include:

- differentiating between hot and cold, wet and dry, rough and smooth;
- recognising some of the properties of materials and how they are used, e.g. waterproof materials, soft materials, transparent materials;
- realising that materials can change when, for instance, they are heated, stretched, mixed or whisked;
- recognising and identifying different materials;
- sorting materials;
- recognising and identifying some animals;
- realising that care should be shown to living things;
- knowing about the changes in the weather and the seasons;
- knowing when it is light and dark;
- knowing that some objects float;
- knowing how to move objects and begin to use the terms, push, pull, swing;
- knowing how we use our bodies to smell, taste, etc.;
- recognising and naming the main parts of the body;
- naming primary colours and knowing that mixing paints makes new colours;
- knowing about melting;
- knowing that some structures are stable and that sometimes high towers of bricks topple over;
- knowing that some objects roll and that some slide;
- suggesting ideas about why things happen;
- using magnifiers and tools correctly and safely.

This list is not exhaustive but the ideas will be familiar to early years practitioners.

The children will have the opportunity to learn some of the science ideas as they work and play alongside the teacher but some will be learned through an independent play situation. The classroom will be arranged so that children can develop ideas as they play in the various areas which have been set up by the teacher.

- There will be an area which is devoted to messy play and here you will probably find the sand and water trays, the painting easels and the mixing tables.
- There will be an outdoor area with large construction toys, a garden or some planters and perhaps climbing frames.
- There will be a quiet area with books, headphones and tapes.
- There will be a writing area with a variety of mark-making equipment.
- There may be a music area with instruments for the children to play.
- There will be a construction corner where children can build large models.
- There will also be tables with jigsaws, malleable materials and some living things.
- There will be a role play area where children can fantasise or be involved in social play.

Many teachers consider that in order for the children to practise skills and learn concepts there needs to be some stability in the location and types of resource which are provided. Children need to be able to repeat their play in order to test out ideas but, on the other hand, new materials and contexts need to be provided from time to time in order to enthuse and stimulate the children. There will therefore, in any early years setting, be a balance between newly introduced materials and those which are familiar to the children. As the seasons change, so will some of the living things in the classroom. Sometimes a new story will be introduced and this may stimulate a new topic for exploring. The role play area will change from time to time in order to introduce the children to new concepts. The outdoor area will be used to develop children's learning in all aspects of the early years curriculum.

Activity 3

Using the list of science ideas and the list of skills which you considered in Activity 1 identify the potential learning in one of the following role play contexts. Figure 5.3 provides an example of how you might do this:

- the garage and petrol station;
- the baby clinic;
- the hairdresser;
- the garden centre;
- the fire station (in outside play area);
- the hospital;
- the castle;
- the shoe shop;
- the space station.

To be set up in covered area — linked to outside play area

collection of small brick
samples (available from local brickworks)
sand, water, trowels, mixing board

- Large construction
- ramps and planks
- box of objects which slide/roll
- wheels from old bicycles
- construction kits with wheels, screwdrivers etc.
- set of large gears
- blocks

The Workshop

pulley system
set up with a
small box attached
— small box and
articles for lifting

Shelves containing
articles to take
apart eg. old clocks

Workbench area *
- small pieces of wood of different types
- sandpaper
- large nails
- short handled hammers

'Office' area with
telephone, paper and
mark-making materials.

* Always closely supervised

Potential for learning

Science concepts	Skills
• objects can be moved by pushing and pulling	• manipulative skills
• recognise and name gears — know that they link together and move together	• ability to select appropriate tools
	• collaboration
• some objects roll when pushed; some objects slide	• observing ways in which materials behave
• we can join materials with nuts and bolts and with nails	• noticing details of events which happen whe they are handling materials
• structures need to be stable so that they don't topple over	
• some wood is easier to 'sand' than others	

Figure 5.3 Outline planning: the workshop

For cross-reference with Study Book see Figure 5.3

Child-initiated and teacher-initiated play

The role play area is set up by the teacher and here children engage in both teacher-initiated and child-initiated play. The area is usually set up for a sustained period of time. Sometimes the teacher will want to put out resources on the carpet or on table tops. These are often provided for a shorter period of time so that a particular skill or concept can be developed. Figure 5.4 shows the roles required for teacher- and child-initiated play.

Child-initiated play	Teacher-initiated play
Teachers provide resources.	Teachers provide the resources.
Adults may join in the play but take the lead from the children.	The teachers take the lead in starting the play and suggest the context.
The teacher's role is to stimulate and encourage the play.	The teacher observes and monitors the learning.
The teacher observes and monitors the learning.	

Figure 5.4 Types of play

For cross-reference with Study Book see Figure 5.4

Consider the following scenario which illustrates teacher-initiated play:

The teacher wants the children to learn that some materials float and some do not and that sometimes the shape of the material affects this. He is not introducing the word sink at this time. He wants the children to play together and test out ideas.

In the water tray he has placed a sheet of aluminium foil which is floating on top of the water. He prods the foil and as it becomes covered in water it slowly sinks to the bottom of the tray. He then tells the children that he is going to make some boats. He shapes his foil into a boat shape and pushes it along the water.

'Oh, look!' he cries, 'It's floating.' He then crumples another identical piece of foil which sinks. He encourages the children to play with the foil and to try to make boat shapes. Some of the children are successful but many are unsuccessful. They do seem to be enjoying the experience and play quite happily, pushing the foil sheets under the water, lying them on top of the water and shaping some. After a few minutes the teacher introduces some foil cartons made of a thicker and firmer foil and he shapes one of these into a boat. He leaves the children at this point with the resources available nearby and suggests that the children might like to play by themselves for a while. He asks if they would like to try and make some boats.

Activity 4

Choose one of the following contexts and suggest how a teacher might plan to develop science skills and concepts through teacher-initiated play. Think about what the children might learn and how you would introduce the play:

- a table with magnets;
- the sand tray;
- the outdoor area with watering cans and water;
- a collection of toy vehicles.

Interactions with young children

In classrooms where very young children are learning, there are usually many adults. Some of the adults will be teachers, some will be trained assistants and some may be parent helpers. It is the teacher's role to plan for all the adults in the classroom. Generally, the curriculum planning is done by the whole team with the teacher taking responsibility for setting and monitoring the learning intentions. It is important that all the adults adopt the same approach when talking to the children, guiding their actions and playing alongside them.

In the photograph in Figure 5.5 you can see Stacey, who is 4 years old, washing the dishes after a cooking session. There is an opportunity here to talk to the child about what she can see and feel. The temptation is to quiz and question her about the temperature of the water, the bubbles or what sponge or cloth is best for cleaning. Very often children do not respond to this approach. They need time to observe as well as the opportunity to think about their response when the teacher is talking to them. On the other hand, talk with children must not be minimal. We need our talk to be a genuine discourse which gives the child the opportunity to feel valued and confident and to engage in thought.

Figure 5.5 Stacey washing up

For cross-reference with Study Book see Figure 5.5

Activity 5

Would you intervene in this situation? If so, what would you say and do? Although questioning is an important part of teaching, it is not always appropriate to question children. Sometimes we can encourage learning, just as much by our actions, as by what we say.

In the photograph in Figure 5.6 you can see Callum looking at himself in a ripple mirror. What would you say and do?

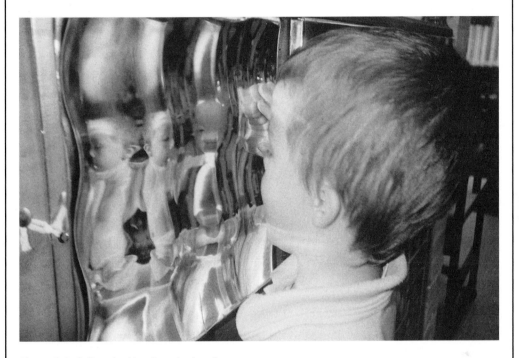

Figure 5.6 Callum looking in a ripple mirror

For cross-reference with Study Book see Figure 5.6

REFERENCES

Drummond, M.J. (1995) 'What are four year olds like? Setting the scene', in *Learning Properly? The Four Year Old in School*, Rochdale: OMEP.

Harlen, W. (2000) *The Teaching of Science in Primary Schools*, London: David Fulton Publishers.

Hartley, K. (2000) 'Encouraging problem solving', *Practical Pre-School*, vol. 23.

Hendy, L. (1995) 'Playing, role playing and dramatic activity', *Early Years*, vol. 15, no. 2, pp. 13–16.

Ishiggaki, E.H. and Lin, J. (1999) 'A comparative study of pre-school teachers' attitudes: towards "children's right to play" in Japan, China and Korea', *The International Journal of Early Childhood*, vol. 1, no. 31, pp. 40–7.

FURTHER READING

De Boo, M. (ed.) (2000) *Laying the Foundations in the Early Years*, Hatfield: Association for Science Education.

Module 6   Meaning and purposes of assessment

MODULE GOALS

- To develop an understanding of the meaning, purposes and methods of assessment as applied to primary science.
- To consider the characteristics and relationship between assessment for formative and for summative purposes (assessment *for* learning and assessment *of* learning).

MODULE OVERVIEW

This module provides a general introduction to assessment and should be studied before attempting Modules 7, 8, 9 and 10. In four main parts it deals with:

- The meaning of assessment. It is important for participants to have an understanding of assessment as encompassing a wide range of activities far beyond tests, which is the view that some will bring to the workshop.
- The purposes of assessment. Although there are many more purposes, we deal here in detail with two, generally known as formative and summative assessment.
- The assessment procedures. There are two aspects to this: the methods for gathering information and the way in which the information is interpreted or turned into a judgement about achievement. Avoid talking loosely of 'methods of assessment' which is ambiguous in meaning because it generally refers to methods of gathering information only which does not fully describe what is done.
- The nature of formative and summative assessment and the relationship between assessment for these purposes in practice.

There are four group activities:

- Activity 1 relates to the meaning and purpose of assessment in specific situations described in five brief vignettes.
- Activity 2 relates to the methods of gathering and of interpreting information used in the same vignettes.
- Activity 3 focuses on the characteristics of assessment for formative and summative purposes.
- Activity 4 involves consideration of the relationship between formative and summative assessment.

Timing

Total time: approximately 2 hours 20 minutes

Introduction		10 mins
Activity 1	Group work	25 mins
	Feedback and discussion	15 mins
Activity 2	Group work	20 mins
	Feedback and discussion	15 mins
Activity 3	Group work	15 mins
	Feedback and discussion	10 mins
Activity 4	Group work	20 mins
	Feedback and discussion	10 mins

Materials required

- flip chart;
- copies of vignettes A to E and Activities 1 to 4 for each participant (if they do not have the Study Book).

INTRODUCTION

Points to make:

- This is an introductory module on assessment and aims to clarify general points and concepts used in discussing assessment.
- Even though teachers have a good deal of experience of assessment for different purposes, it is important that we all share the same understanding of the words used in talking about assessment, including the word 'assessment' itself.
- We start with an activity specifically aimed at this clarification, but this clarification continues throughout the module.
- Some words used and distinctions between them seem like jargon but there are concepts related to assessment for which we need precise words.
- Assessment is going on all the time in classrooms and so we start by examining some instances described in five vignettes.

ACTIVITY 1

Arrange the participants in groups of four for Activity 1. Ask them to read the five vignettes and then to work first in pairs to complete Figure 6.4. After about 15 minutes ask each pair to discuss their responses to the activity with the other pair and prepare a group response (which should indicate areas of disagreement as well as agreed responses). The group should nominate someone to report.

Feedback and discussion

It is probably most effective to take responses across the rows rather than down the columns. Ask one group to give their responses to the first question for all vignettes. Ask other groups for comments or differences. If a group suggests that there was no assessment, ask a group which answered 'yes' to give their reasons. You may well find that the root of disagreement here lies in the meaning being given to the word 'assessment'. Explain that we are using it to include informal as well as formal processes where information is gathered about children's understanding and skills.

Continue down the rows of Figure 6.4, asking one group to lead and others for comments, additions, etc. As far as possible ask groups to substantiate their answers and respond to others who differed. There are no 'correct' answers. However, it is expected that the answer to 'Was there assessment?' is 'yes' in all cases. (See the Study Book p. 84 for further examples of possible responses.)

ACTIVITY 2

As an introduction, refer to the section on the meanings of assessment, which builds on some of the discussion in Activity 1. It is important to recognise that all assessment involves judgement. It is not the same as simply recording what children have done (as in making a video or keeping the entire products of every child); the assessment represents and replaces the work.

Briefly go through the points about purposes and draw attention to the focus of the present study and ask for queries and comments. Then continue to 'procedures'. A point to underline here is that methods of gathering information do not constitute methods of assessment – that is, the same *methods* can be used to gather information for different *purposes*.

The ways in which judgements are made, using different bases for judging, are likely to require most discussion as being less familiar and obvious than methods of gathering information. It is particularly important for the teacher to be clear as to when a child's performance is being compared with his or her previous performance (child-referenced or ipsative) and when it is judged against a standard or criterion that is the same for all children. Both are important but serve different purposes.

Ask participants to work in their previous groups of four to complete Activity 2. Again, one person should be prepared to report (on dissent as well as consensus) from the group.

Feedback and discussion

Ask for one group's responses to the task and then ask each other group to comment on any differences or points they wish to add. The vignettes cover a range of methods of gathering information: studying products (A); observing regular class work (B); discussion of regular work (C); teacher-devised tests (D) and standardised tests (E). They also illustrate different ways of making a judgement: common criteria (A, C, D); child-referenced (B) and norm-referenced (E).

After discussing the responses to this specific activity, spend some time reviewing all the information given about the meaning, purposes, methods of gathering and ways of judging information. Ask participants the following:

- Does it accord with their view of these things?
- What do they want to query or challenge?
- What further clarification would they like?
- What would they like to add?

Where necessary, revisit the relevant points. There is a more detailed treatment of these matters, for those who would like it, in Chapter 8 of Harlen (2000).

ACTIVITY 3

The focus now turns to the two purposes of assessment: formative (assessment for learning) and summative (assessment of learning) which will be considered in this and subsequent modules.

From the discussion of Activity 1 it became clear that vignettes A, B and C described formative assessment and D and E summative assessment. Ask participants to think of one example of formative assessment and one of summative assessment from their own experience. Ask them to work in pairs, to share these examples and then to carry out Activity 3. Explain that the idea is to look across examples and to identify the common characteristics, using the five bullet points and adding others as felt necessary.

Feedback and discussion

Ask for feedback from one pair on formative assessment. Go round other pairs to ask for additions, changes, etc. Write the characteristics identified on a flip chart. Do the same for summative assessment.

Review the lists and eliminate contradictions and repetition. Aim to arrive at a short list, with a brief description relating to each point. For example, for *how the assessment relates to learning*: 'it helps teacher and pupils to identify what has been learned' (formative); and 'it summarises what has been learned at a particular time' (summative).

Since summative assessment is already widely established in practice, it is more familiar than formative assessment and will need less discussion. It will be important to help participants clarify their understanding of formative assessment and the following notes may be helpful:

- Formative assessment is best described as assessment for learning. It is essentially carried out by teachers as part of teaching. This means that it is on-going and a regular part of the teacher's role. However, the fact of it being carried out regularly does not necessarily mean that assessment serves a formative purpose. Regular tests are not always formative in function; it depends on how the results are used and who uses them.

- Formative assessment helps the teacher to decide the appropriate next steps in learning both for those who succeeded in the earlier steps and those who encountered difficulty, so it is an integral part of teaching. It involves identification of where children are in their learning to inform the action to take. It is based on the idea of learning being progressive development.

- The evidence of learning can be interpreted in relation to the progress of the individual child (ipsative) or in relation to goals of learning (criterion-referenced) – often a mixture of both.

- There is an equal emphasis on using the information as on finding what has and has not been achieved.

- In formative assessment children are not being compared with each other.

- To serve its purpose, formative assessment has to be conducted in all contexts where learning takes place (not just in special tasks or situations set up for assessment). This must include hands-on activity, discussion, written work and all other learning situations.

- Learners have a role in assessment for this purpose since it is, after all, they who do the learning. No-one else can really change their ideas or develop their skills. Thus the more they are involved in knowing what they should be trying to do, the more likely it is that their motivation and effort are enlisted in advancing their learning. This means teachers sharing short-term goals with children as well as enabling them to judge the quality of their own work.

A useful source of information about the characteristics of formative assessment is the leaflet/poster *Assessment for Learning: Ten Principles for Guiding Classroom Practice* produced by the Assessment Reform Group (2002) and available on the website www.assessment-reform-group.org.uk.

The emphasis on formative assessment requires some justification. Moreover, if teachers are to make the effort to change practice as needed to implement formative assessment, they need to be convinced of its benefits.

Go through the two reasons given. For more information about the research evidence it may be helpful to obtain the pamphlet *Inside the Black Box* by Paul Black and Dylan Wiliam (1998).

ACTIVITY 4

The discussion of the value and nature of formative assessment raises the question of why it is not more widely practised. Ask participants for their ideas about possible reasons for this and discuss them. One possible reason is that the requirements to conduct summative assessment and the importance given to the results of this assessment dominate teachers' thinking and practice in relation to assessment.

Summative assessment is necessary and has an important role in learning, but it needs to be kept in balance with formative assessment. Go through the main points about the relationship between formative assessment and summative assessment, emphasising:

- Summative assessment dominates when tests and levels are taken as the indicators of effective schools and teachers.
- The more important summative assessment becomes, the more likely it is to be conducted through tests rather than teachers' judgements.
- Tests cannot cover all the important learning goals, so the curriculum breadth tends to be reduced to what is tested.
- Tests can also have an adverse effect on pupils' enjoyment of school, self-esteem and motivation for learning.
- There is solid research evidence for all these points.

It is important for teachers to discuss these points, but also to be positive in response to them. This is the purpose of Activity 4.

Ask participants to work in groups of four to address the three questions in the activity. Ask them to give examples of practice, where possible to back up their opinions. Keep to the 15 minutes suggested and ask each group to be prepared to report on each question.

Feedback and discussion

Consider each question briefly (since it is not going to be possible to change the world by talking but it is useful to exchange ideas and practice). Collect responses from one group for each question and ask the others to add or comment. Turn problems into possible solutions by asking what could be done to change practice.

Read the following five vignettes, A to E. Then, for each one, answer the questions in the following activities.

A

The overarching topic was 'materials' and the teacher of 9 and 10 year olds was embarking on a section about changes in materials. The goal of this section of the work was to enable children to recognise the origin of some materials in everyday use and the ways they have changed to reach their familiar form. She planned to assign groups a different common material (such as silk, cotton, wool, linen, paper) or food (milk, sugar, flour, chocolate) to explore by first-hand investigation and find out further information using books and other sources. They would then share their findings with the whole class.

Before setting up the group work, however, the teacher decided to find out the initial ideas of the children about one of these materials and at the same time show them a way in which they could report their work. She showed them a silk scarf and asked them to produce four sequenced drawings of what the scarf was like before it was a scarf, what it was like before that, and again before that, and before that (as suggested in *Nuffield Primary Science* Materials). They worked in pairs and had a piece of paper for their drawings, as shown in Figure 6.1.

Materials	What it was like before that	and before that	and before that	and before that
The scarf				

Figure 6.1 Pro-forma: production of the scarf

For cross-reference with Study Book see Figure 6.1

The children discussed their ideas and worked on their drawings in pairs for about 30 minutes and then the teacher asked them to pin their drawings on a large board she had prepared for this purpose. Once done, the children looked at each other's drawings and had plenty of questions to ask in the ensuing class discussion.

The collage of drawings gave the teacher an immediate overview of the children's way of tackling this work as well as of their ideas about the origin and changes in this particular material. She noticed that most recognised that the material had been woven from a thread and had been dyed before or after weaving, but few had an idea of the origin of the thread from a living thing, a silk worm. All the materials that she had chosen for them to study originated as living plants, so she was alerted to paying attention to this first link in the chain of changes. She also noted that their drawings were not self-explanatory and so she discussed with them how they could make their drawings clearer. She showed some examples of drawings with labels that helped anyone looking at them to understand what was being represented. The children were then put to work in groups of four, each group being given a different material on which to work.

B

In a different class the children were investigating the dissolving of sugar in water. Some groups were trying different kinds of sugar – icing, granulated, castor, brown, coffee crystals – and some were seeing what difference stirring made to the rate of dissolving. One group was working on the effect of temperature on how quickly the sugar would dissolve. They had some ice cold water, some water at room temperature and some warmer water from the hot tap. They were careful to take the same quantity of the same kind of sugar and to add it in the same way to each sample of water and to stir them all the same amount. However, the teacher noted that they were using different volumes of water. As they were clearly aware of keeping things the same for fair comparison, the teacher asked them if they thought it mattered that there were different volumes of water. They said it wouldn't make any difference, because the sugar would dissolve whatever the amount of water. The teacher realised that this had implications for their understanding of what is going on when a substance dissolves in water. So he asked them to try a separate investigation – of taking a small volume of tap water and adding a large amount of salt. When they found some would not dissolve, even with vigorous stirring, they added more water until it did all dissolve. Without using the word 'saturated' they talked about a certain amount of water only being able to hold a certain amount of salt, so the more water the more salt would be able to dissolve. They then went back to their sugar investigation realising that the volume of water was likely to be a variable they had to control for a fair test.

C

At the end of their investigations of dissolving, the teacher held a discussion with the whole class about what they would need to know about each group's work in order to understand what had been done, what had been found and how it could be explained. They ended up with a list of points that made a good report of an investigation. The teacher wrote these in large print on a chart and pinned them on the wall. While the children wrote their reports of their investigation they were reminded to pay attention to the points listed. When they presented their reports to each other, they used the list to make constructive comments about how the reports (their own and those of others) could be improved.

D

In another class, at the end of the unit on materials the children were given some questions to answer in their notebooks. Here are some of them:

1   What will happen when these things are put in water? Tick 'float' or 'sink' for each one:

	Float	Sink
Metal bottle cap upside down		
Cork		
Apple		
Bottle full of water		
Small coin (5p)		
Large coin (50p)		

Figure 6.2 Questions on floating and sinking

For cross-reference with Study Book see Figure 6.2

2   Describe what you would do to find out which of three different kinds of paper towel soaks up most water.

....

....

3   How can these mixtures of materials be separated? Tick the methods that would work for each one.

Mixture of	Use a magnet	Add water and then filter	Use a sieve
Sand and salt			
Cement and gravel			
Sand and iron filings			

Figure 6.3 Pro-forma: separation of materials

For cross-reference with Study Book see Figure 6.3

E

At the end of each year a school gave a standardised test of study skills to every pupil so that pupils in each class could be compared with the norm for their age group and their progress from year to year could be monitored.

Activity 1

For each of the events described in vignettes A, B, C, D and E, decide whether in your view it involves assessment. If so, identify what information was gathered, by whom, about whom, how it was used and what was the purpose of the assessment, and complete Figure 6.4.

	A	B	C	D	E
Was there assessment?					
What information was gathered?					
By whom was it gathered, about whom?					
Who used it and how?					
What was the purpose?					

Figure 6.4 Assessment features

For cross-reference with Study Book see Figure 6.4

The meanings of assessment

Gathering information about children's ideas and skills in an informal way, as in vignettes A and B, is part of teaching and it is equally part of assessment. The term 'assessment' is used to include a wide range of methods by which information is gathered and appraised. Assessment is more than description; it always involves:

- collecting evidence in a planned and systematic way;
- interpreting the evidence to produce a judgement;
- communicating and using the judgement.

Assessment can be initiated and conducted by those inside the classroom – teacher and pupils – or those outside, as in externally devised tests and examinations or visiting researchers.

Purposes

Assessment can serve a range of purposes:

- to help children's learning (formative assessment);
- to summarise achievement at certain times (summative assessment);
- to evaluate the effectiveness of teaching (where the focus of interest is the class not the individual);
- to monitor the performance of children across a locality, region or country (where only a sample of students is assessed);
- to assist in research or evaluation of curriculum materials.

Our concern here is with teachers and children in primary classrooms where the main purposes of assessment are the first two of these. That is:

- to find out where children are in their learning in order to identify the next steps that are appropriate (formative assessment, or assessment *for* learning);
- to find out what children have achieved at certain points in order to monitor progress and to report this to parents, other teachers and the children themselves (summative assessment or assessment *of* learning).

Everything about assessment – the methods used to gather information, how judgements are made, what use is made of the judgements – should serve the purpose of the assessment. So it is very important to be clear about the purpose when any assessment is planned or undertaken. Indeed, the difference between formative and summative lies not in how the assessment is carried out (for the same methods can be used to gather information for either purpose) but in the use that is made of the information.

Assessment procedures

Information about children's achievements can be collected by:

- questioning in ways that elicit their understanding and skills;
- observing them carrying out their regular class work (observing includes listening, questioning and discussing);
- studying the products of their regular work (including drawings, artefacts, writing);
- introducing special activities into regular class work (e.g. concept mapping, diagnostic tasks);
- giving tests (teacher-made and external; performance and written).

These are methods of collecting evidence, they should *not* be described as *methods of assessment*, for the reason that assessment also involves *making a judgement*. How this judgement is made is an important aspect of an assessment.

Making a judgement means that the information is compared with some expectation, standard or criterion, which can be done in three main ways:

- Sometimes the expectation is specific to a particular child, as when a teacher gives an encouraging response or sign (which can be just a comment or smile) to a child's work because it indicates progress for that child. (This is child-referenced assessment, sometimes described as ipsative.)
- Sometimes the expectation is based on what is normal for children of the same age. (This is norm-referenced assessment.)
- Sometimes the expectation is expressed in terms of certain levels of understanding or skill. (This is criterion-referenced assessment.)

Activity 2

For each of the events A to E identify the main methods of gathering information and the basis used in making judgements about the children's achievements, then complete Figure 6.5.

Event	Method used to gather information	Basis of making a judgement
A		
B		
C		
D		
E		

Figure 6.5 Judgement of children's achievements

For cross-reference with Study Book see Figure 6.5

Activity 3

Formative and summative assessment

The assessment in vignettes A, B and C falls into the 'formative' category, while vignettes D and E describe summative assessment. Think of an example of formative assessment and one of summative assessment and describe it to your group as you begin Activity 3.

Bearing in mind various examples of formative and of summative assessment, identify the defining characteristics of assessment for each of these purposes. Think about, for instance

- how the assessment relates to learning;
- who is involved in what ways;
- when it takes place;
- what special conditions are needed if any;
- what it leads to.

Then write a list of bullet points to describe formative assessment and another to describe summative assessment.

The importance of formative assessment

In this and the other modules on assessment we are paying most attention to formative assessment, although we also refer to assessment for summative purposes. The reason for this emphasis is the recognition of the considerable potential for raising children's achievement by improving practice of formative assessment.

The two most important reasons for focusing on formative assessment are:

1   It is essential to learning and teaching which starts from children's existing ideas and skills. Arguments for this approach are explored in Module 3. When teachers want to take into account the ideas and skills that children bring to a new situation, it is clearly important for them to find out what these are. Only by doing this can these starting points be taken into account and new learning be based on firm foundations. If teachers do not do this, there is a danger of requiring children to take steps that are too large for them, so that they can only follow blindly, without understanding. If the steps are too small, then children are not challenged to develop their ideas and opportunities for learning are missed. But it is not just at the start of new experiences that such information is needed. As ideas and skills develop, there is a continuing need to see how children are conducting their enquiries and making sense of new experiences. Thus gathering information – and importantly using it – need to become part of teaching.

2   There is evidence from research that practising formative assessment is a significant element in raising achievement, especially that of lower achieving children. A review of research in this area (Black and Wiliam, 1998) found that introducing certain practices characteristic of formative assessment had the effect of improving learning to a greater extent than any other intervention. The characteristics of classroom practice associated with these gains in learning are that:

(a) assessment is used by teachers to adapt teaching;
(b) teachers give feedback to children in terms of how to improve their work, not in terms of judgemental comments, grades or marks;
(c) children are actively engaged in learning – meaning that they are active in developing their understanding, not passively receiving information;
(d) children are engaged in self-assessment and in helping to decide their next steps;
(e) teachers regard all children as being capable of learning.

Balancing formative and summative assessment

Summative assessment is needed for reporting what children have achieved, but it does not change that achievement. As the term suggests, it gives a summary of achievement, not a detailed account as is necessary to help learning. This summary can be the result of reviewing a child's work over the relevant period, or the result of giving a test, or a combination of both of these. Often the summary is expressed as achievement at a particular level, or meeting a certain standard or achieving a score in a test. Sometimes – indeed, all too often – the meaning behind the levels, standards or scores is forgotten and achieving the label becomes an end in itself. When this happens, summative assessment tends to dominate teaching and learning and formative assessment is submerged.

Summative assessment is even more likely to come to dominate teaching when the results for a whole class or school are used to evaluate a teacher or the school. This practice is controversial, but widespread. When information from assessment is used in this way, and particularly if it is made public, the assessment has important implications for the status and reputation of the teacher or school (it becomes 'high stakes'). The more that depends on the assessment, the more attention is given to ensuring that the results are as far as possible unbiased. And because there is a widespread assumption that tests are more reliable than teachers' judgements (despite lack of real evidence to support this claim), the desire to make things 'fair' leads to a preference for tests rather than using teachers' judgements to summarise achievement. Now the most reliable tests are the ones that focus narrowly on knowledge that can be assessed as 'correct' or 'incorrect', so the more reliable the test, the less information they can give about skills and concepts that are not so easily tested. When the results are important to teachers they understandably focus on those things that children need to know to succeed, and so end up teaching children to pass tests rather than helping them to achieve the full range of goals of science education.

Activity 4

Consider the points made about formative assessment and summative assessment:

- In your experience, is there a conflict in practice between formative assessment and summative assessment (or assessment for learning and assessment of learning)?
- What do you think can be done to ensure that assessment can serve formative and summative purposes, without the needs of the latter dominating the former?
- In your view, can assessments for these different purposes be combined or should they be kept strictly separate?

REFERENCES

Assessment Reform Group (2002) *Assessment for Learning: Ten Principles for Guiding Classroom Practice*, Cambridge: Assessment Reform Group. See the ARG website: www.assessment-reform-group.org.uk

Black, P. and Wiliam, D. (1998) *Inside the Black Box*, London: School of Education, King's College, London.

Harlen, W. (2000) *Teaching, Learning and Assessing Science 5–12*, 3rd edn, London: Paul Chapman Publishing.

Nuffield Primary Science (1995) *11 Teachers' Guides and 22 Pupils' Books for Key Stage 2*, London: Collins Educational.

Module 7 Assessing enquiry skills

MODULE GOALS

- To describe children's development of enquiry skills in science in a way which can be used in assessing progress and using the information formatively.
- To appraise the use of developmental criteria in the formative assessment of enquiry skills using evidence from practical and written work.
- To consider how developmental criteria can be related to levels of achievement used in reporting summative assessment.

MODULE OVERVIEW

This module focuses on the assessment of enquiry skills, which presents a particular challenge for both formative assessment and summative assessment. Neglect of the assessment of enquiry skills leads to their neglect in teaching. The module deals with gathering information with the help of 'developmental criteria' and deciding the next steps in learning. This is only part of formative assessment; the vital part of using the information to help children take these next steps is the subject of Module 2.

The module is designed to help participants pick up signs of development of enquiry skills during the course of their regular activities. It provides participants with opportunities to consider developmental indicators in theory and in practice, using the indicators to observe a practical activity and to consider some examples of children's written work. It also underlines some of the distinctions between formative assessment and summative assessment discussed in Module 6 and ends by considering how development criteria (or indicators) can be related to normative levels of achievement in national curriculum statements.

The module has four main parts dealing with:

- the notion of progression in the development of enquiry skills;
- the pros and cons of using developmental criteria to gather information for formative assessment from children's practical work;
- the use of developmental criteria in relation to evidence of enquiry skills in children's reports or written work;
- the relationship of developmental criteria to the 'levels' of achievement set out in National Curriculum documents.

There are four group activities:

- Activity 1 calls on participants to use their ideas of development in enquiry skills and to discuss the feasibility and identification of a developmental sequence in these skills.

- Activity 2 provides experience of using developmental criteria in observing a practical investigation carried out by co-participants.
- Activity 3 considers the use of developmental criteria in gathering information from children's written work for formative assessment.
- Activity 4 addresses the use of developmental criteria in summative assessment and asks participants to relate the developmental criteria they have been using to the 'levels' used in reporting children's achievement.

Timing

Total time: 3 hours

Introduction		5 mins
Activity 1	Group work	40 mins
	Feedback and discussion	15 mins
Activity 2	Group work	45 mins
	Feedback and discussion	15 mins
Activity 3	Group work	20 mins
	Feedback and discussion	10 mins
Activity 4	Group work	20 mins
	Feedback and discussion	10 mins

Materials required

- flip chart;
- pro-formae for Observers (X) and Observers (Y);
- copies of Activities 1–4 for those who do not have the Study Book.

For Activity 1

- copies of the statements for the six sets of process skills. Preferably each statement should be pasted on to a separate card so that the statements can be physically moved into different sequences.
- BluTak to place the cards, when sorted, on to a poster.

For Activity 2

For each group:

- large straight-sided container for water (large enough to put a hand into), but *not* graduated;
- large lump of plasticine (about 200 grams);
- ruler;
- paper towels.

Also available, but not for each group:

- paper, sellotape and scissors

For each participant:

- copies of pro-formae for Observers (X) and Observers (Y).

For Activity 3

- copies of children's work, one between two, for those without the Study Book.

For Activity 4

Ask participants to bring their own copies of the National Curriculum, the Scottish 5–14 Guidelines, or other locally used curriculum document.

INTRODUCTION

Points to make in giving an overview and stating the goals of the module:

- Enquiry skills are being used by children in all kinds of science activity, not just when they are investigating and manipulating materials. Using these skills is necessary for learning with understanding (see Module 1) as well as being important goals in their own right.
- There is a development in these skills. Young children can identify the first steps of what to do to find out something by investigation, but later they will be able to produce plans which include controls, identify what is to be observed or measured and how to ensure reliable results.
- If we are to help the development of enquiry skills then we need to know where children have reached and what is the next attainable step for them to take.
- The development of enquiry skills is not as well known and agreed as is the development of some concepts in science. This may be because they do not depend on the content but on the way of working.
- We start from our own ideas of the meaning of development in these enquiry skills. But rather than a blank sheet, we have some statements of observable actions related to skills used in enquiry: questioning; predicting; planning; gathering evidence by observing and measuring; interpreting evidence and drawing conclusions; communicating and reflecting critically.

ACTIVITY 1

Arrange for participants to work in groups of three or four. Although all groups should have access to the statements for the six enquiry skills, ask different groups to start with different skills, so that all skills are considered by some groups if not by all. When a group has finished their first enquiry skill ask them to continue to work on another in the same way.

Ask groups to prepare to report their response to (a) to (d). For (c) they could use BluTak to display their sequence of the statements on cards by sticking them to a poster. A less satisfactory alternative is to use the numbers of each statement and list the order decided by the group.

Set a time limit. (If time is short, ask each group to consider only one set of statements. In this case production of a poster is important in order to share findings with other groups. In this way, between all the groups, there should be a sequence identified for all the skills.)

Feedback and discussion

As a start, ask if any group added to the list. Then take comments briefly from one group in relation to the question (b); ask others for any additions or alternative views. Participants may make the point that it is difficult to identify development because what children do depends so much on what the subject matter is, and whether, for instance, they have chosen it themselves or are required to work on something that may not interest them. These things definitely do influence children's engagement in particular instances. However, in deciding whether there is a development we assume 'all things being equal', that is, that the subject matter is appropriate to the children's interests and conceptual understanding.

There is also a point of view that enquiry skills do not develop, rather, that the change in what children can do just reflects their ability to deal with more complex subject matter. There is research evidence to counter this view, however, and teachers' experience supports the developmental argument. There are dimensions of general changes in skills which apply to all, such as:

- from simple to more elaborate;
- from being used effectively in familiar situations to being used in unfamiliar ones;
- from being used unconsciously to being used consciously and deliberately.

For a discussion of these dimensions of change and of their application to specific skills, see Harlen (2000, pp. 32–42).

Ask all groups to report the order in which they have placed the statements in response to part (c). Take each of the skills in turn. The reports from groups might take the form of just listing the numbers of the statements in the sequence they identified. Alternatively, if they have physically re-ordered the statements and displayed them on a chart, these should be placed on show for all to see. If possible, agreed sequences for all six skills should be produced, as these are needed for Activities 3 and 4.

Points relevant to (d) are likely to have come up throughout the discussion. Bring together the main ones, which may well include the following:

- Children will not show evidence of using process skills unless they have the chance to do so. For example, they may not show that they can plan an investigation if they have not had opportunity to do so because they have always followed instructions.
- Interest and difficulty will also influence whether or not children can use a skill to the extent that they are able. Their skills should therefore be assessed in situations where they are able to engage fully with the content on which the skills are to be used.
- Information should be gathered in a range of activities since not all investigations are of the same kind and some give more opportunity for using particular skills than others.

Round off the discussion of Activity 1 by stating that by arranging the indicators in developmental order we have turned them into something that can be used to identify where children have reached in their progress and what their next steps might be. Next, we see how helpful they are in practice.

ACTIVITY 2

This activity takes some pre-planning so that the written materials and the equipment needed are at hand. If possible, have participants working in groups of six. The idea is that in each group two people conduct an investigation, while the others observe. Two of the observers use developmental criteria to observe and record their observations and two use an open form for making notes of their observations. However, the number of observers can be adjusted in each group (from one to three), but there should always be more than one investigator (so that there is talk between them to listen to).

Assign roles in each group and briefly outline the purpose and procedures of the activity. Give the Observers (X) copies of the two sets of developmental criteria for 'gathering evidence' and 'interpreting evidence'. Two sets are suggested to save on time, although it would be preferable to use all the sets of indicators. These are chosen as being the most relevant for this activity.

Allow 20 minutes for the practical investigation and observations (part 1). Then ask all the observers to discuss together and the investigators to use the developmental criteria (as for

Observers (X)) for self-assessment (10 minutes). Finally, ask observers and investigators to share their experiences and views of the value of using the developmental criteria.

Feedback and discussion

Ask groups to report on the following:

- how the experiences of observing with and without using the indicators compared;
- how useful were the indicators for self-evaluation;
- the extent of agreement among the two groups of observers and the investigators;
- ways in which the procedures could be improved;
- any other points.

Points to make in bringing the discussion together:

- Participants were asked not to interact with the investigators for the sake of the exercise. But not everything can be observed. Children often do things that are difficult to interpret unless you ask them to explain what they are doing. So in practice the teacher would supplement observation with questioning and discussion.
- We do not know what the investigators would have done with a different problem and different material; they may or may not have known a good deal about the investigation before the start. This underlines the point about needing to observe in different activities.
- The pair of investigators was treated as a single entity (and in the classroom the focus of observation may be the group). Whether or not this matters depends on how practical work is organised. If it is in groups, then any decisions about action to be taken will affect the group as a whole. This underlines the purpose of the assessment, which is to help children make progress, not to label them. If decisions are to be made about the progress of individual children, then the observations should focus on the individuals.

ACTIVITY 3

There are two aims to this activity. The first is to show that written work can be a source of evidence about children's enquiry skills, particularly if the children have been encouraged to describe and reflect on what they have done in an investigation. The second is to take the process of formative assessment a stage beyond finding where children are to deciding what are the best next steps to take in developing their enquiry skills.

Participants are likely to work best on this activity in pairs. If all six enquiry skills are used, then it will be necessary to have arranged all of them in developmental order. If this has not been done at an earlier stage in the module, then use the two ordered lists provided (for 'gathering evidence' and 'interpreting evidence').

Ask participants to read the work carefully and to make sure there is evidence for the decisions they make about which of the developmental criteria seem to be met. For some statements there will be no evidence to judge from because we have such a small sample of work. This will lead participants to consider possible next steps for the child. (Although in the real situation that decision would be based on more than one piece of work.)

Feedback and discussion

Take each piece of work and briefly gather findings from various pairs about where the work would be placed in relation to the four sets of enquiry skills. If there are differences of opinion, ask for the evidence which they are using. It may be useful to remind participants that:

- What children write depends on how the task was presented to them, so just because they do not include some aspect does not mean that they are not able to do so.
- It is important to look carefully at work – there is usually more there than first meets the eye (just as we don't always 'hear' all that children say).

Spend more time on how they decided what are the appropriate next steps for these children. The evidence we have for them is very limited, and one would not judge from this alone. But, for this exercise, let us assume that this is typical and that we have more information. As a result, we have found that most statements up to a certain point were met and few were beyond this point. There will always be one or two statements where the evidence is uncertain – where the children sometimes do it but not always.

Ask participants how they would use this information for deciding how to help development of the skill in question. Likely points are as follows:

- For statements of things children do sometimes but not always, identify the situations that favour the use of the skill and use this to help them link to other situations where it is not used.
- For those things that children do not yet do in relation to the skills, support (scaffold) the use by making suggestions, teaching any requisite techniques and modelling the behaviour, but most importantly providing opportunity for using this level of skill. (See Module 2 for discussion of ways of helping children to develop enquiry skills.)

ACTIVITY 4

For this activity participants need to have to hand a copy of the curriculum document relevant to their work. If this is not likely to be available, make copies of the pages relating to the specification of levels for enquiry skills.

This activity relates the formative assessment of enquiry skills to their assessment for summative purposes. Summative assessment is needed for keeping a record of progress, for reporting to parents and the children themselves and providing information to other teachers when children transfer from class to class. This information has to be in a condensed form – if too voluminous it will not be used. It also has to be expressed in a form that is the same for all children. So it should not be child-referenced (that is, judged against a child's previous achievement) but criterion-referenced (judged against criteria that indicate what the child is able to do). The levels of the National Curriculum and similar documents are condensed and insufficiently detailed compared with the developmental indicators we have been using, and cannot effectively be used to decide next steps but that is not the purpose of summative assessment. However, summative assessment does not require the collection of more information than has already been gathered for formative assessment. This activity allows participants to explore the connection between the developmental indicators and the level criteria of the National Curriculum documents.

Feedback and discussion

(a) For collecting findings about levels it is useful to have lists ready of the developmental criteria in sequence (as decided in Activity 1), for example, for gathering evidence by observing and measuring, as shown in Figure 7.1.

Discuss any instances where the levels do not fall in the expected sequence or where there are gaps. Reasons might be ambiguity in the statements or lack of continuity from one level to another.

This exercise might highlight gaps in the developmental criteria either within the six skills or the need to add to them. (Participants should be invited to develop statements to fill such gaps.)

Gathering evidence by observing and measuring	Curriculum level
Identifying obvious differences and similarities between objects and materials	
Identifying points of similarity between objects where differences are more obvious than similarities	
Using their senses appropriately and extending the range of sight using a hand lens or microscope as necessary	
Making an adequate series of observations to answer the question or test the prediction being investigated	
Taking steps to ensure that the results obtained are as accurate as they can reasonably be and repeating observations	
Distinguishing from many observations those which are relevant to the problem in hand and explaining the reason	

Figure 7.1 Developmental criteria

For cross-reference with Study Book see Figure 7.4

(b) On the basis of feedback from (a), ask a group to give the levels agreed for the three pieces of work. Discuss any differences reported by other groups. However, since we did not have sufficient information for determining the levels of working of the pupils who produced the work it is not productive to dwell on this. It is more important to recognise that the information gathered for formative assessment can in principle be used for summative assessment.

(c) Continue the discussion of formative assessment and summative assessment by asking for pros and cons from one group and then additions/differences from others.

Points to emphasise:

- There are considerable differences between formative assessment and summative assessment information in relation to detail. This is necessary on account of the different purposes of the assessment.
- There is the potential for using information gathered and used for formative assessment to serve summative purposes as well by summarising in terms of national criteria.
- There are particular advantages in doing this for the assessment of enquiry skills because the information is derived from a range of activities and thus is more valid than information derived from a test or single investigation.
- While formative assessment information can be summarised to give summative assessment information, this cannot be done in reverse.

INDICATORS OF ENQUIRY SKILLS

The following are lists of possible indicators of six main enquiry skills: questioning; predicting; planning; gathering evidence by observing and measuring; interpreting evidence and drawing conclusions; communicating and reflecting critically.

The statements in the lists are presented in random order. Choose one of these lists initially for Activity 1, then repeat for other lists if there is time.

Raising questions

1   Recognising a difference between an investigable question and one which cannot be answered by investigation.
2   Helping to turn their own questions into a form that can be tested.
3   Asking a variety of questions and participating effectively in discussing how their questions can be answered.
4   Suggesting how answers to various questions (investigable and non-investigable) can be found.
5   Participating effectively in discussing how their questions can be answered.
6   Recognising that only certain questions can be answered by scientific investigation.

Predicting

1   Using past experience or knowledge to make a prediction.
2   Justifying a prediction in terms of relevant science concepts.
3   Explaining the reason for a prediction in terms of patterns in available evidence.
4   Making a reasonable prediction based on an explicit hypothesis (possible explanation of what is going on).
5   Attempting to make a prediction relating to a problem or question even if it is based on pre-conceived ideas.
6   Recognising that a prediction is different from a guess.

Planning

1   Succeeding in planning a fair test using the support of a framework of questions.
2   Identifying what to look for or measure to obtain a result in an investigation.
3   Suggesting a useful approach to answering a question or testing a prediction by investigation, even if details are lacking or need further thought.
4   Identifying the variable that has to be changed and the things which should be kept the same for a fair test.
5   Selecting and using equipment and measuring devices suited to the task in hand.
6   Spontaneously structuring a plan so that variables are identified and steps taken to make results as accurate as possible.

Gathering evidence by observing and measuring

1   Taking steps to ensure that the results obtained are as accurate as they can reasonably be and repeating observations where necessary.
2   Succeeding in identifying obvious differences and similarities between objects and materials.
3   Identifying points of similarity between objects where differences are more obvious than similarities.
4   Taking an adequate series of observations to answer the question or test the prediction under investigation.
5   Using their senses appropriately and extending the range of sight using a hand lens or microscope as necessary.

6   Distinguishing from many observations those which are relevant to the problem in hand and explaining the reason.

Interpreting evidence and drawing conclusions

1   Recognising that there may be more than one explanation which fits the evidence.
2   Identifying patterns or trends in their observations or measurements.
3   Drawing conclusions which summarise and are consistent with all the evidence that has been collected.
4   Using patterns to draw conclusions and attempting to explain them in terms of scientific concepts.
5   Recognising that any conclusions are tentative and may have to be changed in the light of new evidence.
6   Discussing what they find in relation to their initial question or comparing their findings with their earlier predictions/expectations.

Communicating and reflecting critically

1   Comparing their procedures after the event with what was planned in order to make suggestions for improving their way of investigating.
2   Regularly and spontaneously using printed and electronic information sources to check or supplement their own findings.
3   Using tables, graphs and charts when these are suggested to record and organise results.
4   Choosing a form for recording or presenting results which is both considered and justified in relation to the type of information and the audience.
5   Using appropriate scientific language in reporting and showing understanding of the terms used.
6   Talking freely about their activities and the ideas they have, with or without making a written record.

Activity 1

Read the statements of indicators of pupil actions relating to six enquiry skills. The indicators are in random order. For one set of statements initially:

- Decide if you think there are others to add or if some are not relevant.
- Consider whether you think there is a developmental sequence within the statements for a particular skill, that is, that you would expect children to do what is described in some of the indicators before others.
- Try to arrange the indicators in order of development from early stages to later stages.
- Discuss the extent to which the sequence would be generally applicable and, if not, what might influence the extent to which children use certain skills.

It helps to have the statements written on card or separate slips of paper.

These indicators are criteria for use in assessment. They are described as 'developmental' when the statements are arranged as closely as possible, but still necessarily roughly, in terms of the development of the skills.

Having the development of skills in mind enables teachers to do the following:

- know what to look for in gathering information about enquiry skills by observation;
- interpret children's actions in terms of their development of enquiry skills;
- identify the next steps that are appropriate for the further development of children's enquiry skills.

They can also be used for summative assessment, as we will see in Activity 4. In both cases, however, it is necessary to conduct observations on several occasions, since the content of an investigation limits the skills that can be observed and may also influence a particular child's performance (for instance, if the subject matter is familiar or not). This has to be remembered while undertaking Activities 2 and 3 since we can only deal with one example and have to assume that it is typical across a range of activities.

Activity 2

If possible, work in groups of six and give each member a specific role:

- two will be investigators who will undertake an investigation (I);
- two will be observers (X) using the lists of indicators of enquiry skills, rearranged as developmental criteria;
- two will be observers (Y) making notes on what is done in relation to these same sets of enquiry skills.

It is possible to work with only one observer in each group, as long as there is more than one investigator.

Part 1

Investigators (I)

Using the equipment provided (and any other you need) work as a pair to investigate the following:

- What happens to the water level in a container when a large piece of plasticine is totally immersed in the water, and then when the plasticine is made into a shape so that it floats on the water? Do you think there will be any difference in what happens to the water level in these two cases? Will it depend on the shape of the floating plasticine?
- Discuss and write down your predictions before you start.
- Then find out what happens.
- Try to explain what you find.

Observers (X)

Using two of the lists of developmental criteria decide from what you observe which of the statements apply to the skills that they show. Just observe, do not interact with the investigators.

Do this in any way that you find works. You may find the pro-forma (X) in Figure 7.2 of help (the statements for two of the most relevant sets of skills are listed in developmental order as identified by other teachers).

Observers (Y)

Using the pro-forma (Y) in Figure 7.3, make notes of your observations about how the investigators are using the same two sets of skills ('gathering evidence' and 'interpreting evidence'). Just observe, do not interact with the investigators.

Part 2

When the investigation has been completed (after about 20 minutes) spend the next 10 minutes as follows.

Activity 2 *continued*

Gathering evidence by observing and measuring	
Do the investigators:	
(a) succeed in identifying obvious differences and similarities between objects and materials?	
(b) identify points of similarity between objects where differences are more obvious than similarities?	
(c) use their senses appropriately and extend the range of sight using a hand lens or microscope as necessary?	
(d) make an adequate series of observations to answer the question or test the prediction being investigated?	
(e) take steps to ensure that the results obtained are as accurate as they can reasonably be and repeat observations?	
(f) distinguish from many observations those which are relevant to the problem in hand and explain the reason?	
Interpreting evidence and drawing conclusions	
Do the investigators:	
(a) discuss what they find in relation to their initial questions or compare their findings with their earlier predictions/expectations?	
(b) identify patterns or trends in their observations or measurements?	
(c) draw conclusions which summarise and are consistent with all the evidence that has been collected?	
(d) use patterns to draw conclusions and attempt to explain them in terms of scientific concepts?	
(e) recognise that there may be more than one explanation which fits the evidence?	
(f) recognise that any conclusions are tentative and may have to be changed in the light of new evidence?	

Figure 7.2 Pro-forma for observers (x)

For cross-reference with Study Book see Figure 7.1

Activity 2 *continued*

Gathering evidence by observing and measuring	
Interpreting evidence and drawing conclusions	

Figure 7.3 Pro-forma for observers (Y)

For cross-reference with Study Book see Figure 7.2

Investigators

Use the pro-forma for Observers (X) to assess your own performance in relation to the two sets of skills.

Observers (X) and (Y)

Compare your observations among all the observers, focusing on the ease or difficulty of using the method assigned to you.

Finally, discuss as a whole group of six, the different experiences of self-assessment and observing with and without using the lists of indicators. Focus not so much on the performance of the investigators as on the process of assessment and particularly the role of the indicators.

Not all evidence of enquiry skill development takes the form of actions. What children say, write and draw can also provide evidence. This can add usefully to what is observed, particularly because it can be studied after the event, but it is important always to have evidence from what children actually do and not just what they say they have done. Moreover, as you will see, the written work can only give very limited evidence in relation to enquiry skills.

Activity 3

Consider the three pieces of work (Figures 7.4, 7.5 and 7.6). What can you find that is evidence of the six process sets of skills considered here? Where would you place the children in terms of the developmental criteria?

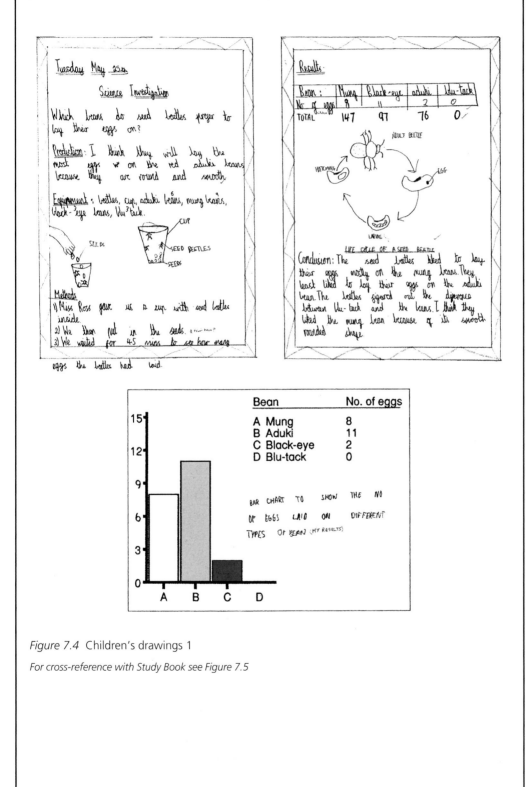

Figure 7.4 Children's drawings 1

For cross-reference with Study Book see Figure 7.5

AN INVESTIGATION

1] What am I trying to find out ?

I wanted to find out that if all the ice cubes melt at the same time but in different places.

2] What do I need ?

I need a tray of ice cubes. They have to be the same because its not fair to have little ones and big ones.

3] What did I do ?

①I put one in the sun②I put one in the class. ③I put one outside④one in my hand⑤one in the freezer⑥one in the fridge⑦one on a heater

4] What happened ?

·The one in the hand and on the heater melted quikest. The one in the fridge was ·the slowest. the one in the freezer won't melt.

5] What have I learnt ?

·The hotter it is the quicker it melts. ·The colder it is the slower it melts.

Figure 7.5 Children's drawing 2

For cross-reference with Study Book see Figure 7.6

Activity 3 *continued*

Upper Junior Science Investigation planning sheet and graph.

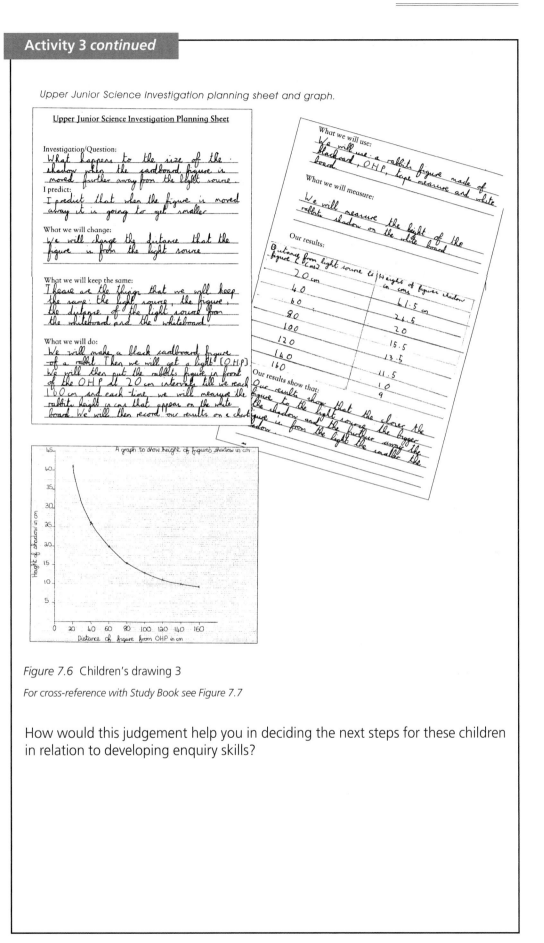

Figure 7.6 Children's drawing 3

For cross-reference with Study Book see Figure 7.7

How would this judgement help you in deciding the next steps for these children in relation to developing enquiry skills?

Using developmental criteria in summative assessment of enquiry skills

Summative assessment, as its name suggests, provides a summary of what has been achieved at a certain time. The observations of actions and study of products made over an extended time can be reviewed against the developmental criteria and used for summative assessment. The summary often takes the form of saying that a child has reached a certain level of performance. Of course a great deal of information is lost in doing this and, most importantly, the answer does not indicate what to do to help learning. But that is not the purpose of summative assessment. This is why it is essential to be clear about the purpose of assessment. Levels are useful in summarising achievement, but they do not improve achievement.

In order to arrive at a summative assessment of enquiry skills we do not need to give a test or make further observations of children's written work. Indeed, the nature of enquiry skills means that to do this would produce a very unreliable judgement. This is because the use of enquiry skills depends a good deal on the content of the enquiry. So we should collect observations across a range of content as part of teaching and combine the findings in making a judgement about the level achieved (using the levels 1 to 8 of the National Curriculum or A to F of the Scottish 5–14 National Guidelines, or other national or local curriculum statements). Activity 4 explores how this process compares with the developmental criteria we have been using.

Activity 4

(a)   For this you will need a copy of the level criteria that apply to the curriculum of your school. Consider the developmental criteria for 'raising questions', 'predicting', 'planning investigations', 'gathering evidence by observing', 'interpreting evidence and drawing conclusions' and 'communicating and reflecting critically' in relation to statements in the curriculum at the different levels.

Does the result confirm your judgement about the sequence of development, in Activity 1?

(b)   On the assumption that the work of the children considered in Activity 3 is typical of their work during the period for which achievement is being summarised, what level does this suggest they were working at?

(c)   Discuss the pros and cons for different purposes of using the more detailed description of skill development in the six sets of criteria compared with the direct use of the curriculum level statements.

REFERENCE

Harlen, W. (2000) *The Teaching of Science in Primary Schools*, London: David Fulton Publishers.

FURTHER READING

Assessment Reform Group (2002) *Assessment for Learning: Ten Principles for Guiding Classroom Practice*, Cambridge: Assessment Reform Group.
Black, P. and Wiliam, D. (1998) *Inside the Black Box: Raising Standards through Classroom Assessment*, London: School of Education, King's College, London.
Harlen, W. (2000a) *The Teaching of Primary Science*, 3rd edn, London: David Fulton Publishers.
Harlen, W. (2000b) *Teaching, Learning and Assessing Primary Science*, 3rd edn, London: Paul Chapman Publishing.

Module 8   Assessing children's conceptual understanding

MODULE GOALS

- To consider the extent to which there is sequence in children's development of scientific concepts and the nature of the changes that indicate progress.
- To discuss the potential of children's written work for assessing progress in understanding of scientific concepts.
- To become familiar with the process of concept mapping.
- To consider the use of children's concept maps for assessing progress in understanding.

MODULE OVERVIEW

This module focuses on ways of assessing children's ideas as a basis for deciding how to help development of conceptual understanding in science. It complements Module 7, which dealt with the development of enquiry skills. Ideas and enquiry skills are developed in every science activity and are dependent on each other for development (see Module 1). It is only for convenience that we deal with them in separate modules. We take a similar approach here as in Module 7 for enquiry skills, looking first at progression and the significant differences between ideas that are typical of early development and later development. We then take a look at ways of collecting evidence about children's understanding, through regular written work and drawings and through concept maps.

There are four group activities. In Activity 1 participants consider the development of ideas about the process of life and the interaction of living things and their environment. Development of particular ideas depends on whether children have encountered them in the subject matter of their activities, but it is important to identify the general changes in the ideas held at different stages of progression.

Finding what children's existing ideas are is the most important step towards deciding how to help their progress in conceptual development. So, in Activity 2 participants consider how information can be gathered from regular work through children's writing and drawings. Activity 3 introduces concept mapping, which is a more direct way of tapping into ideas. In Activity 4, examples of children's concept maps are studied to investigate how they can be used to assess children's ideas and changes in ideas as a result of classroom activities.

Timing

Total time: 2 hours 40 minutes

Introduction		10 mins
Activity 1	Group work	20 mins
	Feedback and discussion	10 mins
Activity 2	Group work	25 mins
	Feedback and discussion	20 mins
Activity 3	Group work	25 mins
	Feedback and discussion	10 mins
Activity 4	Group work	25 mins
	Feedback and discussion	15 mins

Materials required

For Activity 1

- copies of the activity and the list of ideas about 'processes of life' and 'interaction of living things and their environment' for those not having the Study Book.
  It is helpful to have the individual listed ideas on separate cards for ease of sequencing.
- flip chart for recording sequences.

For Activity 2

- copies of the activity and of Figures 8.6 to 8.14 (one set per group) for those not having the Study Book.

For Activity 3

- copies of the activity and paper for drawing concept maps for each participant.

For Activity 4

- copies of the activity and of Figures 8.15 to 8.19 (one set per group) for those not having the Study Book.

INTRODUCTION

Points to make in setting the scene for this module:

- Make it clear from the start that we are assessing children's understanding for the purpose of helping their development. So this implies that (a) we have to know what the course of the development is and (b) where children are in relation to it.
- It is particularly difficult to identify the sequence of development in this case because of the word 'understanding'. The use of this word indicates that we are concerned with children making sense of things, not with the ability to recite facts or phrases.
- The 'problem' is that understanding can be at a variety of levels. For instance, we can 'understand' the concept of dissolving in terms of a solid 'disappearing' in a liquid, although still being there in some form. Or, dissolving can be more broadly conceived in terms of gases going into liquids and liquids into liquids as well as solids into

liquids. We can also 'understand' it in terms of the molecules of one substance being distributed among those of another. At a much more advanced level the graduate chemist would think in terms of the electric charges of groups of atoms that cause some molecules to be brought together and others to be kept apart. Thus there is indeed a progression in the understanding of this concept – although we do not expect children to go as far as the graduate chemist.

- In grappling with this notion we have to distinguish progress in understanding from the knowledge that comes from particular activities. For example, whether the idea that 'light travels in straight lines and shadows are formed when light from a source is blocked' comes before or after 'some materials allow light to pass through and others do not' is dependent purely on the order in which the relevant activities are encountered. Accumulating facts like these is like adding bricks to a pile rather than building a house.
- Therefore, in seeking a way to identify progression we have to consider ideas at the right level of generality. It also helps if we can think in terms of broad changes that can apply to all ideas.
- With this progression in mind, if we then find what ideas children have, we can help them make progress. Sometimes this will be progress in forming the bricks, the 'small' ideas, and sometimes it will be putting ideas together to make 'big' ideas – building the bricks into a useful structure.

ACTIVITY 1

Arrange participants to work in groups of three or four. Each group should consider both sets of ideas. It will help the sharing of ideas if the individual concepts are pasted on to small cards so that they can be rearranged and displayed in a new sequence. Otherwise the groups could report their sequences using the letter labels.

Emphasise that part (a) is a genuine question, and it is open for participants to consider that there is no conceptual progress to be found. They should justify this judgement. In any case they may well find some ideas that could fit anywhere in a sequence, depending on the topics studied. In that case these statements are too topic specific.

Feedback and discussion

Ask one group to report on (a) and (b) together for 'processes of life'. If they cannot put all the ideas into a sequence, they may be able to identify a group of 'early' and 'later' ideas. Invite others to comment on any points of difference, which should be referred back to the first group for their justification. Repeat for 'interaction of living things and their environment'.

In turning to (c) review the sequences and particularly the differences between ideas placed at the 'early' and 'later' parts. Take, for example (from 'interaction of living things and their environment'), the following ideas, which are likely to be at the 'early and 'later' ends of the sequence and put them side by side, as shown in Figure 8.1.

Early ideas	Later ideas
Changes occur in living things in response to daily and seasonal changes in the environment.	Competition for life-supporting resources determines which living things survive where
Different plants and animals are able to live and find food in very different places	Plants are the ultimate source of food for all living things

Figure 8.1 Early and later ideas on interaction of living things and their environment

For cross-reference with Study Book see Figure 8.20

Ask participants if they identified broad differences between these. Collect all the ideas. If these do not include the following, add:

- The early ideas are *descriptive* of experience, while the later ones embody explanations. That is, children can observe living things in their environment and, as a result, form these ideas. On the other hand, the 'later' ideas indicate an *explanation* of observations.
- The early ideas indicate that *simple patterns* have been identified by linking observations of two things together (e.g. difference in the living things and differences in time), while the later ideas require a more complex linking through several *chains of reasoning*.
- The early ideas are more observable and *'concrete'* while the later ones are more *abstract*.

Take the full list and see if it applies to the ideas for 'processes of life'. Discuss the extent to which these dimensions of change indicate a view of progress in understanding across a range of scientific concepts.

There are two further points worth noting. First, that the 'early ideas' will have been derived from a limited number of observations of particular living things, for example, that worms are found in soil and are able to live there, while fish would not be able to live in soil but only in water. Thus, although the early ideas are not expressed as relating to particular living things, they are only a step away from the 'small' ideas that refer to specific objects or events. There is, therefore, a change from smaller to bigger ideas within the progression.

The second point is a philosophical one that teachers should be aware of, but is not intended for the children. It is that the generalisations about living things are, like all scientific generalisations, hypotheses that can never be proved 'right'. (See the quotation from Steven Hawking in Module 1 of the Study Book). We have not yet found a living thing that does not 'produce its own kind' but there is always the possibility! Until that time we are happy to live with and use this idea because it is the best way we have of making sense of our present experience.

ACTIVITY 2

In setting the scene for this activity, point out that the children were asked to express their ideas about particular phenomena, e.g. how a drum makes a sound and how we hear the sound. But the point in this activity is to use the products to identify what ideas the children have, not whether they answered correctly the question they were asked. For some participants this will be a new way of looking at children's work – trying to understand children's thinking behind the work rather than whether the children have correctly reported what they did.

It is particularly important for participants to consider the further information that the teacher would need since some of the listed ideas are 'bigger' than the particular ones that the children show in their drawing or writing.

The participants work in pairs or groups of three and should be encouraged to agree their group answers, since this involves them in sharing and justifying their views. All groups should be able to work on all three sets of work about sound, light and materials in the time available (25 minutes).

Feedback and discussion

Ask one group to report on the ideas about sound, including what the teacher would do to gather the additional information. Give others the opportunity to disagree or query. Repeat for 'light' and 'materials' with different groups leading.

Recall that we are concerned in this module with gathering information and deciding what the next steps are in developing understanding in relation to particular science concepts. (For ways of helping children to develop their ideas, see Module 2.)

After gathering responses, ask participants about how easy or difficult they find it to identify children's ideas from these pieces of work. Points emerging from this discussion are likely to include:

- Single pieces of work are not enough to indicate the grasp of general ideas, so, as in the case of enquiry skills (see Module 7), it is necessary to accumulate information over several instances.
- The value of the product for assessing ideas depends on the way in which the task was given to the children. In most of these cases the children were asked specifically to show or write about 'how you think you hear the drum' or 'how you think you see the light from a torch that is behind your head, using a mirror'. If the tasks had been given in terms of 'drawing a picture to show what you did', then the thinking might not have been revealed.
- In almost all cases, discussion with the child is necessary to clarify their thinking, and particularly in trying to assess the extent to which they apply the idea in other than that specific situation.

Some of these points suggest that more information can be obtained by setting tasks specifically designed to require the children to make explicit their ideas. Concept maps are one important way of doing this and therefore are explored in the next two activities.

ACTIVITY 3

Concept maps may need some introduction for many participants. They are schematic ways of representing relationship among concepts. If we take the two concepts 'green' and 'leaf', we can relate them to each other in terms of the relationship that we understand links them, as is shown in Figure 8.2.

Figure 8.2 Concept map

For cross-reference with Study Book see Figure 8.1

The arrow indicates the direction of the relationship and the words written beside it form a proposition about how the two are related. That is, 'leaves may be green', but not 'green may be leaves'. We can add to this by linking to other words, thus forming a map of inter-related concepts.

Although a map can be drawn by asking for all the concepts that the person drawing it finds relevant, the result is more useful if the concept words to be used are specified. In the classroom context, the teacher might 'brainstorm' with children all the 'idea' words relating to a particular topic and then ask them to draw maps to show how they see them connected.

So in Activity 3, participants are asked to draw their own maps using the words specified. Draw attention to the need to show the direction of the relationship by arrows and to label the arrows. Participants should do this individually first (about 15 minutes), then form pairs and exchange maps. Participants should compare the links and the labels on the arrows and discuss differences.

Feedback and discussion

First collect impressions of the process of drawing a map. Often this experience causes some concern among participants about their own grasp of the concepts involved. In doing so, this underlines the value as a way of finding out people's ideas about these things.

Then ask about the similarities and differences found between maps. Also ask for feedback on:

- How easy was it to 'read' a map made by someone else?
- What differences in understanding were revealed?
- How were these identified?

Then move the discussion to the use of concept mapping with children.

For those not previously familiar with concept maps, the technique may seem too difficult to use with children. However, there is overwhelming experience that children as young as six find the idea easy to grasp and indeed enjoy making the maps (see Further Reading). Various suggestions have been made for making the process easier for young children, such as having the concept words written on cards and arrows also on cards for children to move around. In Activity 4 we look at some examples of children's maps and what they can tell us about the children's ideas.

ACTIVITY 4

Parts (a) and (b) of this activity concern the use of concept maps in formative assessment. Suggest that one way of analysing a map is to turn it into a narrative. Participants might try, for example, expressing David's ideas as ' the bean needs air, soil and water, then sun. When seeds fall on the soil, they grow, . . . etc.'

Part (c) indicates some ways in which children's maps can be analysed for the purposes of summative assessment.

Participants work in pairs or groups of three and should create agreed responses to all three parts.

Feedback and discussion

(a) Collect views on David's and Debbie's initial ideas. It would appear that these children have already learned a good deal about the parts of plants which may indicate a confusion between the requirements of growing plants and of germinating seeds and what seeds need to grow. It is noteworthy that both include air as needed for plants to grow. They also include 'sun', although it is not clear in David's map whether this refers to the bean seeds or the bean plants and this may indicate a confusion between the requirements of growing plants and of germinating seeds. What implications do participants see for appropriate next steps for these children?

(b) Collect views on the usefulness of the 'before' and 'after' maps for the teacher to see where ideas have developed and more links have been created (often an indication of the formation of 'bigger' ideas). What significance might be attached to the two separate, but not connected maps, that Kathy and Claire drew after the activities?

What role might these maps play for the pupils in self-assessment? Stow, in an article in *Primary Science Review* (1997) suggests that 'before' and 'after' maps can be used by children to reflect on how their ideas have changed and what they have learned.

(c) Collect views on how children's maps can be compared with a 'level' or standard. Ask participants how easy it was to compare their map with Claire's. Would Claire's map, turned into a narrative, enable her 'level' of understanding of ideas about heat and temperature to be judged?

Finally, note other ways of assessing children's understanding of ideas:

- Setting specific 'application' questions. It is important for these to seek application in a context different from that already discussed.
- Using concept cartoons (see Further Reading). These are enjoyable for children and teachers, but the ideas discussed are the ones presented and may not tap into the particular ideas that children have.
- Setting up a discussion among children and listening to the words they use and how they relate one idea to another (i.e. an oral concept map). Concept cartoons can be used for this, especially if children are encouraged to add their own ideas to those given in the cartoon.

Activity 1

Understanding of ideas shows in pupils' ability to apply them rather than just recite them. Here are some ideas about living things – one set relating to the processes of life and the other to the interaction of living things and their environment. They are presented in random order. For each set:

(a) Consider whether there is a developmental sequence within each set of ideas, that is, would you expect children to be able to understand, and apply, some before others?

(b) Try to arrange the ideas in order from early stages of development to later stages.

(c) Discuss the extent to which the sequences indicate broad differences between ideas placed towards the beginning and the end of the sequences.

Ideas about the processes of life

(a) There are organs within the bodies of mammals arranged in systems which carry out the major life processes.

(b) Living things produce their own kind.

(c) There are different kinds of living things called plants and different kinds called animals, which include human beings.

(d) Animals and plants depend on each other in various ways.

(e) All living things are made of cells.

(f) Human beings need certain conditions to promote good health and body maintenance.

(g) The basic life processes are common to plants and animals.

Ideas about the interaction of living things and their environment

(a) The remains of living things will, in most circumstances, decay and this process releases substances that can be used as nutrients by other organisms.

(b) Changes occur in living things in response to daily and seasonal changes in the environment.

(c) Human activity can interfere in the balance between resources and the plants and animals depending on them.

(d) Competition for life-supporting resources determines which living things survive and in which location.

(e) Human activities can produce changes in the Earth's surface and atmosphere that can have long-term effects.

(f) Plants are the ultimate source of food for all living things.

(g) Different plants and animals are able to live and find food in very different places.

Activity 2

How much can you tell about children's understanding of scientific concepts from their written work?

(a)　Look at the pieces of work on pages 123–8 and decide which of the ideas, listed in (i), (ii) and (iii), they give some information about.

(b)　In order to decide the extent to which the child has grasped an idea, you no doubt want to have more information. So suggest, in each case, what the teacher might do to find the extra information.

(i) Ideas about sound

What does this tell us about the child's understanding	Figure 8.6	Figure 8.7	Figure 8.8
Of how to produce sound			
Of the difference between pitch and loudness			
Of how the sound produced by an instrument can be changed			
About sound being produced when objects vibrate			
Of how to change the pitch and loudness of the sounds produced by musical instruments			
That sound travels through solids, water and air			
Of how the pitch of a sound made by a particular instrument can be raised or lowered			

Figure 8.3 Pro-forma: child's understanding of sound

For cross-reference with Study Book see Figure 8.2

What the teacher needs to do to get more information:

....

....

Activity 2 *continued*

(ii) Ideas about light

What does this tell us about the child's understanding	Figure 8.9	Figure 8.10	Figure 8.11
Of light being essential for seeing things			
That there are many sources of light			
That the Sun is the source of light for the Earth			
That shiny objects are not light sources and need a light source if they are to shine			
That we see objects when light from them goes into our eyes			
That light is reflected off objects			
That the position, shape and size of a shadow depend on the position of the object and the light source.			

Figure 8.4 Pro-forma: child's understanding of light

For cross-reference with Study Book see Figure 8.3

What the teacher needs to do to get more information:

....

....

Activity 2 *continued*

(iii) Materials

What does this tell us about the child's understanding	Figure 8.12	Figure 8.13	Figure 8.14
That there is a great variety of materials			
Some materials are natural and some are made by chemical processes			
The uses of materials can be related to their properties			
Materials can be changed into different forms			
Some materials can be changed permanently by heating and changes in other materials can be reversed by cooling			

Figure 8.5 Pro-forma: child's understanding of materials

For cross-reference with Study Book see Figure 8.4

What the teacher needs to do to get more information:

....

....

Activity 3

(a) Working alone, draw a concept map which shows your ideas about how these things are connected. Make sure that you show a direction on the linking lines and label them to indicate the relationship.

Hot	Candle	Metal
Cold	Oven	Wood
Temperature	Fire	Plastic
Air	Draught	Insulation
Thermometer	Burn	Heat

(b) When you have finished, exchange maps with a partner and compare your ideas. You should ask for explanations of links that you do not understand and be prepared to justify the links in your own map.

Activity 4

Concept maps can be used to reveal children's initial ideas before an activity, to identify changes in ideas after an activity compared with beforehand, and to assess a child's level of understanding. Refer to the maps in Figures 8.15 to 8.19 for the various parts of this activity.

(a) The maps in Figures 8.15 and 8.16 were drawn by top infants at the start of activities on growing seeds. What can be found about the children's initial ideas? How might the teacher use this information in planning the focus of the work?

(b) In Figures 8.17, 8.18 and 8.19 compare the 'before activities' maps with the 'after activities' maps. The activities the children were involved in between these times were

- using a thermometer to measure the temperature of a variety of things in the classroom;
- heating food (chocolate, bread, eggs) and observing the effect;
- discussing winter clothing to keep them warm;
- using their hands to assess temperature.

Identify the nature of the changes in terms of, for example, integrating new information into their ideas, creating more relationships, changing previous misunderstandings. List the changes for each one.

(c) To assess the level of understanding, some basis for comparison is needed. One such basis is a map showing the links that you consider would be appropriate for a child of that age and experience. To try this, compare the map you drew in Activity 2 with the ones drawn by Claire in Figure 8.19. Another way is to express the child's links in words and compare them with the statements in the curriculum document for different levels of achievement.

Drawings for Activity 2

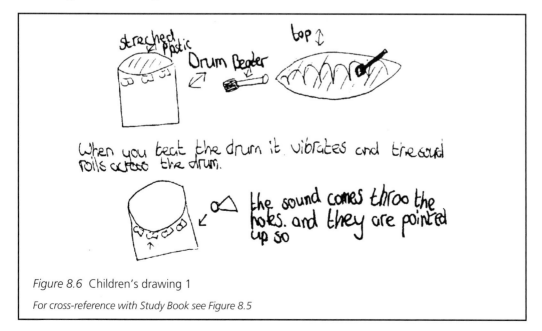

Figure 8.6 Children's drawing 1

For cross-reference with Study Book see Figure 8.5

I think I hear the sound by listening hard and I think it could be because the drums sound is very loud.

Figure 8.7 Children's drawing 2

For cross-reference with Study Book see Figure 8.6

I noticed that when I plucked the rubber band it made a low noise. If I stretched the band tighter the pitch of the noise was higher. The more I stretched the higher the noise became.

(Age 9 years)

"*I noticed that when I plucked the rubber band it made a low noise. If I
stretched the band tighter the pitch of the noise was higher. The more I
stretched the higher the noise became.*"

Figure 8.8 Children's drawing 3

For cross-reference with Study Book see Figure 8.7

sun   moon.   mirror

torch   Fire   Heater

'Things that give off light'

Figure 8.9 Children's drawing 4

For cross-reference with Study Book see Figure 8.8

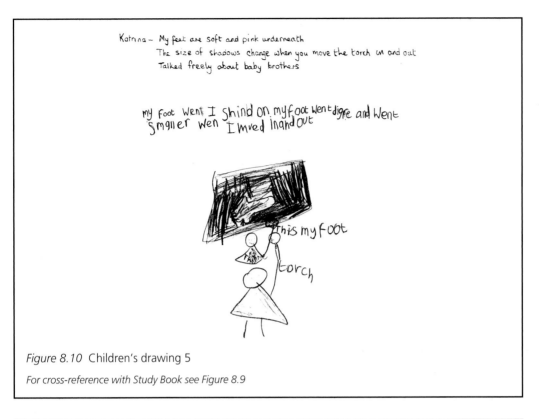

Katrina – My feet are soft and pink underneath
The size of shadows change when you move the torch in and out
Talked freely about baby brothers

my foot went I shind on my foot went digre and went smaller wen I mved in and out

this my foot

torch

Figure 8.10 Children's drawing 5

For cross-reference with Study Book see Figure 8.9

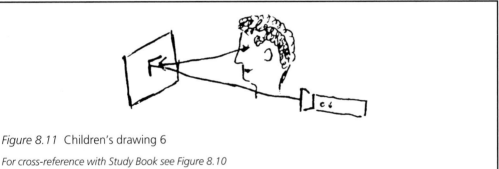

Figure 8.11 Children's drawing 6

For cross-reference with Study Book see Figure 8.10

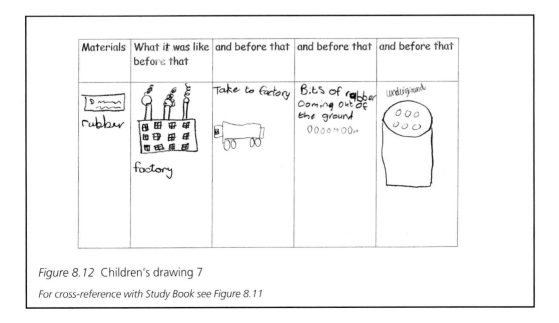

Materials	What it was like before that	and before that	and before that	and before that
rubber	factory	Take to factory	Bits of rubber ooming out of the ground	underground

Figure 8.12 Children's drawing 7

For cross-reference with Study Book see Figure 8.11

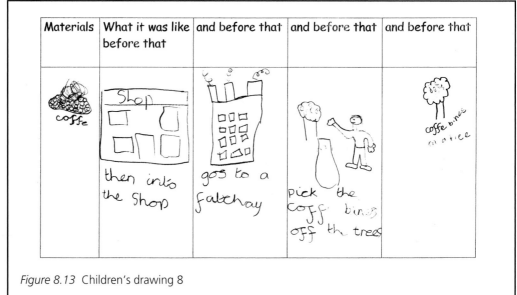

Figure 8.13 Children's drawing 8

For cross-reference with Study Book see Figure 8.12

Figure 8.14 Children's drawing 9

For cross-reference with Study Book see Figure 8.13

Drawings for Activity 4

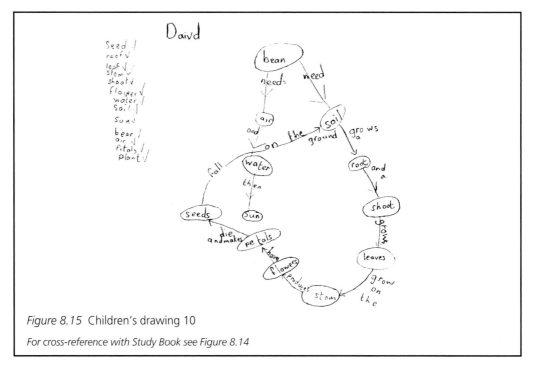

Figure 8.15 Children's drawing 10

For cross-reference with Study Book see Figure 8.14

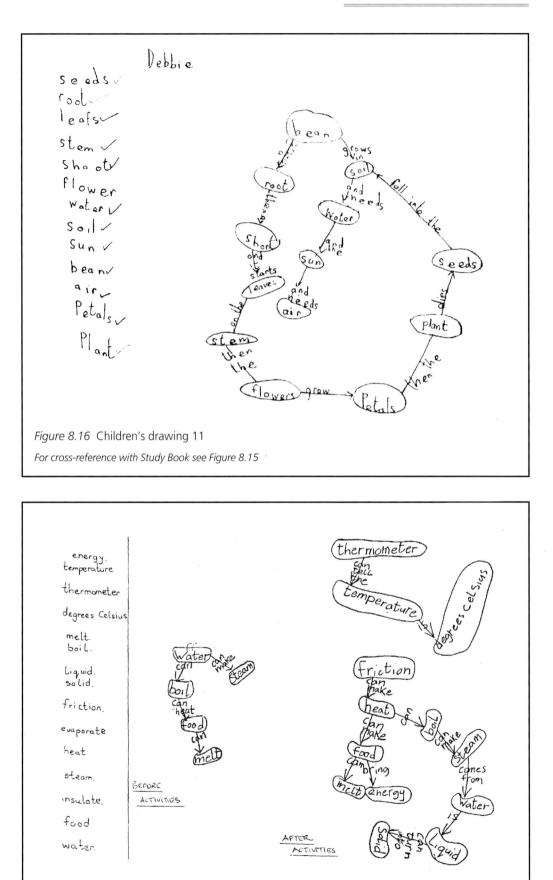

Figure 8.16 Children's drawing 11

For cross-reference with Study Book see Figure 8.15

Figure 8.17 Children's drawing 12

For cross-reference with Study Book see Figure 8.16

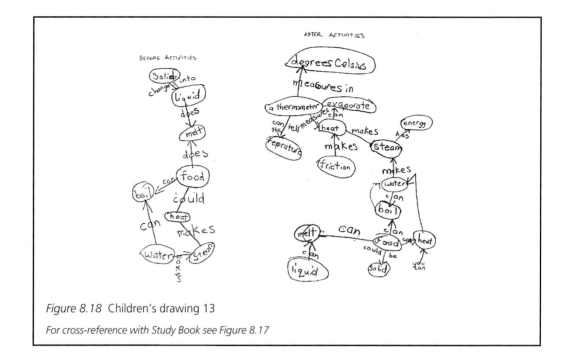

Figure 8.18 Children's drawing 13

For cross-reference with Study Book see Figure 8.17

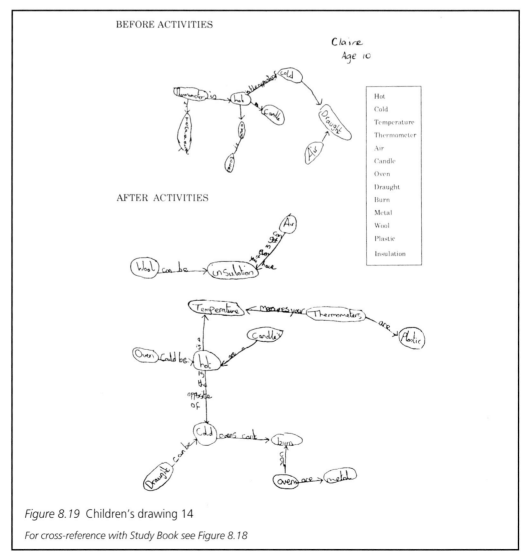

Figure 8.19 Children's drawing 14

For cross-reference with Study Book see Figure 8.18

REFERENCE

Stow, W. (1997) 'Concept mapping – a tool for self-assessment?', *Primary Science Review*, No. 49, pp. 12–15.

FURTHER READING

Atkinson, H. and Bannister, S. (1998) 'Concept maps and annotated drawings', *Primary Science Review*, No. 51, pp. 3–5.

Cross, A. (1992) 'Pictorial concept maps: putting us in the picture', *Primary Science Review*, No. 21, pp. 26–8.

Harlen, W. (2000) *The Teaching of Science in Primary Schools*, 3rd edn, London: David Fulton Publishers.

Kilshaw, M. (1990) 'Using concept maps', *Primary Science Review*, No. 12, pp. 34–6.

Millar, L. and Murdoch, J. (2002) 'A penny for your thoughts', *Primary Science Review*, No. 72, pp. 26–8.

Naylor, S. and Keogh, B. (2000) *Concept Cartoons in Science Education*, Crewe, Cheshire: Millgate House Publishers.

Willson, S. and Willson, M. (1994) 'Concept mapping as an assessment tool', *Primary Science Review*, No. 34, pp. 14–16.

Module 9   Involving children in assessing their work

MODULE GOALS

- To understand the reasons for and the importance of sharing learning goals with children.
- To consider how goals of different kinds can be conveyed to children of various ages.
- To discuss ways of helping children to understand and use criteria for assessing the quality of their work.
- To consider the possible application of different ways of involving children in assessing their own work.
- To discuss the relevance of peer assessment in science.

MODULE OVERVIEW

Involving children in the formative assessment of their own work and in peer assessment means that they can be in control of their learning and take responsibility for recognising the steps they need to take to make progress. An essential prerequisite for this is that the children understand what it is they are intended to learn from their work that is wider than answering the particular questions they are investigating. With this understanding they are in a position to focus their efforts on how they are working as well as on what results they achieve.

Self-assessment and peer assessment also require recognition of the qualities of 'good' work and how 'less than good' work can be made better. The teacher's role is to help them understand and use the quality criteria and then enable them to take the next steps that are indicated.

This module is designed to support teachers in realising the importance of pupil self- and peer assessment and to provide them with some ways of implementing these aspects of learning. It has four main parts, each with a group activity.

- The first part focuses on sharing goals with children and Activity 1 asks participants to work out how they would share, with children of specified ages, the goals the teacher has for particular activities.
- The second part concerns the communication of quality criteria and Activity 2 considers the pros and cons of an example of doing this and brings together other ideas.
- The third part provides some examples of ways of involving pupils in self-assessment that teachers have used and Activity 3 involves considering their suitability in different situations and for different age groups.
- Finally, the fourth part deals with peer assessment and Activity 4 asks participants to discuss the extent to which they consider this is appropriate in different circumstances.

Timing

Total time: 2 hours 35 minutes

Introduction		10 mins
Activity 1	Group work	20 mins
	Feedback and discussion	15 mins
Activity 2	Group work	25 mins
	Feedback and discussion	15 mins
Activity 3	Group work	25 mins
	Feedback and discussion	15 mins
Activity 4	Group work	20 mins
	Feedback and discussion	10 mins

Materials required

- flip chart and pens;
- copies of Activities 1–4 for those not having a copy of the Study Book.

For Activity 1

- OHT with quotations from Pollard *et al.* (see below);
- OHT with quotation from Harlen (2001).

For Activity 2

- copies of the vignette of Mrs B.

For Activity 3

- copies of Approaches A to E.

INTRODUCTION

Points to make in giving an overview and stating the goals of the module:

- One of the significant points emerging from the review of research into formative assessment by Paul Black and Dylan Wiliam (1998) was the value of helping children to assess their own work.
- At the same time they recognised that one of the reasons for this practice not being widespread, despite its benefits, was that pupils that did not have a sufficiently clear picture of the learning goals of their activities.
- However, there is evidence from detailed classroom observations of children that they do assess their work, but they do not do this in relation to the learning goals.

For example, when the PACE (Primary Assessment and Curriculum Experience) project asked children how they felt about their teacher looking at their work, some responses were:

> If I've done something not quite right I feel nervous. We show each other our work. If theirs is better than mine I feel really worried.

I don't like giving my book in 'cause it's a mess – I hide it at the bottom of the pile.

Sometimes I don't want her to look at it because I haven't tried. I haven't put enough effort into it.

It depends what book she's looking at. I like it when she looks at my science and my English because I always get them finished – and maths. I don't like her looking at the rest.

(quotes from Pollard and Triggs, 2000)

It is useful to have these on an OHT.

These quotations indicate that children are making some judgement of their work, although they do not always know how the teacher will judge it. They are worried when they do not know the criteria the teacher will use. Children generally judged their work in terms of its quantity, correctness, neatness, whether it was finished and how much effort was put in. However, these were not necessarily the goals of the particular piece of work and it appeared that generally the children (years 5 and 6 in this case) were unaware of the *learning* that was intended.

This emerged also in a class which was observed as part of the Association for Science Education and King's College, London (AKSIS) project, when some boys spent three lessons finding out which of three kinds of paper was the strongest. Afterwards they were interviewed:

Interviewer: What do you think you have learned from doing your investigations?
Robert: . . . that graph paper is strongest, that green one.
Interviewer: Right, is that it?
Robert: Um . . .
Interviewer: You spent three lessons doing that, seems a long time to spend finding out that graph paper is stronger.
James: Yeah, and we also found which . . . paper is stronger. Not just the graph paper, all of them.

(Harlen, 2001, p. 132)

Again it will be helpful to have these on an OHT.

The boys appeared to be unaware of the process of investigation as a learning goal, in contrast with their teacher. Would the boys have reflected more on their way of investigating had they known that this was a major goal?

Children should know what are the educational aims of their work so that they can focus their effort and judge whether or not they are achieving them. So the first activity is about sharing goals with children.

ACTIVITY 1

Ask teachers to work in pairs or threes, mixing age groups taught if possible. Emphasise that the purpose is to consider the language in which learning goals can be communicated to children. So in this exercise, it is important that they work out the exact words they would use – not just a vague indication. But this cannot be done unless they are clear in their own minds as to the learning goals.

So the first thing is to complete the middle column of Figure 9.1, stating the goals they would have for this activity with the indicated age group. It is anticipated that these would include enquiry skill goals and conceptual understanding goals at the least.

Ask participants to add at least two further pupil activities to Figure 9.1 and specify the age group in each case.

Feedback and discussion

Invite one group to say what the learning goals were that they specified for the first two activities and to read out the words they would use for communicating these to children. Ask another group to do the same and judge the extent of consensus. If there is a considerable difference in level of language, ask these groups to comment on why they chose the words they used. Otherwise, ask for comment from others on any major differences and for suggestions of changes they would make.

Look out for statements that in effect tell the children the specific idea or the conclusion that you hope they will reach. This is not the purpose. What the teacher says should indicate what they will learn *about*, or learn *how*, not the outcome of the activity. *This is the important difference between the aim of the activity and the learning goals.* The teacher may well have to tell the children what they should do, but this should not be confused with sharing the learning goals.

Collect from other groups some examples of the goals of activities that they added. Since there is a lack of good examples of ways of expressing goals for children, it may be helpful to collect a range and either put them on a poster for display or, after the session, type them out for copying to all participants.

Make the point that it is not enough to state the goals at the start; it is important that comments made by the teacher throughout the activity reinforce these goals and that they are revisited at key points, such as when the children are preparing to report their work.

ACTIVITY 2

In the case of some goals, it is necessary to go further, to help children know how to judge whether they have succeeded in producing work of the quality intended. In the children's comments at the beginning of this module, there was a recurring theme that children were anxious 'If I don't know if I've done it right'. This is particularly relevant to the products of the children's work, such as the way they set out their findings, or report their investigation, or explain things. A child can produce an account of their work, but is it a 'good' account?

Being told that one of the goals of an activity is to produce a plan for an investigation that will help them find out, for example, which material is best for keeping an ice cube frozen the longest, is not enough to enable them to judge whether they have a good plan. So there are two aspects to consider – the kind of learning and the criteria to be used in assessing successful achievement. In this activity we are considering the second of these.

Ask participants to read the vignette about Mrs B and then, in groups of three, to discuss parts (a) and (b) of Activity 2. They should prepare to give a structured answer to these questions. Draw attention to part (c). Sharing experiences and other approaches is an important part of collaborative learning in the group.

Feedback and discussion

Ask for reasons why participants think it is (and why some may think it is not) important for children to recognise the criteria of quality that apply to their work. Collect reasons given in response to part (a) on a flip chart and display them. Consider the importance *vis-à-vis* the understanding of goals. The danger has to be avoided of reinforcing the children's use of surface features as quality criteria. The important aspects of quality concerned here are related to content: clarity of expression; sequencing; details of evidence, etc.

The approach Mrs B used meant that the features used to identify quality came from the children and they were, therefore, expressed from the start in language that the children used. This had the advantage of ensuring the children's ownership of the criteria. There could be the disadvantage of including less important, and leaving out more important, aspects. However, by careful questioning and reminding the children of the purpose of the activity the relevant can be given preference over the less relevant. For example, if a child refers to the colouring, the teacher could probe with 'but is that really important if the idea is to let us know what happened and to explain it?' So the discussion reinforces attention to the learning goals of the activity and the children themselves will be more discriminating about what it is important to include.

By contrast, had Mrs B plucked criteria out of the air (as it would seem to the children) and imposed them, then there may not have been the same commitment and understanding in the children.

Collect and discuss other approaches that participants suggest. Examples of the criteria used, as well as how they were reached, will be useful to share and offer as examples for others to try.

ACTIVITY 3

In the last activity we discussed part of what is needed for children to be involved in assessing their own work. Here we take that a stage further, where children apply criteria (implicitly or explicitly) and then use the information this gives to decide what they need to do next (or next time) in relation to improving their work.

One point to bear in mind is that introducing the process of self-assessment for the first time to children needs to be a gradual process. This is a point well made by Shirley Clarke in her book *Unlocking Formative Assessment* (2000). She suggests starting with some questions displayed on the classroom walls to stimulate self-assessment at the end of lessons. These include: 'What do you need more help with about learning to . . . (whatever the learning goal was)?', 'What are you most pleased with about learning to . . . (learning goal)?' Other useful points she makes are: (a) it is helpful for the teacher to model how to answer these kinds of question; and (b) during the period of learning how to self-assess, the teacher might choose one question and relate it to the learning goal of the lesson and then give a period (15 to 30 seconds) for children to think about their answer. Then the teacher either collects responses in a whole class discussion or has the children working in pairs and exchanging their thoughts.

Clarke also makes the point that children can be encouraged to be honest about any problems they are having, if the teacher welcomes comments from those who say they were 'stuck' because this is an essential step in the teacher being able to help them.

Go through the examples A to E and make sure that they are understood. They vary in sophistication and thus in appropriateness to children of different maturity.

Groups of three or four are suitable here. Suggest that some groups begin with B, others C, or D, etc. so as to ensure that all are discussed by some in detail in the time available.

Feedback and discussion

Take each approach and ask one group to share their views on age group and context suitability and on possible modification for other age groups and contexts. Ask for comments but not full reports from other groups before moving on to the next approach.

Points that can be added if not emerging from the feedback:

- A does not seem to go beyond identifying criteria for assessment. However, for very young children it is a good starting point. If the discussion with the teacher takes place some time after the work was carried out, children are more likely to be prepared to discuss improvements. The teacher can then ask, 'You did this some time ago, do you think you now could make it even better?', 'What could you do to improve it?'
- B is valuable as long as it does not become part of boring routine. Make sure there is time to do this thoroughly and to give the child the individual attention he or she needs; less often but more focused is better than hurried and superficial treatment. (This is where peer assessment can come in, to provide more opportunities for pupils to talk about their work to another.)

- C requires some preparation, particularly where children are new to this way of reflecting on their work. It may be helpful to 'model' the discussion of the piece of work in a way they could do with their parents. Even some paired role play is a good use of time if it also helps the children to look more carefully at their work in relation to the criteria of quality.
- D is best used occasionally and if it takes the form of a practical activity. For instance, in one class some pupils set up simple circuits that did not work and asked others to find out why. They were quite ingenious in concealing a piece of a non-conductor in the circuit – but by doing this they tested their own understanding of materials and circuits.
- E has been developed and used with lower secondary pupils, but has potential at the upper primary level. It is particularly applicable to the conceptual understanding in an activity and clearly requires a classroom climate where it is acceptable for pupils to discuss what they do not understand.

ACTIVITY 4

Several of the approaches above require individual children to interact with the teacher. Clearly, opportunities for this are limited. However, children can more frequently discuss their work with each other and help each other to improve. Such discussion needs to be structured, at least when it is new to the children. For example, the children can be arranged in pairs, asked to exchange work and then think of two or three questions about it reflecting the criteria of quality. If it is a conclusion following on something that has been observed or found from an investigation that is being assessed, the questions might be 'Can you tell what was found?', 'Does the conclusion help to answer the question that was being investigated?', 'What would help to make it clearer (a diagram, or series of drawings)?' After such a discussion one child said about having her work assessed by another: 'She said it was hard to understand my investigation so I asked her what sort of thing I should have put to make her understand. Next time I will make sure that I describe things more clearly.'

The discussion can usefully continue in the groups for Activity 3. It is particularly valuable for participants to learn from each other's experience, so make sure that they include this in discussing part (a). Ask them to list appropriate and inappropriate situations in response to (b).

Feedback and discussion

Go briefly through A to E again and ask for comments on relevance for peer assessment. Collect and share any new approaches that participants have used.

Bring together on a flip chart the points made about appropriateness and inappropriateness. There may well not be agreement on these, since those with experience of peer assessment will probably judge it more widely appropriate than those who have not tried it. As long as we are considering assessment for helping learning, there are few circumstances where it cannot be used. There are issues, however, about how to pair children (similar or different attainment; mixed or same sex, etc.).

Points to add if not covered:

- Teacher time is not the only reason for encouraging peer assessment. Having children talk to each other about their work requires them to think through the work again and find words to describe it without the pressure that comes from the unequal relationship between the child (novice) and the teacher (expert).
- It is also consistent with the understanding of learning as being the development of ideas through social interaction as well as through interaction with materials.
- It can help children to respect each other's strengths, especially if pairs are changed on different occasions.
- The class atmosphere – of co-operation and collaboration, and not competition – is an important prerequisite.

Activity 1

For the two activities given in Figure 9.1 and two more that you choose, write down what your goal would be for the children to learn and then how you would convey this to the children (please write the exact words you would use).

Activity and age group	Your learning goals	What to say to the children
Owl pellet dissection (age 8/9)		
Toy cars rolling down a ramp (age 6/7)		

Figure 9.1 Pro-forma: learning goals

For cross-reference with Study Book see Figure 9.1

Developing criteria for judging the quality of work

Here's how one teacher helped her class to identify what makes a good report of an investigation:

Mrs B gave each group of children two examples (presented anonymously) of accounts of an investigation written by children in the same class in earlier years. One was a clear account, well set out so that the reader could understand what had been done, although the writing was uneven and there were some words not spelled correctly. There were diagrams to help the account, with labels. The results were in a table, and the writer had said what he or she thought they meant. However, it was admitted that the results didn't completely answer the initial question and there was a comment about how things could have been improved. The other account was tidy, attractive to look at (the diagrams were coloured in but not labelled) but contained none of the features in the content shown in the other piece.

She asked the children to compare the pieces of work and list the good and poor features of each one. Then they were asked to say what were the most important things that made a 'good' report. The class brainstormed their ideas and Mrs B collected them and later made copies for all the children to keep in their science folders. But she also went on to explore with the children how to carry out an investigation in order to be able to write a good report. These points too were brought together in the children's words and printed out for them.

Activity 2

Discuss in your group (or think about, if you are working alone):

(a) How important is it for children to understand the criteria of quality of their work in science, as well as the learning goals?

(b) What are the pros and cons of the method used by Mrs B? Would it be suitable for all age groups? Would it allow for a development in the expectations of quality as children get older?

(c) What other ways have you used, or can suggest, for helping children to understand what is expected in terms of the quality of their work?

Encouraging children to assess their own work

Self-assessment is not something that can be introduced all at once to children who are not used to it. Shirley Clarke, in *Unlocking Formative Assessment* (2000), suggests starting with some questions displayed on the classroom walls to stimulate self-assessment at the end of lessons. These include: 'What do you need more help with about learning to . . . (whatever the learning goal was)?', 'What are you most pleased with about learning to . . . (learning goal)?' Clarke suggests, for one to three weeks, spending some time at the end of each lesson to model some answers children might give. After the modelling period, the teacher might choose one question, relate it to the learning goal of the lesson and give a period (15 to 30 seconds) for children to think about their answer. Then the teacher either collects responses in a whole class discussion or has the children working in pairs and exchanging their thoughts, or he or she discusses with a group at a time, while other groups do other things.

Clarke makes a useful point about encouraging self-evaluation by responding to children who say they were 'stuck' by welcoming this as an essential step in finding out how to help the learning. By the same token she suggests that a teacher might respond to children who find no problem by telling them that this is worrying because they may not be learning anything new. Activity 3 lists some other ways in which teachers have engaged children in self-assessment of their work.

Activity 3

Some examples of approaches to self-assessment:

A   Selecting their 'best' work from their folder or note book and explaining to the teacher why these pieces have been chosen.

B   Taking any piece of work and answering the questions: 'What have I done well?', 'What could I have done better?', 'What do I need to do to improve?'

C   As B, but presenting this to their parents/guardians on parents' evening.

D   Asking children to set a task for their peers designed to show if they have understood a concept.

E   Using 'traffic lights', that is, children mark their own work in terms of their understanding, using a green spot is they are confident that they understand, yellow if they are not totally confident and red if they feel that they don't understand something about their work.

For each of these approaches to encouraging self-assessment and for others that you have used, decide the age groups and circumstances in which they may be most appropriate and suggest how they might be modified for other age groups, then complete Figure 9.2.

Approach	Age group and context suitability	Modification for other age groups and contexts
A		
B		
C		
D		
E		
Other		

Figure 9.2 Age group and context suitability

For cross-reference with Study Book see Figure 9.2

Activity 4

(a) Which of the approaches in Activity 3 can be adapted to peer assessment? Can you add any other approaches to peer assessment from your experience?

(b) In what circumstances (age group, context, purpose) is peer assessment appropriate? In what circumstances do you consider it would be inappropriate?

REFERENCES

Black, P. and Wiliam, D. (1998) *Inside the Black Box*, London: School of Education, King's College, London.

Clarke, S. (2000) *Unlocking Formative Assessment*, London: Hodder and Stoughton.

Pollard, A and Triggs, P. with Broadfoot, P., McNess, E. and Osborn, M. (2000) *What Pupils Say: Findings from the PACE (Primary Assessment, Curriculum and Experience) Project*, London: Continuum.

FURTHER READING

Goldsworthy, A., Watson, R. and Wood-Robinson, V. (2000) *Investigations: Targeting Learning*, Hatfield: Association for Science Education. Publication of the AKSIS (Association for Science Education and King's College, London) project.

Harlen, W. (2001) *Primary Science: Taking the Plunge,* 2nd edn, Portsmouth, NH: Heinemann.

Lindsay, C. and Clarke, S. (2001) 'Enhancing primary science through self- and paired-assessment', *Primary Science Review*, No. 68, pp. 15–18.

Module 10 Providing effective feedback to children

MODULE GOALS

- To help participants recognise that it is important to be clear about the evidence in children's work before making inferences about their thinking.
- To identify the features of effective feedback on children's written work.
- To consider how to give feedback that helps children take the next steps in their learning.
- For participants to reflect on the purposes of marking and whether every piece of work requires the same detailed attention.

MODULE OVERVIEW

This module is about giving feedback to children of the kind that will help their learning. It includes feedback given orally and in writing. Written feedback, or 'marking', is often seen as a chore by teachers that helps them check that work has been done by children but may not always have a significant part to play in the children's learning. The module activities are designed to enable participants to consider how feedback can be more effective and thus make better use of the time spent on marking.

There is often more in children's work than appears on first – and fast – reading. So before deciding how to respond it is important to be clear about the evidence. Activity 1 takes participants through a structured exercise in which they are asked to suspend judgement on some children's work until they have looked at it carefully and described what is there. In Activity 2 participants consider some examples of teachers' feedback on children's work and reflect on the principles that might guide marking practice. In Activity 3 these guidelines are applied in considering oral and written feedback on particular pieces of work.

Timing

Total time: 2 hours 30 minutes

Introduction		10 mins
Activity 1	Group work	50 mins
	Feedback and discussion	15 mins
Activity 2	Group work	20 mins
	Feedback and discussion	15 mins
Activity 3	Group work	25 mins
	Feedback and discussion	15 mins

Materials required

For Activity 1

- a copy of Figures 10.1 and 10.2 for everyone (as they may want to make notes on them during the group work);
- a copy of Activity 1 for those who don't have the Study Book;
- flip chart or overhead with questions for discussion of part (b).

For Activity 2

- copies of Figures 10.3, 10.4 and 10.5 for each group;
- copy of Activity 2 for those without the Study Book;
- copy of points by Evans (2001) on an OHP;
- flip chart to record guidelines for effective feedback.

For Activity 3

- copy of Activity 3 for those without the Study Book;
- OHP transparency of Thomas's work in Figure 10.7.

INTRODUCTION

As we have noted in other modules, it is the child who has to do the learning, so the teacher has to help the children to recognise how their ideas match up to what is expected and thus to realise what they need to do to take the next step in their learning. Involvement in self-assessment (see Module 9) can provide some of this information, but some comes from the teacher. The purpose of this module is to consider *what kind of teacher feedback is most useful*?

Points to make:

- We are concerned here with feedback (i.e. marking, when it is written work) that has a formative purpose, that is, to help learning.
- Feedback should help children's understanding in several ways: by indicating further steps to take in learning, by helping to show children how they can take these steps, by motivating further learning.
- Feedback has both a short-term and a longer-term effect. In the short term it contributes to the next steps in learning; in the longer term it contributes to the pupils' view of how successful they are in undertaking certain kinds of task. The feedback they obtain from success or failure on previous tasks accumulates to influence their

future motivation for learning. This is an important reason for ensuring that children are not continually faced with tasks which are too difficult and that feedback is non-judgemental.

- What is suggested in the module activities might well seem to be too onerous for teachers to incorporate in their regular work. One of the points to consider in addressing this is the purpose of marking in particular cases. Some purposes, for example to check on whether work has been done, can be achieved in other ways. In other cases children can mark their own work (see Module 9) and in others, again, it may not be necessary to mark every child's work.
- Children should be given time to consider the feedback from teachers and, if necessary, time to respond to it. Then both teacher and child will see the marking as important.
- Seen in this way, marking is an additional opportunity for children to receive individual attention from their teacher.

ACTIVITY 1

Introduce this by emphasising that it is a professional development exercise that is not intended as a suggested procedure for regular practice, although there are messages from it that should influence how participants look at children's work. Children's work gives valuable clues to their thinking. If we consider it only superficially, then the feedback cannot be as useful for helping learning as it otherwise might be.

(a) For this activity participants should be in groups of no less than four (and probably no more than five). One person in each group is nominated as the 'chairperson'. You should identify these before the activity and if possible go through the procedures with them. In particular, give them the following information about the two pieces of work to be considered, so that they can introduce the work to the group.

- Lee is 5 years old. The class was undertaking activities about feet after the teacher had read them a story called *Alfie's Feet* (by Shirley Hughes). In groups, the children were investigating different kinds of footwear to see if it was waterproof, drawing round their feet, measuring them, casting shadows of their feet and drawing the shadows. While Lee was investigating the shadow of his foot, his teacher noted that Lee 'noticed the concentric circle pattern made by the torch; noticed the size of the shadow changed when the torch was moved'.
- Tony is 10. His class had been studying various environments, including polar regions. They became very interested in how icebergs float. They floated some ice cubes in water and the teacher asked them to continue at home, using blocks of ice of different size and measuring the amount of ice above and below the water. Then they were asked to write up their investigation.

Make sure that all the participants read the procedures in Activity 1 before starting and explain, if necessary, that the purpose of the structure is to experience careful study of the work before making an interpretation. Ask chairpersons to keep the focus at each phase on what is prescribed, that is, accept only observations (points about what is there) in phase 3 and keep inferences to phase 5.

Chairpersons should keep to time and in phase 4 summarise all the observations that are agreed. In phase 6, there may be alternative interpretations, which participants should be able to justify.

(b) After both pieces of work have been considered using these procedures, ask all groups to spend 10 minutes 'debriefing' and preparing to report on their views of the experience. You might suggest these questions (written on a flip chart) to guide this discussion:

- To what extent did the exercise change your insights into the children's work?
- What were your reflections on the process of considering pupils' work?
- What insights into these pupils' thinking might such study provide for their teacher?
- Are there any implications for routine marking – how likely is it that evidence available in children's work may remain unused?

Feedback and discussion

There is no need to collect details of each group's response to the pieces of work. Any relevant points are likely to emerge in illustration of points about the participants' perceptions about the activity. Use the questions suggested above to collect reactions.

Bring together the points made, recalling that the activity was a professional development, not a regular procedure for considering pupils' work. Bring out the implications there are for regular work and ask participants to bear them in mind in the following activities.

ACTIVITY 2

Participants should preferably work in pairs or groups of three for this activity. Ask them to read the work carefully, as in the last activity, and make their own interpretation of the work based on the evidence before commenting on the teacher's comments. They should spend no more than 10 minutes on the children's work and the teacher's feedback. Then spend the rest of the time reflecting on their reasons for their reactions to the teacher's responses and using these to identify principles for giving effective feedback.

Feedback and discussion

Ask for some responses to (a) and (b) from one group and ask them from reasons for their comments on what the teacher wrote. Briefly collect from other groups additional points or different points of view. Then move to collect ideas for 'guidelines' for effective feedback.

List the points on a flip chart, taking one from each group until all have been collected. Compare these with the following 'do's and don'ts' based on ones proposed by ex-HMI Neville Evans in an article in *Primary Science Review* (2001).

1 Plan the task for the children so that there are worthwhile learning outcomes.
2 Identify one or two aspects of the work that are of particular interest as the foci of the marking.
3 Comment only on the science-specific aspects of the work (unless the task was specifically set for careful presentation and accuracy in using language, for instance).
4 Avoid judgemental comments and, above all, scores, marks or grades, since these divert children's attention from what they have done.
5 Pinpoint weak aspects, such as misuse of terms or conclusions that are not based on evidence.
6 Don't pose rhetorical questions ('Do you think so?', 'I wonder why?').
7 By all means pose questions, so long as the child understands that a response will be expected and will be read.
8 Don't waste effort and time on marking tasks that are mainly about reinforcement.
9 Manage marking by clearly identifying what work is worth marking for its science. Any other work should be acknowledged by signature, not by the ubiquitous tick, which is often interpreted by pupils (and parents and others) as commendation.

To these we might add the useful suggestions from Goldsworthy *et al.* that it is important to give pupils time to read and react to comments. Their suggestions include:

> When you hand the work back allow pupils to work in small groups and ask them to look at one another's work and your comments. Ask them to work out what each of them

needs to do to improve. You could try focusing on a group containing higher achievers, another average group and a group containing slower learners.

(2000, p. 38)

This is an approach that is suggested with older juniors in mind, but the idea could well be adapted for younger children.

Use this list to add to what the participants have produced, if it suggests points that participants wish to include, but don't impose it on them. They should feel ownership of their guidelines and be able to justify them from their own thinking. Write them on a chart and display on the wall for all to see (or make copies if this is possible in the time). Participants will apply them in the next activity.

ACTIVITY 3

This activity takes the discussion of feedback to the point of deciding the wording appropriate for particular work and particular children. To set the scene for the first set of work, show Thomas's drawing (Figure 10.7) on an OHP. Thomas was a young child and feedback would be oral. Nonetheless the participants should try to identify the exact form of words they would use. For the second set of work the participants should consider the written responses that they would make.

Participants should work in twos or threes, completing one set of agreed answers. In the first column they should write down what they infer about the children's ideas or skills, having looked carefully at what is there. Then, with their 'guidelines for effective feedback' in mind they identify the content and form of the feedback they would provide for the children.

Feedback and discussion

Collect the comments of one group on the pieces of work in the first set, focusing on their interpretation of the children's thinking. Then pick one child's work (e.g. Thomas) and ask for the wording of the oral feedback. Write this on the flip chart and ask for variations from other groups. There is likely to be a good deal in common for the different children, and so it may not be necessary to go through the full set.

In the second set there are important differences between the children's work which will be reflected in the feedback. Spend some time on the participants' interpretations of the work. Did they, for instance, note that Daryl used water instead of soup? Would Mary and Yasmin really use soup? So have they thought through their plans sufficiently? Neither Mary nor Daryl has said how they would decide which was best. Yasmin has not considered how to set up a trial and none of them has mentioned that the quantities of soup or water need to be the same. Find out what other differences the participants noted before they decided how to respond to each one.

As you collect comments and ideas for feedback, question the participants about the evidence on which they are basing their responses. Emphasise that effective feedback is informed feedback and can be an important part of teacher–pupil interaction if both parties take it seriously.

As with other aspects of education, in respect of marking 'less may mean better learning'; a smaller quantity of work thoroughly considered is worth more than all work treated super-ficially. Participants may well point out that there is a strong expectation from parents and sometimes from the school management that all work has to be marked. However, schools are increasingly recognising the need to review marking practices, particularly in the light of the research that shows that many existing practices need to be changed. The purpose of the marking of children's work has to be carefully identified. Just as there are different aims of assessment, there are different aims of marking. We have been considering here marking for helping learning, rather than for accountability. The extent that what has been discussed can serve other purposes, such as communicating with parents, depends on how well the reasons for adopting guidelines for effective feedback are disseminated in the school and to parents.

Activity 1

This is a structured exercise for professional development, not intended as a regular teacher activity.

(a) Work in groups of four. One of the group is nominated as the chairperson for the discussion. In this role he or she introduces the pieces of work, keeps time and makes sure that everyone makes a contribution. Each group follows these procedures:

1   The chairperson introduces the work and the procedures (2 minutes).
2   All read the work carefully in silence (3 minutes).
3   Each person has 2 minutes to describe what (s)he notices about the work.
4   The chairperson brings the points together as an agreed statement about the evidence.
5   Each person has 2 minutes to weigh what (s)he infers about the child's thinking – what is understood and what is not understood.
6   These ideas are brought together to consider what the next steps for the pupil might be.

Apply these procedures, first to the work of Lee (Figure 10.1) and then to that of Tony (Figure 10.2).

Figure 10.1 Lee's drawing of his foot

For cross-reference with Study Book see Figure 10.1

Activity 1 *continued*

(b) Finally, prepare to report on the experience of paying careful attention to the evidence before making inferences about the children's work.

Icebergs in water

Tony

Each time the iceberg floated with most of it under the water. It was only the surface above the water. I tried it with a flat circle, a round cylinder shape and a small ball of ice Each time mostly the same thing happened, it floated to the top with only the surface showing the rest was under the water.

I measured it with a tape measure.

The cylinder was 1 inch $\frac{1}{4}$ of that was above the water.

It was hard to measure it under the water.

Figure 10.2 Tony's discussion of icebergs

Source: Primary Science, No. 42, p. 2

For cross-reference with Study Book see Figure 10.2

Activity 2

Look at the examples of children's work in Figures 10.3, 10.4. and 10.5. The children were 8 or 9 year olds. They were exploring evaporation by leaving small quantities of various solutions exposed in the classroom and by putting wet paper towels in various places. The goal was to learn about water vapour in the air.

(a)   Read carefully what the children wrote and the teacher's comments. Given the purpose of the activity, what is your view of the teacher's comments in each case?

(b)   How would you respond to this work? Complete Figure 10.6.

(c)   In your group, devise some guidelines for marking children's work so that the feedback helps their learning.

Last week the coffee was he dry it was wet
but now it is dry up
the coffee is dryed up and it looks liake toffe
it has drays up

Why has it dried up? I think because we left it
for a week
Where has the water gone? it has gone to the air

Figure 10.3 Child's view of evaporation 1

For cross-reference with Study Book see Figure 10.3

Stacey
Tuesday 10th November
Me and Stephen wet a peice
of paper. we wet it the same
time. I shut My desk and
Stephen left is open a little
way we could not find out
which one dried up first
So we had to wet it a again
but the paper was so slimy
It riped so we got a new
piece but we wet it at
10 o'clock. it never dried
while we were at home it
never dried. today we checked
if it was dry Mine was wet
Stephens peaice was dry so
we wet it again we wet
the same time we have Just
seen if they were dry Mine
was wet Stephens was dry
now we are righting about it

Stacey

Why do you think your paper
is still wet and Stephen's paper
has dried? Stephens paper has
been getting air Mine ds not
because My Desk was shut.

Figure 10.4 Child's view of evaporation 2

For cross-reference with Study Book see Figure 10.4

Activity 2 continued

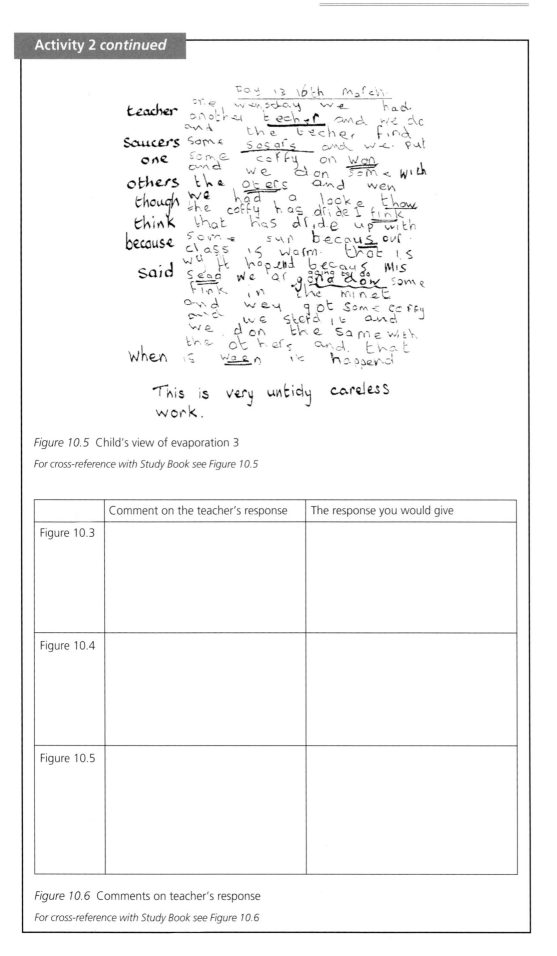

Figure 10.5 Child's view of evaporation 3

For cross-reference with Study Book see Figure 10.5

	Comment on the teacher's response	The response you would give
Figure 10.3		
Figure 10.4		
Figure 10.5		

Figure 10.6 Comments on teacher's response

For cross-reference with Study Book see Figure 10.6

Activity 3

For the two sets of work described below, use your 'guidelines for effective feedback' to decide how to respond, orally for the first set and in writing for the second set.

Set 1

Context: 6 and 7 year olds were investigating 'materials'. After a discussion about what their (wooden) chairs were made from and where that came from, tracing the wood back to trees, the teacher asked them to do the same thing for other objects: a handkerchief, a cup, a leather belt, etc. She suggested they could use books to find out what they didn't know.

The children drew a series of pictures (see Figure 10.7) and also wrote about each stage. Figure 10.8 shows what six children wrote by their drawings (the children's spelling has been corrected).

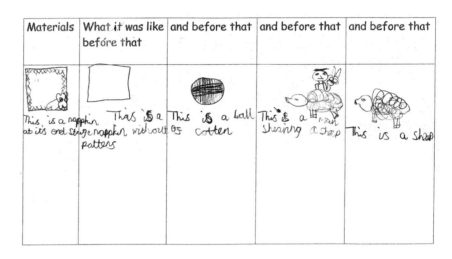

Figure 10.7 Thomas's ideas about the origins of a handkerchief

For cross-reference with Study Book see Figure 10.7

	Object	What it was before that	. . . and before that	. . . and before that	. . . and before that
Thomas	Handkerchief	This is a handkerchief without its patterns	This is a cotton ball	This is a man shearing sheep	This is a sheep
Paul	Cup	Plain cup	Fire it in a kiln to make it hard	Clay	Dig clay from the ground
Lucy	Cotton cloth	Cotton thread	Cotton being cleaned	Cotton factory	A sheep
Katie	Leather belt	Strip of leather	Wash the skin	This is the skin of a cow	This is a cow
Elish	Cotton	A factory	Spinning wheel	Thread	A sheep

Figure 10.8 Children's views of original states

For cross-reference with Study Book see Figure 10.8

For each of these, write your own comments in Figure 10.9 and then what you would say to the children in response.

	Your comments/ interpretation	What you would say to the children
Thomas		
Paul		
Lucy		
Katie		
Elish		

Figure 10.9 Comments to children

For cross-reference with Study Book see Figure 10.9

Set 2

Context: the plans in Figure 10.10 were written by 11 year olds in answer to being asked what they would do to see which kind of container would keep soup hot for the longest time.

	'This is what I will do'	Your comments/ interpretation	What you would write in response
Mary	I would take some soup and pour it into the different cups and take the temperatures and see which was best.		
Daryl	I would take the three containers and fill each one with water at the same temperature and put lids on them all. I would put a hole in the lids and put thermometers through them. Then I would leave them and read the thermometers every minute. I would draw a graph of the centigrade at each minute.		
Yasmin	I would see how hot they were after a certain time. The best one would be the one that was hottest for the longest time.		

Figure 10.10 Children's views on keeping soup hot

For cross-reference with Study Book see Figure 10.10

REFERENCES

Evans, N. (2001) 'Thoughts on assessment and marking', *Primary Science Review*, No. 68, pp. 24–6.
Goldsworthy, A., Watson, R. and Wood-Robinson, V. (2000) *Investigations: Targeted Learning*, Hatfield: Association for Science Education. Publication of the AKSIS (Association for Science Education and King's College, London) project.

FURTHER READING

James, M. (1998) *Using Assessment for School Improvement*, Oxford: Heinemann.
Leakey, A. (2001) 'Fantastic feedback', *Primary Science Review*, No. 68, pp. 22–3.

Module 11   Science and other subjects

MODULE GOALS

- Teachers can plan more economically for learning, using on occasions an integrated approach to achieving learning outcomes, linking subjects appropriately rather than in a way which loses the integrity of the subject.
- Children see their learning in an holistic way and can see the links between different areas of learning.
- Teachers are able to make cross-curricular links in their planning which are relevant and meaningful.
- Learning objectives and outcomes are clear for the different activities, those for each curriculum area being clearly defined and pertinent to the subject.

MODULE OVERVIEW

Although many schools teach science as a separate subject, there are some who integrate science with other subjects, particularly with the younger children. However, even if subjects are taught separately, there are many opportunities for developing skills and ideas which cross subject boundaries. In this module we consider how a story can be a starting point for cross-curricular activity with some very young children and think about how geography, history and science can be taught through a study of the local area. Opportunities for developing literacy and numeracy in science contexts are also explored.

There are six group activities:

- Activity 1 is focused on a story which has been used with young children. The cross-curricular links are explored and the learning objectives are discussed.
- Activity 2 considers science and citizenship.
- Activity 3 involves looking at some roofs and thinking about how scientific enquiry can be developed alongside history and geography.
- Activity 4 is focused on the development of writing. A range of genres is presented and participants are asked to consider how these can be used in a scientific context.
- Activity 5 considers the use of non-fiction science-based texts.
- Activity 6 looks at the use of measurement in science.

Timing

Total time: circa 3 hours

Introduction		5 mins
Activity 1	Group work	20 mins
	Feedback and discussion	15 mins
Activity 2	Group work	10 mins
	Feedback and discussion	15 mins
Activity 3	Group work	15 mins
	Feedback and discussion	15 mins
Activity 4	Group work	15 mins
	Feedback and discussion	15 mins
Activity 5	Group work	20 mins
	Feedback and discussion	15 mins
Activity 6	Group work	10 mins
	Feedback and discussion	15 mins

Materials required

For Activity 1

- copies of the story and the activity.

For Activity 2

- copies of the activity.

For Activity 3

- copies of the activity;
- copies of the photograph and the sketch of a cross-section of a roof.

For Activity 4

- copies of the task and the pro-forma (Figure 11.4).

For Activity 5

- a selection of non-fiction science-based books or texts;
- copies of the pro-forma (Figure 11.5).

For Activity 6

- copies of the activity.

INTRODUCTION

General points to make:

- the appropriateness of cross-curricular work, with the move towards subjects being taught separately;
- whether this approach is more suitable for younger or older children;
- planning issues and keeping track of which aspects of the curriculum are being covered;
- the need for clarity about what is being taught and that learning objectives are clearly identified;
- the importance of links between subjects and how learning can be enhanced;
- the importance of the order of teaching in different curriculum areas so that pupils have the prerequisite knowledge, understanding and skills they need.

ACTIVITY 1

This activity involves participants in considering how a story can be used as a starting point for learning in different curriculum areas. Participants work in pairs or threes to list the possibilities for activities which may be generated by the story and then list some possible learning outcomes resulting from these activities. Ask each group to take one or two curriculum areas to feed back as a starter, with other groups adding extra ideas.

Feedback and discussion

Possible areas that may arise from reading the story are as follows.

Science

- Properties of materials, wet and dry sand, materials for the shelter and boat, water-proofing, similarities and differences.
- Healthy eating – what makes a healthy diet? Is the picnic they put together healthy?
- How quickly do different blocks of ice melt? Wrapping ice cubes in different materials to compare how quickly they melt. Exploring with ice-balloons.
- Comparing different boat shapes or sail shapes to see which moves fastest.

PSHE

- Empathy, understanding feelings, caring for others.
- Consider the dilemmas of the characters. What are their needs? How do they feel?
- Have the children ever felt like this? What did they do?

English

Any story has the potential to be used in many ways, so any list here would be extensive. One possibility to link with the PSHE would be to look at adjectives that describe feelings.

Design Technology

- Building a shelter, repairing the boat, making a smaller raft from the original boat.
- Can children design and make an island in the sand tray? What would the island need?
- Methods for attracting attention of other boats.
- Following on from healthy eating in science, designing and making sandwich fillings.

Mathematics

Measuring.

Geography

- Draw a map of the island from the description.
- Mark on the map the features described in the story.

The possible learning outcomes from the story are as follows.

Science

- Pupils are able to recognise common materials and understand why they are chosen for particular purposes.
- Pupils are able to describe some similarities and differences between materials, e.g. wet and dry sand.
- Pupils are able to use scientific terminology to describe materials, e.g. rigid, flexible, strong, waterproof.
- Pupils understand that eating the right kind of food helps to keep us healthy and which food should be eaten less often and why.
- Pupils can explain that ice melts when left at room temperature, and that some materials are more effective than others at keeping things cold.
- Pupils know that different shapes of boat travel at different speeds.
- Pupils know that sail size and shape can affect how fast a boat can travel.

The investigation using boats could result in the acquisition of many enquiry skills, as could that on the insulating properties of materials.

PSHE

- Pupils recognise the need to care for each other.
- Pupils learn to work co-operatively.
- Pupils are able to recognise feelings and learn how to cope with them.
- Pupils recognise that we all have different talents and how each person can contribute.

English

Pupils have an increased range of vocabulary to describe feelings.

Design Technology

The activities again give rise to a range of learning outcomes including:

- the ability to generate ideas;
- communicating their ideas by drawing and making models;
- selecting tools and materials;
- measuring, cutting and shaping materials;
- joining and combining materials in different ways;
- using finishing techniques;
- the hygiene procedures associated with preparing food;
- talking about their ideas and saying what works well and what they would change.

The activities give the opportunity to work with a range of materials including food and textiles.

Mathematics

- Pupils measure using non-standard or standard units.
- Pupils choose suitable measuring instruments.
- Pupils read the scales to the nearest labelled division with appropriate accuracy.

Geography

- Pupils are able to ask geographical questions.
- Pupils can express their views about the island environment.
- Pupils can make maps.
- Pupils can use geographical vocabulary.

ACTIVITY 2

This activity involves participants in identifying ways in which science might provide a context for developing skills in citizenship.

PSHE has always had an important part in primary education; however, the aspect of Citizenship has received increased emphasis, particularly with its statutory introduction at Key Stages 3 and 4.

The following is an extract from the National Curriculum *Handbook for Primary Teachers Key Stages 1 and 2*:

Key Stage 1

Pupils should be taught:

- to take part in discussions with one other person and the whole class
- to take part in a debate about topical issues
- to realise that people and other living things have needs, and that they have responsibilities to meet them
- what improves and harms their local, natural and built environments and about some ways people look after them
- to realise that money comes from different sources and can be used for different purposes.

Key Stage 2

Pupils should be taught:

- to research, discuss and debate topical issues, problems and events
- that there are different kinds of responsibilities, rights and duties at home, at school and in the community, and that these can sometimes conflict with each other
- to reflect on spiritual, moral, social and cultural issues, using imagination to understand other people's experiences
- to resolve differences by looking at alternatives, making decisions and explaining choices
- that resources can be allocated in different ways and that these economic choices affect individuals, communities and the sustainability of the environment
- to explore how the media present information

Feedback and discussion

Since 'science' can have a 'bad press' it provides a fruitful area for controversy – genetic engineering, cloning, depleting the Earth's resources, polluting the atmosphere – the list continues. How much of this is science rather than applied science or technology, or economics is debatable, however, since a degree of comfort has become the norm for significant proportions of the globe, many do not understand the cost of these, the implications for their continued availability, and would not wish their comforts to be removed. The other side of the 'bad press coin' is exactly that, the benefits which accrue from scientific endeavour in prolonging life, relieving suffering, improving standards of living and leisure.

At an early age children can understand the needs of living things, including themselves. They are particularly quick to identify with environmental issues – the threat of pollution, litter and threats to species.

Even young children can study through other subjects, e.g. geography and history, the lifestyle of children in other countries and in other times. They can understand the need for an adequate and varied diet and as they get older, the importance of particular types of food. They can compare life in previous times with life now, including the quality of life for children, what they were expected to do in terms of child labour and the conditions in which they lived. They can discuss the introduction of medicines. Poor sanitation and the lack of clean water, and low levels of rainfall can all be related to the need to care for people on a global scale. Filtration, water treatment, evaporation, condensation as topics will all arise. Flooding, both in England and elsewhere can be discussed, along with what can be done to alleviate suffering.

In discussing changes in materials, burning, and in particular the burning of forests, can be discussed and the impact upon the climate and local economy. Local issues, such as the siting of a landfill site or factory, can provide useful material for debate on the environment. How the media report on scientific and environmental issues can be examined.

Looking at roofs: linking geography, history and science

Although in many schools the older children have separate lessons for history, geography, science and other areas of the curriculum, teachers often make links between subjects so that children can see their learning as an holistic experience. In a study of the local area this is particularly appropriate. In the case of Mickland School, Caversham, the Micklands estate is an easily recognisable enclave (see Figure 11.3). The houses of Micklands are easily identifiable because of the distinctive feature of the sharply angled roof line.

As you would expect, an area where the houses are noticeably unique has an interesting history. The estate was founded in the 1930s by a movement of labour from Wales under the Land Development Association and many local people remember calling it the 'Welsh Colony'. The design of houses in a particular area is often influenced by the people who first settled there. When we study the history and geography of any local area, the buildings provide a stimulating starting point.

The roof lines of buildings in various locations can provide not only a link to the history of the area but also to the geography. The climate of the country and the type of terrain have an influence on the design of the buildings. In Malta people are encouraged to build houses with flat roofs so that they can place water-collecting tanks there and, in places which have a great deal of snow, houses have particularly steep pitched roofs so that the snow will slide off.

Teachers should encourage children to be curious and to ask questions which they can investigate. This is true whether the questions are of a geographical, historical or scientific nature.

ACTIVITY 3

In this activity, teachers are asked to look at a photograph of some houses and to think of questions which might be answered by scientific enquiry. Children who raise these questions would be encouraged to find out answers for themselves and these answers might help them to understand why certain materials are used for a variety of purposes and why buildings are designed in particular ways.

Feedback and discussion

Observation of the photograph will reveal:

- steeply pitched roofs and a flat roof over the garage extension;
- a 'lean-to' roof at the side of one of the houses.

Questions which may be raised might be:

- What happens to rain and snow when they fall onto the roofs?
- Why do houses have gutters?
- Why are flat roofs covered with roofing felt?
- Are 'flat' roofs really flat or do they have a slight slope?

Investigations which might be carried out by practical activity:

- Make model houses from shoe-boxes. Make some with flat roofs, some with slightly sloping roofs and some with steeply sloping roofs. Cover the roofs with plastic film and test to see what happens when simulated snow made from tiny polystyrene balls, which can be collected from packaging material, is dropped onto the roofs.
- Do the same with 'rain' produced by pouring water from a watering can.
- Observe roofing felt and try to make a similar product with a variety of materials. Test to see which of the home-made roof coverings are the most waterproof.

There will probably be some discussion about the advisability of taking children out into the local area and giving them the opportunity to observe roofs. They will then be able to observe the different types of roofing tiles. Old houses may have slate roofs but most modern houses have tiles which are made of concrete. Building suppliers may be able to provide small samples of these materials for children to observe and to test for strength and porosity.

If it is possible to view a house under construction, then children can prepare sketches such as the one in Figure 11.1 which will help them to think about how the roofs are joined to the buildings, how the tiles are attached to the rafters and how the fascia board and the soffit board support the gutters. A collection of materials which are used in the construction of roofs can very often lead to further questions for investigation.

Children can be encouraged to carry out research into the types of materials used for gutters. In the lifetime of their great-grandparents and grandparents there will have been wooden gutters, metal gutters and plastic gutters and the reasons for the changes are nothing to do with fashion but to do with the availability of new materials and their properties. Perhaps children could find out for themselves that plastic will not rust or rot.

Possible learning outcomes of these experiences might be (see Module 1):

- to predict what might happen;
- to plan and carry out a fair test;
- to make relevant observations;
- to interpret evidence and to draw conclusions;
- to compare materials on the basis of their properties;
- to understand how the design of a house is influenced by the weather.

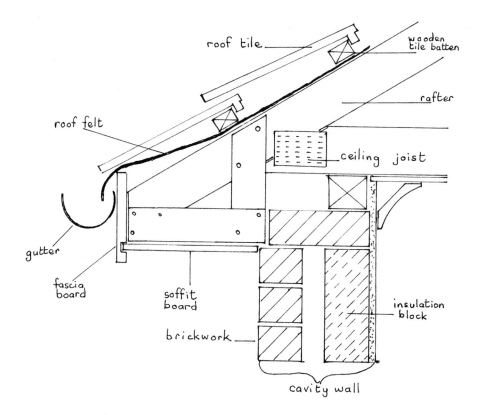

Figure 11.1 Sketch of cross-section of a roof

For cross-reference with Study Book see Figure 11.4

Perhaps the discussion will be extended to a consideration of the design of other homes. Older children could be encouraged to use the Internet to search for images of different types of houses and there could well be some discussion about how the design is influenced by the climate in different places. If you consider the need to collect rainwater in Malta, there could well be some investigation into the best materials for making a water storage tank and the best shape for the tank.

Perhaps children could be asked why they think that the walls of houses in very hot countries are often painted in very light colours and whether or not cave dwellers would be hot or cold in their caves. Questions of this type can be answered by carrying out practical investigations and yet help children to understand the influence which the weather has on our lives. Further research about the natural resources of a geographical region might also lead to some ideas about why homes are built using certain materials.

ACTIVITY 4

Numeracy and literacy links

No-one would dispute that if children are to take their place in society, then the skills of literacy and numeracy are very important. However, there are many ways in which literacy and numeracy skills can be developed while at the same time providing children with opportunities to develop scientific ideas.

There are three activities in this section. The first part focuses on the different forms of writing with which children need to be familiar and the second part on the way in which information books about science can be used. The final part considers measurement in science.

The focus in Activity 4 is on suggesting a variety of ways in which children's writing skills can be developed as they think about and record their science investigations and observations. You will probably want to stress the importance of being quite clear about the learning objectives of the lessons. Some might be science-focused and the writing will be a way of reinforcing understanding of the science ideas or a means of recording results. At other times the main focus will be on developing the skills of writing using a science-based context. Give each group a copy of the pro-forma Figure 11.4 and ask them to identify contexts for the various forms of writing.

Feedback and discussion

Ask the group to present their ideas and collate these on a flip chart so that a wide variety of contexts can be shared. You may want to consider giving each person another copy of the pro-forma so that they can make notes during the presentations from the groups.

Perhaps the ideas might be similar to those presented in the example in Figure 11.2.

Type of writing	Science context
Sequencing events	Make a flow chart to show the sequence of events when you carried out an investigation into which fabric was the most waterproof.
Writing instructions	Make chocolate crispy cakes and observe the changes as the chocolate melts and hardens. Write a series of instructions so that someone else can make the cakes.
Writing verses	Imagine that you are a sugar lump which has been put into a cup of hot water. Write a verse to describe how you feel and what happens to you.
Preparing glossaries	Prepare a glossary including words such as melt, dissolve, separate, etc. and explain the meanings
Letter writing	After an investigation to find the most absorbent paper towel, write to the headteachers of the school requesting that the 'best' brand be used in the school cloakrooms
Note making	Read non-fiction books about rubber, cotton or silk and make notes from a variety of sources.
Writing stories	Imagine that you are a candle on the dining room table. You are smart and red. Write a story about what happens to you as you burn away. Think about the colours in your flame and what happens to you when a boy in the house blows out the flame.
Writing in charts and tables	Make water filters from sand, paper, gravel and pebbles. Test out the filters as you try to clean dirty water. Write down the results of your observations in a chart.
Describing events or observations	Write a descriptive account – what you observe when you put ice cubes into a shiny can.

Figure 11.2 Examples of writing in science contexts

For cross-reference with Study Book see Figure 11.5

ACTIVITY 5

For this activity you will need a collection of non-fiction books. You might like to concentrate on one area of science such as living things, materials or Earth in space. If you have enough books, it is more effective if people work in pairs but this will depend on the resources which you have available. The activity is suitable for children and is often carried out as a way of encouraging pupils to use indexes, glossaries and content pages to help them to develop research skills.

Give each pair a copy of the pro-forma (Figure 11.5) and ask them to fill in the first column. Supposing you were going to give them a book about snails, they would write in the first column all that they knew about snails. They then fill in the second column to indicate what they would like to find out. Finally, you will give them the book to read and they search for the information they need to complete the third column which shows what they have learned.

Feedback and discussion

If you ask each group or pair to report back on what they have learned by doing the exercise you will perhaps be able to extend the subject knowledge of some of the teachers. The main point though is to examine the strategies which they used to find the relevant information. You will also want to emphasise that although this was primarily an activity to develop literacy skills, nevertheless some science ideas were developed.

ACTIVITY 6

Activity 6 is concerned with measurement in science. Spence (1998) suggests that being numerate involves 'gathering numerical information by measuring and being able to present this information in graphs, charts and tables'.

Doing science investigations often involves the collection of data. Sometimes this is collected by observing, such as when we describe the results of decay after certain periods of time, but very often some form of measurement is involved. By helping children to understand that accurate measurements will help them to answer questions which they want answered, we are making mathematics real and worthwhile. Children also need to be able to estimate and to think about whether their results are realistic. This, too, is an important part of helping children to solve problems accurately. Many young children are taught to repeat their measurements two or three times in order to make sure that they are accurate and teachers will help children to see the links between the maths which they meet in numeracy lessons and the mathematics which is used in science.

In Activity 6, teachers are asked to consider the ways in which measurement is used when children are carrying out some investigations as part of their study of sound. They are investigating to find out if adults or children have the best hearing and about the effectiveness of ear trumpets.

Feedback and discussion

Finding out whether children or adults have the best hearing

The teacher will discuss with the children how they might find out the answer to this question. Probable suggestions might include dropping a small object such as a paper clip onto a hard floor. People should be blindfolded and should stand with their backs to the person doing the dropping and raise their hand if they hear a sound. The children will need to decide whether the people being tested should move away from the 'dropper' or whether the dropper moves away from the people being tested. They will also have to make decisions about how far away from the sound source people should be each time they are tested. Would this be every metre, every 50 cms or less? The person with the 'best' hearing would be the person who could hear when they are a long way from the source and when all the other people being tested had failed to hear the object drop.

Children and their teacher would also need to discuss how results would be recorded and design a chart to show results.

Making and testing ear trumpets. Do ear trumpets help us to hear better?

Teachers will probably want to help children towards an understanding of how quantitative data can help us to interpret results and draw conclusions. The teacher in this example would give the children the opportunity to talk about how they might answer the question and there will probably be some discussion about why ear trumpets might have been used in the past and why they might be thought to be effective. Perhaps the teacher could show a picture of an ear trumpet, as it would be most unlikely that children would be familiar with them.

The suggestions for answering the question might involve making ear trumpets of different lengths or of different diameters and testing these in a controlled way. The children would have to measure the diameters and the length of the trumpets and also decide what to measure in order to judge which was most effective. This could involve measuring distances from a sound source in a similar way to the previous investigation, although the course participants might have other ideas.

The main points here are that children should be encouraged to use measurement in science and to understand how numerical data which we collect can help us to draw conclusions.

Activity 1

A particularly effective way of approaching science for younger children is through the medium of stories. These can be used as a stimulus in part for older children, but care needs to be taken to ensure that the science is not lost or links contrived.

Read the story 'Polly and Humpty' which has been used by some teachers of 5 and 6 year olds.

Polly and Humpty

One day Polly and her friend Humpty decided to go for a picnic. They were staying at the seaside for their holidays and Polly thought that the sea looked exciting.

She had seen the boats bobbing up and down in the water and had watched the children laughing as they put their hands into the water and splashed their fingers.

'Let's go for a sail and take a picnic,' Polly said to Humpty.

'Oh, yes, but please can we row the boat?' asked Humpty.

'Row the boat?', said Polly 'What do you mean . . . row the boat?'

'I want to pull the oars like the big girls and boys do,' said Humpty. 'That makes the boat go along in the water.'

'Oh that!' replied Polly. 'Of course you can. I want to put my fingers in the water and splash and splash,' she said jumping up and down.

'Come on, then, let's make some sandwiches and then we can go and get a boat.'

Polly and Humpty made some jam sandwiches and got two cans of Coke and four chocolate biscuits from the cupboard in the kitchen.

They put the food and drinks in a plastic coolbox with some blocks of ice and set off for the beach to see the man who looked after the boats.

They had to pay £1 for the boat and Mr Salty, the man who looked after the boats, told them to bring the boat back after one hour.

'Oh yes, we will,' said Polly, 'We only want to sail a little way and eat our sandwiches.'

Mr Salty gave them some little red jackets to put on. The jackets had air inside them just like balloons, and were to keep them from sinking if they fell into the water.

Polly and Humpty got into their boat. Humpty felt very important because he was using the oars, and he told Polly to sit very still in case she fell out.

Polly trickled her fingers in the water and sang a song. Humpty was very tired so he closed his eyes and went to sleep. Polly had a rest too, because the sun had made her sleepy. The little boat floated away on the sea, and Humpty and Polly slept on and on.

'Ummmm!' said Polly.

'Ooh!' said Humpty.

'Snnnzz', snored Humpty.

'Snnnzz', snored Polly.

Suddenly there was a crash and a bump. They both woke up. Humpty looked around. Polly looked around.

'Where are we?' said Polly.

'Where are we?' said Humpty.

The little boat was not in the sea any more. It was stuck in the sand and had a hole in the bottom.

Humpty and Polly could not see any people. They could see some sand. They could see the sea. They could see a big hill made of sand, but they couldn't see any people. They were on an island.

Humpty began to cry. 'Oh, I want to go home,' he cried. He didn't feel important any more and wished that he hadn't decided to go for a sail. Polly didn't want her friend Humpty to feel sad so she tried to be brave. She went to look at the boat. There was a big hole in the bottom, but the sandwiches were still in the coolbox and so was Mr Salty's big toolbox and rope.

'Let's climb the hill and see what is on the other side,' said Polly. 'There may be some people there.' So Humpty and Polly climbed the hill. On the other side there were some trees, and hanging on the trees were some juicy oranges. There were no people to be seen.

'Well,' said Humpty, 'We could build a little house on this side of the hill and we have oranges to eat. I like oranges.'

'Oh, yes!' said Polly, 'We'll be quite safe here and someone will be sure to find us. It will be an adventure, won't it?'

Consider how this may be used in a cross-curricular approach. Which curriculum areas could be covered? List some possible learning outcomes for each area.

Activity 2

Look at your curriculum for science and identify some areas that would provide a good context for the development of skills in citizenship. Try to draw on historical as well as topical issues, since history does on occasion repeat itself, particularly with respect to environmental issues, and this may be an area for looking at how scientific ideas are based upon evidence.

Activity 3

(a) Look at the picture in Figure 11.3 and write down as many questions suggested by the picture which could be answered by scientific enquiry. Concentrate particularly on the roofs.

(b) Consider how children might answer these questions by practical activity.

(c) Be prepared to discuss these ideas and to identify the opportunities for learning science.

Figure 11.3 Micklands houses' roof line

Source: Sue Malvern

For cross-reference with Study Book see Figure 11.1

Activity 4

Imagine that you are the teacher of 7 and 8 year olds who are learning about the properties of materials. Fill in the pro-forma in Figure 11.4 to provide examples of how science observations and investigations can be used to develop writing skills.

Type of writing	Science context
Sequencing events	
Writing instructions	
Writing verses	
Preparing glossaries	
Letter writing	
Note making	
Writing stories	
Writing in charts and tables	
Describing events or observations	

Figure 11.4 Pro-forma: types of writing in science contexts

For cross-reference with Study Book see Figure 11.2

Activity 5

You have a non-fiction science book. Look at the title of the book but don't open it! In the first column of the pro-forma in Figure 11.5 write down all you know about the area of science which is included in the title of the book. For example, it could be snails or forces or the moon. When you have completed this, then identify in the second column what you would like to find out. When this column is completed, then you can use the book to find the answer to your questions.

Think about the strategies which you are using as you search for the information which you need.

What I know about	What I would like to know about	What I have learned about ......

Figure 11.5 Pro-forma: What I know, want to know and have learned

For cross-reference with Study Book see Figure 11.3

Activity 6

Mr Jones and his class of 9 year olds are learning about sound. They will be finding out whether children or adults have the best hearing and making and testing ear trumpets and trying to find out if ear trumpets help us to hear.

Identify the opportunities for the use of measurement as the children carry out the investigations.

REFERENCES

National Curriculum *Handbook for Primary Teachers: Key Stages 1 and 2*. Department for Education and Employment and the Qualifications and Curriculum Authority, London 1999.

Spence, M. (1998) 'Measurement in primary science and maths', *Primary Science Review*, No. 53, p. 6.

FURTHER READING

Feasey, R. and Gallear, R. (1999) *Primary Science and Literacy*, Hatfield: Association for Science Education.

Feasey, R. and Gallear, R. (2000) *Primary Science and Numeracy*, Hatfield: Association for Science Education.

QCA (2002) *Citizenship: A Scheme of Work for Key Stages 1 and 2*, London: QCA.

Module 12 Planning for continuity and progression in science activities

MODULE GOALS

To help teachers, planning for work in science, to do the following:

- to identify criteria to ensure that planning is thorough and provision is appropriate;
- to recognise the importance of curriculum continuity;
- to cater for individual differences and to ensure progression in learning;
- to evaluate their plans.

MODULE OVERVIEW

This module invites teachers to produce detailed plans for a series of activities with children. The first stage (Activity 1) involves identifying the important considerations for teachers. These are then applied, as a framework, to planning in a specific area of work (Activity 2). Evaluation of the plans of another group forms the basis of Activity 3.

Timing

Total time: approximately 2 hours 30 minutes

Introduction		10 mins
Activity 1	Group work	25 mins
	Feedback and discussion	20 mins
Activity 2	Group work	25 mins
	Feedback and discussion	25 mins
Activity 3	Group work	20 mins
	Feedback and discussion	25 mins

Materials required

- flip chart and pens

For Activity 1

- copy of vignette and questions (Activity 1) for those who do not have the Study Book.

For Activity 2

- copy of Activity 2 for those who do not have the Study Book;
- copy of Figure 12.1 for each participant.

For Activity 3

- copy of Activity 3 for those who do not have the Study Book.

INTRODUCTION

Points to make:

- Although the preoccupation of teachers is often: 'What will the children *do*?' this module is designed to encourage thinking about the process of planning, starting with questions about what the children might *need*, and *why*.
- Continuity applies to provision and is important between schools and between classes in a school. Here, we concentrate on within-school continuity. It is assumed that teachers' normal practices derive from a whole-school plan of work. Issues about liaison, for curriculum continuity purposes, between schools are not specifically addressed here.
- Continuity is important to avoid repetition. Nothing is wrong with 'something completely different', but it is important to make references to and link it to work that has gone before.
- Progression applies to learning. There is nothing wrong with planning for reinforcement of ideas or skills but steps in learning can be planned to broaden understanding and to extend the skills repertoire. However, it is important to ensure that the 'steps' are of an appropriate size, in order to cater for the different needs of individuals.
- Continuity and progression apply to planning for conceptual understanding and for skill development.
- Since teaching does not always lead to learning, there is a constant need for assessment and review.

ACTIVITY 1

This activity considers teachers' planning. Teachers work in groups of three or four. The vignette is fairly long, so allow teachers about 5 minutes to assimilate the details. Essentially, this puts 'flesh' on the enquiry framework described in Module 1. They then need 20 minutes to address the questions which are designed to focus their thinking on the important steps in describing a 'planning framework'. Figure 12.1 describes a complete planning framework.

Feedback and discussion

Some teachers might have found it difficult to avoid describing the content of activities that children might do and have wanted to make plans for this. Keep the discussion focused towards the steps in the planning framework. This is important for Activity 2.

General aim	Need to consider
Continuity	*Age* of children
	Experience of children
	Context of work
Progression in skills development	Children's levels of performance
	Appropriate *learning objectives*
	Resources and equipment needs
Progress in developing understanding	Children's current ideas
	Appropriate *learning objectives*
Differentiation	How to group children
	Individuals' needs and *capabilities*
Assessment	*Opportunities and Evidence*

Figure 12.1 Planning framework

For cross-reference with Study Book see Figure 12.1

The *age* and *previous experience* of the children are the first consideration. It is important to consult the school plans and the children's records in order to acknowledge the work that went before, in considering continuity of experience.

In extending children's understanding, an appropriate *context* for the work should be selected. In this case, it is a different one (Growing Food) to that previously studied. An additional advantage of the context for this particular work is that children are able to make their own contributions from the outset, by bringing samples of soil from their own gardens.

Children's individual records, examples of their work and evidence from discussions all contribute to the teacher's ability to identify appropriate *learning objectives*. The development of key skills is facilitated by addressing every stage in the enquiry framework. The nature of the children's ideas about growing plants will emerge in the discussions that accompany the design of the investigations. In this way, reinforcement and appropriate development of ideas will be provided.

As the children's questions and ideas become focused on particular investigations, the teacher, in monitoring how each group is working, can make appropriate interventions, according to *individual needs and capabilities*.

By anticipating the sorts of investigation that they might undertake, the teacher has an idea of the likely need for *resources* and specific pieces of *equipment*.

The children's descriptions of their findings, their reflection on what happened and the teacher's questions will provide *opportunities and evidence* for assessing what progress has been made.

Groups will have summarised this in different ways. Use Figure 12.1 to draw together the important steps in a planning framework.

ACTIVITY 2

In this activity, teachers use the planning framework from Activity 1 to produce plans for a topic on 'keeping fit'. Using the same groups as in Activity 1, allow teachers 20 minutes to plan and 5 minutes to summarise, on flip chart paper.

Feedback and discussion

Again, it is important that the age group of the children is defined. In finding out about children's previous experience, not only are school plans and records important but it is likely to be of concern to some teachers that children who are new to the school could present more of a challenge. Acquiring information on their experience and ability will depend on the existence of effective liaison procedures.

Several contexts for work on 'keeping fit' are likely to be identified. Teachers will recognise that *investigations* on diet are not practicable and the use of secondary sources is more appropriate. Investigations relating to exercise, fitness and pulse rate, are feasible but have different resource implications. The context of this work will depend on whether the chosen focus is predominantly on diet or on exercise, for example.

As with practical activities, children's willingness or ability to engage with secondary sources will vary and careful consideration to the grouping of children must be given. It follows, then, that outcomes of the work will be different according to a child's contribution to the group so the teacher will need to anticipate using different sorts of evidence to assess each child's achievement.

ACTIVITY 3

This activity provides an opportunity for the participants to evaluate each other's work. Groups exchange planning summaries from Activity 2 and spend 20 minutes evaluating the plans, using the questions in Activity 3.

Feedback and discussion

Before each group reports, emphasise the importance of constructive criticism. It is important to encourage members of the reporting group to ask questions about the plan, for clarification. Note any common themes emerging from the reports.

Restrict the feedback to 15 minutes. In the final 10 minutes, ascertain to what extent participants are normally able to engage in review, reflection or evaluation, either on their own or with colleagues at work. Endeavour to elicit and collate examples of good professional practice in this area.

Activity 1

The vignette describes a teacher's approach to planning a series of science activities.

Chris was introducing science activities within an overall topic about growing food, to a class of 9 and 10 year olds. The previous year, the group had studied germination and plant growth, as part of their work in science. Chris planned that the children should now discuss and investigate the differences between types of soil. The idea was that the children should undertake some investigations of sandy, loamy and clay soil, so samples of each of these were provided, to which some of the children contributed samples that they brought from gardens at home. Chris wanted the investigations to advance the children's ideas and therefore to start from their ideas and questions. It would have been easy to ask the children to find out, for example: 'Which soil holds most water?', 'Does water drain through some soils more quickly than others?', etc. and to start the children's investigations from these questions. These are perfectly good questions for children to investigate and likely to be among those the children ended up investigating, but Chris wanted to hold back such questions, in order to try to find out what the children would ask and what ideas they had.

The first part of the work was an exploratory phase of looking at the different soils. In groups, the children were given samples of the three main types, some hand-lenses, sieves, disposable gloves and some very open instructions:

- Separate the different parts that each of the soils contains
- Find out what is contained in all the soils
- Find out what is different in each soil
- Think about how these differences might affect how well plants grow in the soils.

This task required children to use their ideas about soil in making their observations. It encouraged them to look closely at the soil and to think about the differences they found. During this activity the teacher visited each group to listen in to what the children were saying about the types of soil. Many of their statements at this stage contained hypotheses and predictions. The children were quick to say which they thought would be best for plants to grow in (for example: 'The darkest coloured one') and to identify the ability to hold water as a property that was needed.

There was then a whole class discussion, pooling findings and ideas from different groups. Chris said that they would test their ideas about which was best for growing plants when they had found out more about the soils and the differences that might make one better than another. What do plants need to grow? Water was the most popular answer. Some mentioned 'fertiliser' and there was a discussion of what this meant in terms of the soils they had looked at and it was eventually identified with the bits of leaves and decayed plant material they had found, particularly in the loam. Chris introduced the word 'humus' to describe this part of the soil. No-one mentioned the presence of air in the soil until the teacher asked them to think about the difference between soil that was compressed and the same soil in a loose heap. They were challenged to think about whether there was the same amount of air between the particles in each soil and whether this was likely to make a difference to how well plants would grow in it.

The discussion identified four main differences to be investigated: the differences in the amount of water held in the soil; how quickly water drained off through each one; the amount of humus in each; and the amount of air. Each of the six groups in which the children were working chose one of these and set about planning how they would go about their investigation. Although having different foci, the investigations of all the groups were relevant to developing understanding of the nature and properties of soil so that, when they did the trial of which soil enabled plants to grow best, they would be able to explain and not just observe the result. Chris monitored how the children were working together in their groups: there were some who were inclined to 'take a back seat' and one or two who would rather be a scribe than participate in any practical work.

The investigations provided opportunities to help the children develop their enquiry skills, in order to carry out systematic and fair tests through which they would arrive at findings useful in developing their ideas. The teacher asked them first to plan what they would do and identify what they would need in terms of equipment. Their thinking was probed about what variables to control and what to observe or measure by questions such as: 'How will you be sure that the difference is only caused by the type of soil?', 'How will you be able to show the difference?' Chris had ideas, gathered from various sources, about useful approaches but kept these from the children, only to be introduced if they did not produce ideas of their own. The children were encouraged to make notes of what they found as they went along and then use these notes to prepare a report. Each group reported to the whole class. The teacher told them that they should report what they did and what they found, but also say whether it was what they had expected and to try to explain the differences they found.

At the end of the practical work and after a period for bringing their ideas together in their groups, each group in turn presented a report, while other children were given the opportunity to ask questions. Chris refrained from making comments at this stage and asked questions only for clarification. When all the reports had been given, the findings were listed for each soil and the children were asked to decide which might be best for growing some seedlings. The choice was not as obvious as some children had initially thought, so they were very keen to try this next investigation and find out what really would happen.

Attention then turned to the samples of soil that the children had brought from home. In order to compare them with the three soils they had investigated, Chris suggested mixing some of each with enough water to loosen the parts from each other and allow the constituents to separate as they settled to the bottom. The children then used these observations and what they had found about soil to predict which might be 'good growing' soils. These samples were then included in the seedling trials.

Before going on to set up the next investigations, Chris asked the children to reflect on which parts of the work just completed they had enjoyed most, which would they do differently if they could start again and what they now felt they could do better than before.

(Adapted from Harlen, 2000, pp. 2–4)

Activity 1 *continued*

(a)   Identify the key steps taken by the teacher that helped to ensure that the plans were thorough.

  (i) How was curriculum continuity addressed?
  (ii) How were individual differences catered for?
  (iii) How was progression built into the aims?

(b)   Describe, for each step, what the teacher did and what children did.

(c)   Using your notes, draft a planning framework on flip chart paper and appoint a spokesperson to describe the framework to the other groups.

Activity 2

Use the planning framework from Activity 1 to prepare a topic on 'keeping fit'. The focus should be on exercise, diet and lifestyle.

For each heading in the 'need to consider' column, identify what the teacher needs to know and how to find out. Exemplify the teacher's planning by anticipating some activities that the children might undertake. Begin by defining the age group of the children.

Summarise your planning using the framework headings, on flip chart paper. Appoint a spokesperson to describe your planning.

Activity 3

Take one of the other group's plans from Activity 2. Using the planning framework as a guide, analyse and critically evaluate the plans. Ask yourselves the following questions:

- How well is each of the steps in the framework taken into consideration?
- Are aims and objectives clear?
- Are the aims and objectives justified and appropriately matched to the children's age and experience?
- Is there anything you would like to add?
- Is there anything over which you would exercise caution?

Appoint a spokesperson to summarise your evaluation of the planning.

REFERENCE

Harlen, W. (2000) *The Teaching of Science in Primary Schools*, 3rd edn, London: David Fulton Publishers.

FURTHER READING

Progression and continuity

Asoko, H. and Squires, A. (1998) 'Progression and continuity', in R. Sherrington (ed.), *ASE Guide to Primary Science Education*, Cheltenham: Stanley Thornes, pp. 148–55.

Progression and differentiation

Naylor, S. and Keogh, B. (1998) 'Progression and continuity', in A. Cross and G. Peet (eds), *Teaching Science in the Primary School*, Book Two, Plymouth: Northcote House, pp. 34–58.

Progression

Naylor, S. and Keogh, B. (1997) 'Progression in learning in science', in A. Cross and G. Peet (eds), *Teaching Science in the Primary School*, Book One, Plymouth: Northcote House, pp. 51–63.

Differentiation

Naylor, S. and Keogh, B. (1997) 'Differentiation in teaching science', in A. Cross and G. Peet (eds), *Teaching Science in the Primary School*, Book One, Plymouth: Northcote House, pp. 64–75.
Naylor, S. and Keogh, B. (1998) 'Differentiation', in R. Sherrington (ed.), *ASE Guide to Primary Science Education*, Cheltenham: Stanley Thornes, pp. 140–7.
Qualter, A. (1996) *Differentiated Primary Science*, Buckingham: Open University Press.

Module 13   ICT and science (1)

Using ICT to collect data

MODULE GOALS

- To consider how ICT can be used in the teaching and learning of science.
- To consider how children can collect data by using sensors and to evaluate the benefits of collecting data in this way.
- To evaluate branching databases and to consider progression.
- To suggest how spreadsheets might be used in the teaching and learning of science.

MODULE OVERVIEW

The module should be read in conjunction with Module 14 which also deals with ICT in science. This module provides opportunities for teachers to evaluate opportunities for using ICT in science and to consider whether or not the use of ICT would be beneficial in the planned programme of learning. It deals with the following:

- identification of opportunities;
- the evaluation of branching databases and spreadsheets;
- the opportunity to consider how sensors can be used to collect data and how the use of sensors can be introduced.

There are five group activities:

- Activity 1 relates to an outline plan of a teaching programme for 8 and 9 year olds. Participants are asked to suggest whether or not ICT should be used in the programme and in what context.
- Activity 2 is focused on the introduction of sensors to a class of 6 year olds (Module 14 considers the use of sensors with older children).
- Activity 3 is concerned with the introduction of branching databases and a range of these is evaluated.
- Activity 4 considers progression in the use of branching databases and the opportunities for using them.
- Activity 5 addresses the use of spreadsheets and here participants are asked to set up a spreadsheet and to evaluate the effectiveness of an example.

Timing

Total time: approximately 3 hours

Introduction		5 mins
Activity 1	Group work	20 mins
	Feedback and discussion	10 mins
Activity 2	Group work	20 mins
	Feedback and discussion	15 mins
Activity 3	Paired work at the computer	20 mins
	Feedback and discussion	15 mins
Activity 4	Group work	20 mins
	Feedback and discussion	15 mins
Activity 5	Paired work at the computer	25 mins
	Feedback and discussion	15 mins

Materials required

- flip charts and pens;
- computers so that participants can work in pairs;
- a range of branching databases for Activity 3;
- a spreadsheet program for Activity 5;
- copies of the module activities for each participant if they do not have copies of the Study Book.

INTRODUCTION

Points to make:

- State the aims of the modules.
- Stress that the module assumes that teachers have used ICT in their teaching and are familiar with some of the software, websites and CD-ROMs.
- The aim of the activities is to think about how the use of ICT enhances the learning of science. The activities are not designed to introduce teachers to specific software, but rather to think about the teaching and learning.

ACTIVITY 1

No computers are needed for this activity. You will probably want to introduce the activity by collecting together some ideas from the group about the various applications which could be used in science. Alternatively, as an *aide-mémoire*, you might like to give the participants a list similar to the one below to help them to make decisions about the use of ICT in the sample programme.

Some ICT applications which could be used in science:

- word processing, e.g. reports of investigations or poems to describe observations;
- using graphics to illustrate reports or using presentation software such as Powerpoint;
- use of the Internet to research information;
- branching databases;
- databases;

- spreadsheets;
- sensors;
- control systems;
- using CD-ROMs either to search for information for a report or to develop interrogation skills;
- simulations;
- the use of digital cameras and computer microscopes.

Allocate groups to the various topics and, if possible, make sure that there is coverage of all the areas of study. Give out details of the topics to be covered in each term. The participants work in groups of three or four to suggest whether or not they would use ICT and to justify their decisions. Stress that we are primarily concerned with the learning of *science* and that the ICT should be a tool to facilitate the science learning.

Feedback and discussion

Go through the outline science programme and collect the ideas from the teachers. They will perhaps suggest something similar to this.

Term 1: Building circuits and testing materials to see which are insulators and conductors

Children could add their results to a chart which has already been prepared. They could then interrogate the chart to look for patterns and to notice that it is metals which are conductors. However, the use of ICT would not necessarily enhance the science learning in this case. A concept keyboard could be a useful tool for children with learning difficulties as this would reduce the time spent on writing the names of the materials. An overlay such as the one in Figure 13.1 would perhaps be appropriate.

Identifying the features of solids and liquids and classifying certain materials as either liquids or solids

Children could use a branching key as this would encourage close observation. The questions could relate to the particular features of solids and liquids as well as to the particular details of the materials.

Enter	Delete		
Wooden ruler	Metal scissors	Spoon	Rubber
Plastic plate	Nail	Does not allow electricity to pass	Allows electricity to pass

Figure 13.1 Example of a concept keyboard overlay

For cross-reference with Study Book see Figure 13.2

Term 2: Examining bones and learning how the skeleton supports the body. Learning how muscles help movement

The use of a CD-ROM could enable children to identify bones and learn how the muscles work to allow movement. You will have your own ideas about suitable CD-ROMs. Teachers may also have their own suggestions about software which could include:

- The Ultimate Body from Dorling Kindersley www.dk.com
- My World: Skeletons from Semerc Granada Learning www.granada-learning.co.uk
- How the body works: Bone and Muscle from Aims-Multimedia www.aims-multimedia.com

You may want to spend a few moments considering how the use of these CD-ROMs could fit into the teaching programme. Would the teacher use an interactive whiteboard and use the video clips and pictures as a direct teaching aid? Or would teachers prefer to have the children using the software in small groups as part of individual research? There are organisational issues here which you may want to discuss.

Learning about friction and forces

Teachers will probably identify the opportunities for first-hand investigation. Children could use force meters to measure the force needed to pull an object along a table or up a ramp. If the ramp or table is covered with different materials, each time they test children will be able to observe the effects of friction. Another common investigation, which illustrates the same concept, is the testing and timing of various sports shoes as they slide down a ramp.

Results can be entered into a database or simple graphing program. You will probably want to stress here that it is the analysis of the data which helps the learning process. Children can see patterns in results very clearly when they are in graph form.

Term 3: Learning to use and read thermometers. Finding out which materials are good thermal insulators

If the teacher wants the children to learn to use thermometers then there is obviously no substitute for repeated practice. He or she will probably also want children to use the thermometers in an investigation.

However, this may also be an opportunity to discuss how scientists in manufacturers' laboratories would use temperature probes and computers when testing designs (e.g. for vacuum flasks or insulated teapots). It would perhaps be possible and appropriate to compare the readings of the thermometers with those obtained by the temperature probes.

Investigating three habitats

The three habitats to be investigated are:

- a small wood which is close to the school;
- the school garden;
- the pathways around the school.

ICT could be used in a variety of ways in this topic. Obviously not all of these would be used at the same time with one class. Teachers will justify their selection of suitable applications.

- Using a digital camera to take pictures of the various habitats. Back in the classroom children can scrutinise the pictures and make notes about the features which they notice.

- Using branching databases to make keys for identifying plants and animals found in particular places.
- Using databases to present data about the plants, animals, soil conditions, amount of light, temperature, etc. which were noted during the visits to the different habitats. Children could present a report about the habitats which they have studied. Here they could import clipart and use word processing programs. Their graphs and the interpretation of the patterns noted could also be included in the reports.

You may want to suggest that children pose questions for their friends which could be answered by scrutinising the graphs or sorting the data which they have collected.

Sensors could be used to measure the amount of light and the temperature of the soil in the various habitats either using the head teacher's laptop computer or a remote data-logger.

CD-ROMs could also be used to collect information about the plants and animals which were found in the habitats. If you have access to suitable on-line resources, children could use key words to search for information. You may want to consider how on-line resources may be used, although this is discussed in more detail in Module 14. You might like, at this point, to collate a list of CD-ROMs which the course members and you recommend. These could include:

- *Garden Wildlife* from Anglia www.anglia.co.uk
- *My World 2 More about minibeasts* from Semerc Granada Learning www.granada-learning.co.uk
- *My World 2 Garden* from Semerc Granada Learning. www.granada-learning.co.uk.
- *Picture base World habitats* from AVP www.avp.co.uk
- *Eyewitness Encyclopaedia of Nature* from Dorling Kindersley www.dk.com

However, it is worth noting that all information sources should be evaluated carefully by the teacher before they are used by children. In many cases books provide more useful and accessible information. It is the interactivity of some ICT resources which can be a motivating influence on children's learning.

ACTIVITY 2

There are no computers used in this session but it is assumed that participants are familiar with the appropriate software and at least one sensor package. The teachers are asked to suggest a teaching sequence for a teacher who wants to introduce sensors to a class of 6 year olds. It is not the intention here that teachers prepare detailed plans for the lessons which they suggest, but, rather, that they consider how and why sensors might be used and the learning outcomes at each stage.

Feedback and discussion

Point out that it is very difficult to measure the amount of light which comes through different materials. We can judge subjectively but sensors can do this more accurately. Perhaps the teacher would begin by talking to the children about how they could set up an investigation to test out predictions about the best materials to use to keep out the light. If it is appropriate, a model house could be constructed and different materials could be placed over the window. Mr Bold would then ask the children about the best way to judge the effectiveness of the different materials. It would be at this point that he would introduce the sensors.

He would perhaps teach this lesson in the computer classroom where the interactive whiteboard is situated. He could then demonstrate, with children as assistants, how the light sensors could be used. It would be important to stress aspects of fair testing as they recorded the results. The advantages of measuring the amount of light in this way is that children can see the results immediately. As the children are young, Mr Bold would probably select either a numerical display or a large format block graph to show the results. He would spend time helping the children to interpret the results.

During the following two weeks children could work in pairs at the classroom computer to test a variety of fabrics with their model house. They would be able to print out their results and these could be compared in order to find the 'best' fabric. He would help children to understand the terms opaque, translucent and transparent.

ACTIVITY 3

You will need access to computers for this activity. Teachers work in pairs to evaluate at least two different branching databases. You will probably introduce this activity by collecting ideas abut why this type of software is so useful in science. Stress that it is only by observing carefully and structuring questions carefully that children are able to make effective 'keys' which can be used by their friends. Many teachers begin by playing a 'Twenty Questions'-type game so that children know which type of question to begin with. Alternatively, there is the 'What am I?' game where children have a picture of a plant, animal or inanimate object stuck to their forehead which also helps children to think about the structure of questions which are used to make keys. Discuss the way in which focused questions can help children to observe in detail. When the children are used to asking appropriate questions, many teachers ask children to make a branching key on paper or with cards so that they can see the way in which the questions and answers branch out.

Allocate pairs of participants to computers and if possible have a wide range of software to evaluate. These could include:

- Flexitree from Flexible software www.flexible.co.uk
- Retreeval from Kudlian e-mail sales@kudlian.demon.co.uk
- Granada Branch from Granada Learning www.granada-learning.co.uk
- Decision from Black Cat www.blackcatsoftware.com
- Infotree from Semerc Granada Learning www.granada-learning.co.uk
- Tree from Semerc Granada Learning www.granada-learning.co.uk

Feedback and discussion

Use the suggested criteria to evaluate the software. It may be that some of the teachers have used one or more of these programs with children and can share their experiences. Ask teachers what science they think children might learn from using the database. Ask also what science skills are being used.

ACTIVITY 4

This activity can be done without computers. The aim here is for teachers to decide whether or not the use of branching databases would be useful for certain topic areas. There is the opportunity for teachers to identify key ideas as they prepare the list of 'items'.

Feedback and discussion

It will be interesting to compare the lists which the teachers produce. You might like to discuss how the list could be used to assess the children's understanding as you analyse the questions on the database.

You may want to consider how children progress from using branching databases to sort and identify objects which are essentially very different, for instance, a lemon and an apple, to looking very closely at a collection of invertebrates or leaves. Underwood and Underwood (1990) showed from their research that, while younger children asked few questions which were concerned with the testing of ideas, older children showed a more logical questioning approach.

ACTIVITY 5

When introducing spreadsheets to children, teachers usually begin with simple calculations involving addition. This is a very simple example. Teachers are asked to evaluate this format of the spreadsheet and to consider what, if any, science learning would have taken place when children were filling in data and looking for patterns. (There is a further examination of the use of spreadsheets in Module 14.)

Feedback and discussion

Collect the ideas about the questions which could be asked about the data. These will be focused on comparisons of amounts of carbohydrate eaten by different people or on the most popular form of carbohydrate eaten by the individual children. It is not possible, from a quick analysis of the data, to compare the total amounts of the different carbohydrates eaten over the three days. Another drawback with this particular example is that the completed totals have to be added before the sub-totals can be calculated. The teachers may decide that there would not be much science learning taking place while the children were using the spreadsheet. If children were to learn about healthy eating, then a spreadsheet which calculated amounts consumed from the different food groups would be more helpful. This example does not enable the user to graph total amounts eaten from different food groups. It is the consideration of what headings to set up which will be the focus of your discussion, particularly if the teachers want to graph the results. An example such as the one in Figure 13.2 would enable the results to be graphed and would provide more opportunities for analysis.

Name	Fruit	Vegetables	Protein	Carbohydrate	Dairy products	Total grammes
Sam						
Bill						
Fred						
Mary						
Tariq						
Ali						
Total grammes						

Figure 13.2 Suggested spreadsheet: food groups: amount of food consumed

THE ACTIVITIES

We live in an age where technological advances are made almost daily. Digital cameras, video recorders, the sending of e-mails, Internet shopping, mobile phones and text messages are commonplace to most of our children.

The children we teach in school are very familiar with computers. Many have computers at home and often use these to play games. We would be doing our pupils a disservice if we did not teach them to use ICT (Information and Communication Technology) in their learning of science. However, teachers have to be very clear about the benefits of using ICT. The software and hardware can be *tools* to develop the *learning of science* but we need to evaluate the provision very carefully before we decide to use ICT. The ICT must enable the children to learn more effectively than they would if ICT were not used.

Naturally we would expect the children's IT skills to be developed as they work in science, but when planning for science learning, the objectives for the lessons should be focused on the science skills and concepts.

Activity 1; Identifying opportunities

In order that a school can plan for continuity in the science curriculum teachers must identify, at the initial planning stage, what the possible uses of ICT might be. They must evaluate the opportunities and consider if ICT would enhance learning.

Here is an outline of some of the science work which a school has planned for the 8 and 9 year olds:

Term 1

Building circuits and testing which materials are insulators and conductors.
Identifying the features of solids and liquids and classifying certain materials as either liquids or solids.

Term 2

Examining bones and learning how the skeleton supports the body. Learning how muscles help movement.
Learning about friction as a force.

Term 3

Learning to use and read thermometers. Finding out which materials are good thermal insulators.
Investigating three habitats:

- a small wood which is close to the school;
- the school garden;
- the pathways around the school.

The school has a computer suite where there are ten networked computers with Internet access. The head teacher has a laptop computer and each class has two additional computers. There are also two digital cameras, a scanner and sensors to measure temperature, sound and light. The school has recently purchased a computer control interface but the staff have not yet had time to learn how to use it. A range of CD-ROMs which provide information about science-related topics is also available as are three tape recorders.

The network programs include:

- a simple pictogram program suitable for very young children;
- a simple word processing program for younger children;
- a word processing program for children aged 8 and older;
- a spreadsheet;
- a database;
- a branching database;
- a graphics program;
- a program to support the use of sensors;
- a program which enables children to prepare a multimedia presentation.

Activity 1

Select one of the topics and then do the following:

- consider whether or not the use of ICT would enhance the teaching of science;
- state what software or application you would use;
- think about what the children might learn;
- consider whether the ICT might be used in an investigation, for collecting information or for interpreting information.

Activity 2; Using sensors

Sensors are often used to collect data in science investigations. The most common sensors used in primary schools are those which monitor light, sound and temperature. Usually sensors are attached to a small box which is plugged into the serial or analogue port of the computer; although, in some packages, the sensors are attached directly into the serial ports. Children can measure the effects of placing the temperature probes into hot and cold places and substances. They can test materials to see which is the best thermal insulator and they can use the light sensors to see which materials allow most light to pass through. Sound sensors can help children to find out which materials muffle sound most effectively or which of a series of drums makes the most noise. The sensors can also be used away from the computer and then connected to the computer so that the data can be interrogated at a later date.

The advantages of using sensors are:

- children can see the results on the screen immediately;
- the information can be presented in a variety of ways such as tables and graphs;
- pupils and teachers can decide how often to take measurements and then these are taken automatically.

Consider the following scenario.

Mr Bold wants to introduce sensors to his class of 6 year olds. His work in science is focused on the topic of materials and he has chosen to do much of the scientific enquiry through the context of homes. The children have made collections of materials which are used in building homes and have observed which are flexible, which are waterproof and which are porous. They have considered why certain materials are used for particular purposes and have been involved in sorting and classifying. He wants the children to learn that some materials are transparent, some are translucent and some opaque. He also wants the children to develop some of the skills of scientific enquiry. He has asked the children: 'How could we decide which fabric would be the best to make curtains which would keep out the light?'

The school has a computer suite where there are ten networked computers and an interactive whiteboard but the teacher has access to this room for only 1 hour each week. However, he also has two computers in the classroom and three light sensors which can all be attached to the computers by interfaces.

It is assumed that before you begin Activity 2 you will have used temperature sensors, light sensors and sound sensors and that you are familiar with the associated software.

Activity 2

What would be the teaching sequence which you would plan if you were Mr Bold? You can assume that he is proposing to spend two one and a half hour sessions on the work over a period of two weeks but also that there will be several 15-minute periods during that time, when small groups or pairs of children can work independently. When planning, consider the anticipated learning outcomes at each stage of the teaching sequence, exactly what Mr Bold and the children might be doing during the lessons and what key questions might be asked.

Activity 3; Using branching databases

Children use branching databases when they are observing and classifying materials, objects and plants and animals. These programs are often introduced when the teacher wants children to learn to use and make classification keys. As children have to ask questions which can be answered by a 'Yes' or 'No' answer, they have to think very carefully about how to frame appropriate questions. Usually, when beginning this type of work, children start with about six simple objects such as pieces of fruit or a collection of pictures of animals and make a sorting key on paper before moving on to work on the computer.

Activity 3

For this activity you will need access to a computer and at least two different branching databases. Imagine that you are working with a group of 7 year olds and that this is their first introduction to branching databases. They have in front of them small pictures of the following:

- cat
- horse
- fly
- blackbird
- fish
- snail.

Try to make a branching key using first one of the programs and then the other. Evaluate the software using the following criteria:

- Ease of use.
- Would children be stimulated by the graphics?
- Are children alerted if they make errors of procedure?
- Is it possible to print out the finished key?
- Would other groups of children be able to use the completed key easily?
- Is there the opportunity for children to add items to the completed key?

Activity 4 Progression in using branching databases

As children become proficient in both their observation skills and their ability to make and use keys, teachers will encourage them to make very detailed observations when classifying. For example, when describing and classifying different types of common insects they may observe features such as body shape, number of legs or the position of antennae. They will make very close observations in order to describe the approximate size of the insects and the colours and patterns on the bodies. They will also develop the ability to make subsets within their classification keys and will deal with greater numbers of items.

In which of these areas of study could branching keys be used?

- Materials including solids, liquids and gases
- Earth and Space
- Plant reproduction
- How the heart works
- Healthy eating

If so, could you suggest between six and ten items which could be included in the various keys?

If you do not think that children would benefit from using and making a branching key when studying any of the topics, then do not select a list of items for that particular area. Be ready to justify your decisions.

Spreadsheets

Spreadsheets are used when calculations have to be made. At first, the teacher will set up the spreadsheet and the formula to be used for the calculation. Children then add the data into a matrix of cells and, after the calculations have been made, they can use the information to find answers to questions which they and their teachers have posed. The programs can be used to graph data in several forms such as bar charts, pie charts and scattergraphs. As children become more proficient in the use of spreadsheets they will decide for themselves what formula to use and how the data should be arranged in the cells. The spreadsheet can be cut and pasted into other programs to present reports.

Figure 13.3 is a section of a spreadsheet which a group of children and their teacher have set up as part of their investigation into how much carbohydrate children have eaten over a period of time. The teacher set up the headings and the columns and the children keyed in their names and the data.

- What questions could the children ask which could be answered by inter- rogating the data?
- Is this a good example of the use of a spreadsheet? Would you arrange the column headings in a different way?
- If you were working with your class on a topic concerned with healthy eating, what information would you like the children to collect?
- How could the headings be set up so that the children could sort the infor- mation and interrogate the data so that they could learn about the importance of a balanced diet?
- Would you want children to collect data about eating over a long period of time?
- Would you want children to collect data from people of different ages?

If you have access to a computer and spreadsheet software, then perhaps you could set up the column headings of your choice and enter some data which you could collect from colleagues. By doing this you will be able to evaluate the software and the opportunities which it presents for learning science.

Activity 5 *continued*

Name of person	Food eaten	Day 1	Day 2	Day 3	Total
Sam	potato	100	50	50	200
	pasta	0	30	0	30
	cereal	0	0	30	30
	bread	150	25	25	200
				total	460
Fred	potato	0	50	50	100
	pasta	50	0	0	50
	cereal	30	0	0	30
	bread	100	50	50	200
				total	380
Harry	potato	50	25	25	100
	pasta	75	0	0	75
	cereal	0	28	28	56
	bread	25	75	25	125
				total	356
Mary	potato	70	75	0	145
	pasta	0	0	40	40
	cereal	30	35	28	93
	bread	50	25	25	100
				total	378
Susan	potato	0	0	0	0
	pasta	40	0	0	40
	cereal	28	60	25	113
	bread	50	25	35	110
				total	263
Elizabeth	potato	60	35	0	95
	pasta	0	0	30	30
	cereal	25	25	25	75
	bread	30	30	30	90
				total	290
	totals	963	643	521	2127

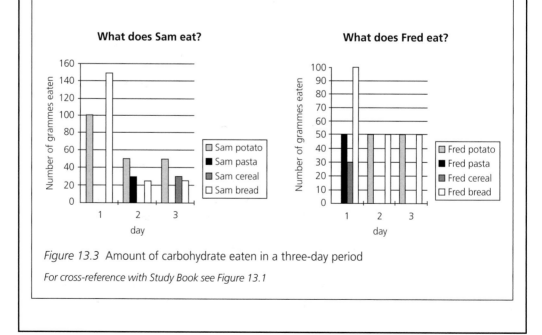

Figure 13.3 Amount of carbohydrate eaten in a three-day period

For cross-reference with Study Book see Figure 13.1

REFERENCE

Underwood, J. and Underwood, G. (1990) *Computers and Learning*, Oxford: Basil Blackwell, p. 97.

FURTHER READING

Cross, A. and Peet, G. (1997) 'Information Technology as essential in primary science', in *Teaching Science in the Primary School*, Plymouth: Northcote House.

Feasey, R. and Gallear, R. (2001) *Primary Science and Information Communication Technology*, Hatfield: Association for Science Education.

Frost, R. (1996) *IT in Primary Science*, Hatfield: Association for Science Education.

Newton, L. and Rogers, L.T. (2001) *Teaching Science with ICT*, London: Continuum.

Straker, A. and Govier, H. (1996) *Children Using Computers*, Oxford: Nash Pollock Publishing.

Teacher Training Agency (1999) *Using Information and Communications Technology to Meet Teaching Objectives in Science Initial Training*, London: Teacher Training Agency.

Websites

www.kented.org.uk/ngfl/teaching/qca.htlm
www.rogerfrost.com
www.becta.org.uk
www.vtc.ngfl.gov.uk/resources/cits/science/prfocus

Module 14 ICT and science (2)

Using ICT to interpret data and communicate findings

MODULE GOALS

- To consider how children might interpret information which has been collected by the use of sensors.
- To think about how to help children to use databases and graphs in order to present information and to consider how children might learn by analysing the information.
- To evaluate and compare two CD-ROMs and to consider how these might be used by children.
- To appraise some Internet sites and to think about the learning opportunities.

MODULE OVERVIEW

There are two parts to this module. The first two activities deal with the way in which children can use information which they have collected from sensors and databases. There is then a consideration of how young children can use simple graphing programs to present results and interpret information.

The second part of the module is focused on information gathering from CD-ROMs and the Internet.

Opportunities are provided in this module for participants to consider children's work and to think about what children might have learned. There is emphasis on planning tasks which will enable children to interact with information obtained from the Internet and CD-ROMs. The activities should provide a stimulus for discussion about the ways in which such materials might be evaluated.

There are five group activities:

- Activity 1 calls on participants to look at a child's work and to consider what might have been learned. There are opportunities here for participants to discuss how they would help children to interpret information and discuss ideas.
- Activity 2 is focused on the setting up and use of a database. The importance of selecting appropriate fields is considered as is the interpretation of data.
- Activity 3 is a short activity which considers how young children might record and analyse the results of an investigation using simple graphing programs.
- Activity 4 provides experience of evaluating the learning opportunities of CD-ROMs and asks participants to prepare critiques of two similar resources.
- Activity 5 is focused on the way in which the Internet is used to search for information, the learning opportunities which might be provided and the importance of scrutinising sites used by children.

Timing

Total time: 3 hours

Introduction		5 mins
Activity 1	Group work	15 mins
	Feedback and discussion	10 mins
Activity 2	Group work	20 mins
	Feedback and discussion	20 mins
Activity 3	Group work	15 mins
	Feedback and discussion	15 mins
Activity 4	Paired work at the computer	30 mins
	Feedback and discussion	15 mins
Activity 5	Paired work at the computer	20 mins
	Feedback and discussion	15 mins

Materials required

- copies of the activities for those who do not have the Study Book;
- copies of the children's work.

For Activity 4

You will need a selection of CD-ROMs which have been designed for children aged between 4 and 11. Each pair will need access to two CD-ROMs which provide information on the same topic, for instance, forces, materials, etc. You may have access to a network or intranet which can enable participants to compare two resources.

For Activity 5

- each pair will need access to the Internet.

INTRODUCTION

Points to make in giving an overview and stating the goals of the modules:

- When children are interpreting graphs and tables they are engaging in part of the process of scientific enquiry. The skill of interpretation is important if children are to learn from their investigations or from the analysis of prepared data. They need to consider what they have learned from the analysis of the data and should be given opportunities to express their own ideas (see Module 3).
- We experience the effects of the use of sensors in our everyday lives. Children can be given the opportunity, not only to collect data using sensors, but to evaluate the effectiveness of the sensors as opposed to other methods measuring and monitoring changes.
- Sources such as CD-ROMs and the Internet can help children to access information but we need to make sure that the children are given every opportunity to develop their own understanding. In order to do this, we must devise activities which enable them to respond to the materials and to think about what they are learning.

ACTIVITY 1

Allow participants time to read the scenario and to talk to others about the skills and concepts which the children might have learned and about the way in which *they* might have arranged the work with the sensors. Ask them to list the main points from their group discussion and the questions which they might have asked the children.

Feedback and discussion

You perhaps need to begin by asking if any group had comments to make about the way in which Mr Smith had planned and organised the work. Comments about the learning might include reference to children:

- knowing about the part which sensors play in our everyday life;
- realising that these particular sensors pick up light from all parts of the room and thinking about how to solve the problem;
- noticing that dark colours reflected least light;
- comparing other colours.

Some teachers might suggest that questions such as 'Which colour reflects most light?' or 'Why do you think that the lime green felt reflects almost as much light as the white sample?' would focus thinking. Others may suggest that, at first, children should be free to present their own report before going on to answer the teacher's questions. Teachers will also emphasise the part which sensors play in our everyday life and refer to how they can help children to understand this.

ACTIVITY 2

It is assumed that participants will be familiar with the use of databases. Arrange the participants in groups of about four to six and begin by discussing with them the use of databases. If the participants are trainee teachers, you will probably want to consider the importance of selecting the appropriate fields so that the learning objectives of the teaching programme can be met. Most teachers, at this stage, ask the children what they want to find out about the chosen area of study and consider carefully the types of questions which will need to be answered by the data. If you want children to be given the opportunity to express their ideas, then you have to make sure that the data collected will provide enough information in an accessible way. Discuss also how some information is collected by observing and measuring, e.g. the colour of flowers or the shape and size of leaves, but that some data can be collected as a result of practical investigation.

Allocate each group two or three of the subject areas to discuss. This number will depend on the time available and the number of participants who will be giving feedback. Try to make sure that all the areas are covered so that participants can reflect on their own practice during feedback time.

Feedback and discussion

Here the focus will be on sharing ideas about contexts and a discussion about whether or not the fields chosen will provide enough information for children to learn from the analysis. For instance, if you were taking feedback from the group who were considering the 10 year olds involved in the study of air resistance, you might find that participants suggested that children make and test a variety of autogyros or parachutes. Obviously the size of the parachutes would be important in a study of air resistance as would the type of materials from which the parachute was made. Suggested fields might be:

size of canopy	shape of canopy
time taken to fall to the ground	material from which the parachute is made
whether or not there was a central hole	weight on the end of the strings
length of strings.	

Consider and discuss how these fields might be named, as most databases which are used by children have a limit on the number of letters which can be used in a field name.

Questions which could be asked might be:

- Do the parachutes drop more quickly if there is a hole in the canopy?
- Does the weight on the end of the strings affect the time taken to fall?
- Do the bigger parachutes fall more slowly than the smaller parachutes?
- Does the material from which the parachute is made affect the time taken to fall?

Obviously the teacher will have given the children the opportunity to raise their own questions as they observe the parachutes falling but he or she might want to add questions of his own which could challenge the children's thinking. Children will be able to graph two fields if one of them is numeric and will be able to answer the questions by looking at the graphs, but it is the explanation of the results which will enable the teacher to gain knowledge about the children's ideas and help him or her to challenge misconceptions.

ACTIVITY 3

Consider how simple graphing programs might be used. Explain the context in which the work was done and make sure that each of the participants can see a copy of the children's work. Share any ideas which teachers have about the contexts in which they have used programs such as these. Emphasise that this type of software is useful for recording results of an investigation where one of the variables, usually the dependent variable, is numeric.

Feedback and discussion

The teacher has asked the children to interpret the results and to give explanations. It could be that all the participants are in agreement that the teacher asked appropriate questions. Perhaps he or she might extend the thinking by asking Charlie and Andrew if they thought that the weight of the object was significant or whether they thought that the shape of the object might have an effect on the force needed to pull it along the table. Teachers will want children not only to suggest explanations but also to think about ways in which the explanations might be tested.

Move onto the feedback about possible investigations or explorations for very young children which could be recorded using a simple graphing program. The number of ideas will depend on the experience of the participants but activities such as testing the absorbency of disposable nappies when studying the topic of babies, the measuring, using non-standard measures, of seedlings as they grow, counting the number of people who recognised certain smells in smelly pots or investigating the stretch of materials could all be appropriate.

The use of word processing, using multimedia presentation software and the use of tape-recorded reports might all be suggested as other ways of using ICT to communicate the results of the enquiry.

ACTIVITY 4

As an introduction to this activity you might discuss the importance of evaluating the CD-ROMs before using them with children. Points to stress will be the importance of children becoming actively involved with the materials and the danger of wasting time by printing out extracts from text which children do not understand. Discuss the ways in which teachers can help children to engage with the materials.

Allocate two people to each computer and provide them with two CD-ROMs. If this is not possible, then people can circulate so that they have the opportunity to view more than one resource, preferably with the same subject focus, so that direct comparisons can be made.

Feedback and discussion

The key points to bring out here will be that:

- It is important that the resource provides opportunities for children to *think*. The CD-ROMs provide information which could help the children in their learning of concepts but there needs to be some challenge and some opportunity for the children to relate the knowledge gained to their own existing ideas (see Module 3). Sometimes the resource guides children through this process, but if it does not, then the teacher must prepare to do this by providing a forum for the exchange of ideas in order to promote learning with understanding.
- Teachers will have to think carefully about what the children do with the information which they find by their searches on the CD-ROM.

ACTIVITY 5

Computers with access to the Internet are needed for this activity. Arrange the participants so that they can work in pairs at the computers. If you have your own favourite sites these can be used instead of those suggested here. It is the consideration of how they are to be used which is the issue for discussion.

Before the evaluation of the sites takes place you may want to consider the following points:

- We do not want children to be involved in unproductive browsing.
- Teachers should preview the sites and check for accuracy before children use them.
- We need to make sure that children are clear about the purpose of their search and the way in which they will interact with the material.
- Teachers may have to produce worksheets or a list of questions so that children are cognitively involved with the text which they read or the simulations which they observe.
- Some sites provide information and some suggest investigations or activities.

Feedback and discussion

The discussion will be focused on what children might learn by accessing the site and selecting the appropriate information. As with the CD-ROMs the teacher will need to ensure that the time spent collecting the information is fruitful and encourages thinking. The teacher will have previewed the materials which are to be used and will have devised ways in which children will present the information which they have learned in order to encourage the development of ideas. There will probably be some comment about the readability of the text and the accuracy of the graphics.

For instance, if you were discussing the insecta site there may be some comment about the limitations of the site. The range of insects which are discussed is limited and the text is not extensive. On the other hand, there is a possibility of using differentiated worksheets to give children when they explore the information. Those children who find reading difficult will be able to look at the pictures of the insects and answer questions about the colour, the number of legs or why they think that there are hairs on some of the legs.

Other questions which might be asked and which would help children to learn might be concerned with the following:

- why people do not like cockroaches;
- why ladybirds are brightly coloured;
- what the insects eat;
- how long they live;
- how many eggs they lay;
- when the eggs are laid;
- why farmers like ladybirds.

There may be a discussion about some of the vocabulary. European children may not understand what is meant by 'the fall' and there may need to be explanations of terms such as pupate.

THE ACTIVITIES

When children are using ICT in science, they have to interpret results and evaluate the scientific evidence. They also have to communicate their findings in a variety of ways. The first part of this module looks at how children interpret finding and communicate their results. The second part looks at how the Internet and CD-ROMs are used to gather, interpret and communicate ideas.

Activity 1   Interpreting data collected from sensors

Consider this scenario:

Mr Smith's class of 8 year olds are learning about light. They have done investigations into how shadows are formed and are now learning about how light is reflected. They have explored mirrors and are thinking about how light is reflected off different coloured materials and fabrics. Last week they watched a video about the way in which the lights in a lighthouse are switched on when it becomes dark and this led to a discussion about how sensors are used in everyday life. They discussed the way street lights and intruder warning lights are operated and the part which sensors play in the process. Mr Smith has planned to do an investigation involving children planning a test to find out about the rate at which water warms up if it is placed into plastic bottles which are wrapped in felt samples of different colours and placed near a powerful lamp. He wants the children to understand the distinction between the reflection of light and the absorption of light. He hopes that the investigation will help children to understand why we wear light-coloured clothes when the weather is warm.

He thought that this would be a good opportunity to show the children how light sensors could be used as a tool to collect data and so he arranged his teaching so that he could take one-third of the class at a time into the computer suite to carry out an investigation into the way in which coloured samples of felt reflect light. He had only one computer in the classroom and so he enlisted the help of the head teacher who worked with the rest of the class while he was in the computer suite. The children and the teacher discussed how to carry out the test and decided to hold the sensors 6 cms from different coloured felt samples and to take readings using the sensors. They were very disappointed in the results which showed very little difference between the samples. They thought that perhaps the light from the classroom was interfering with their readings so they decided to try putting the felt around the inside of a beaker and placing the sensor inside. They were pleased to see that this was much more effective.

When all the children in the class had carried out the investigation and had printed out the tables and graphs, they compared their findings. The children realised that this investigation would not have been possible without the use of the sensors, although one child suggested that he brought his father's light meter into school to see if it would do a similar job. Another child pointed out that even if this piece of equipment were used, they would not have been able to draw graphs and tables of results so easily and quickly.

Look at the children's work in Figures 14.2 and 14.3 and consider what the children might have learned by carrying out this investigation. Complete the pro-forma to show in Figure 14.1 (a) what might have been learned and (b) what questions you might ask.

There are a variety of packages available which enable children to carry out similar investigations:

- Ecolog from Data Harvest www.dataharvest.co.uk
- RM Detector with Number Magic from RM www.rm.com
- LogIT available from Griffin and George with Junior Insight from Logotron www.logo.com

Activity 1 *continued*

- RM Investigate software used with LogIT
- First Sense from Philip Harris www.philipharris.co.uk

What might have been learned	What questions might be asked

Figure 14.1 Using sensors: identifying and developing learning

For cross-reference with Study Book see Figure 14.1

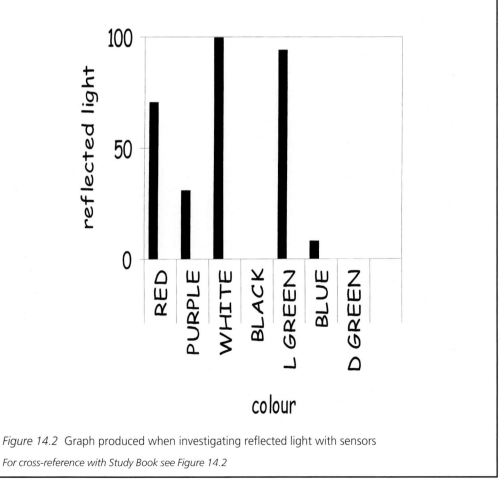

Figure 14.2 Graph produced when investigating reflected light with sensors

For cross-reference with Study Book see Figure 14.2

Activity 1 *continued*

This is a colour reflection sheet that shows which colours shine through a plain water tub. As you see dark green and black had less light going through them, White had the most light in. To do this we had to put a material of felt in the plain water tub then you put a light called a sensor inside the felt, then press Snapshot and the reflection of light will show up in a box. (on computer) If you can see, the lighter colours had more light in the felt but the darker colours only had a tiny bit of light reflecting through.

By Stephanie Neill.

Figure 14.3 Child's account of her investigation with sensors

For cross-reference with Study Book see Figure 14.3

Figure 14.4 Using sensors to find out about reflected light

For cross-reference with Study Book see Figure 14.4

Activity 2 Searching, sorting and graphing information

Children will need to learn how useful computers can be at searching for information. You can introduce prepared data-files which store information on a wide range of topics such as plants, insects, planets or birds. It is possible to search and sort information very quickly when using these databases whereas using books would take time. Most schools have database software which provides the opportunity for children not only to search ready-made files but also to create their own.

When children are creating a database, they have first of all to decide what sort of information they are going to collect. The information is arranged in categories which are called fields. So, for instance, if they were making a database about plants found in the school garden, they might set up fields such as name, colour, where found, leaf shape, flower colour, berries, etc. When the children have filled in all the details about a particular plant they have completed a record. There will be a record for each of the plants and when all have been completed the data can be displayed in a table.

Figure 14.5 is a graph showing the comparative heights of some of the flowers which they might have in the school garden. The teacher will have shown the children how to highlight the area of the table which they want to graph, how to select the type of graph which is most suitable for the purpose and how to label the *x* and *y* axes.

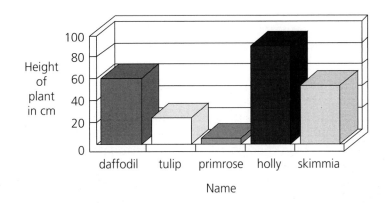

Figure 14.5 Height of plant

For cross-reference with Study Book see Figure 14.5

He or she will also have shown the children how to *search* for information so, for example, they could find all plants which were yellow and all plants which are above or below a certain height. They will also learn to *sort* information. In our example they might sort the plants by height or perhaps in alphabetical order. However, perhaps some people might say that there could be more opportunities for learning if children had compared the height of plants of the same type which grow in different places. This would give them the opportunity to consider the effect which light has on plants.

When the teacher is planning to work with databases with the class, he or she has to be mindful of what he or she wants the children to learn. The fields will be

Activity 2 continued

chosen with care and after discussion with the children about what they want to find out. Although many databases are compiled as a result of surveys and explorations, sometimes information may be added which is collected as a result of a controlled investigation.

There are many databases to choose from. If possible, evaluate them before you buy so that you choose those which are most suitable for the various age groups in school. The height of plants graph was produced using *Information Workshop* which operates on different levels for the different age groups. These are suitable for young children:

- First Workshop from RM   www.rm.co.uk
- Information Workshop from RM or Black Cat   www.rm.co.uk
                                                                        www.blackcatsoftware.com
- Junior Pinpoint from Longman   www.logo.com
- FlexiDATA form Flexible Software   www.flexible.co.uk

Imagine a group of teachers are planning the use of databases with classes of different ages.

6 year olds	garden plants
7 year olds	invertebrates
8 year olds	ourselves
9 year olds	rocks and soils
10 year olds	air resistance
11 year olds	nutrition

Select two or three of the subject areas and show the following:

- In what particular context the databases could be used.
- What fields could be set up for each of the contexts.
- What questions could children ask as they interrogate the database.
- What specifically the children might learn.
- Whether any of the information could be collected as a result of an investigation.

Activity 3 Communicating results

Sometimes a teacher might want the children to use a simple graphing program to display results of an investigation. This makes the analysis of results easier and the children spend less time on the actual recording. Figure 14.6 shows the work of Charlie and Andrew, 8-year-old boys who had been investigating forces. They used a Newton meter to measure the force needed to pull objects along a table and also to pull open a cupboard. The teacher asked them to draw conclusions and to explain their results. When he went home, Charlie used a spreadsheet on his home computer to draw a similar graph (Figure 14.7).

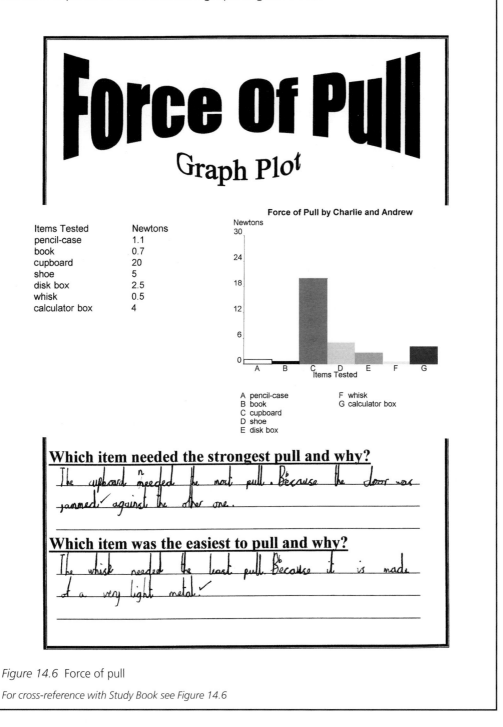

Figure 14.6 Force of pull

For cross-reference with Study Book see Figure 14.6

Activity 3 *continued*

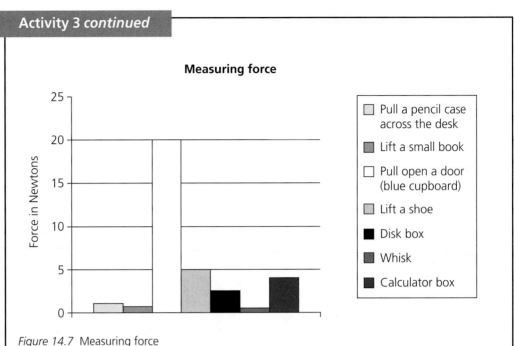

Measuring force

Legend:
- ☐ Pull a pencil case across the desk
- ▨ Lift a small book
- ☐ Pull open a door (blue cupboard)
- ▨ Lift a shoe
- ■ Disk box
- ▨ Whisk
- ■ Calculator box

Figure 14.7 Measuring force

For cross-reference with Study Book see Figure 14.7

The simple graphing programs are particularly suitable for use with young children. Some produce pictograms and have the facility for the teacher to use graphics. If we are to encourage the type of scientific enquiry which involves controlling variables then, even at an early age, we can encourage children to interpret simple graphs which they make as a result of their own enquiries.

Here are details of simple graphing programs for younger children:

- Starting Graph from RM www.rm.co.uk
- Counter from Black Cat www.blackcatsoftware.com
- Pictogram from Kudlian Software e-mail to sales@kudlian.demon.co.uk

Now do the following:

(a) Examine Charlie's work. He is enthusiastic about the use of ICT and enjoys learning. After the investigation, would you have asked him the same questions as those which his teacher asked? Could you suggest other questions which might probe his understanding of forces?

(b) Imagine that you are working with 5 year olds. Can you think of two simple investigations where results could be displayed easily using a simple graphing program?

(c) Can you think of other ways of using ICT, apart from graphs, databases and spreadsheets, that might be used to communicate the results of enquiry?

Activity 4   Using CD-ROMs

CD-ROMs are often used as a source of information but they may also encourage children to investigate, predict and suggest explanations. These are the skills which are essential in young scientists. The CD-ROMs present the information in a variety of ways, not only as text but with graphics, video clips and animation. As with all ICT applications, the teacher has to decide whether it will be more beneficial for the children to use the CD-ROM or whether a book would be more useful. The ICT may be amusing and may motivate children but 'aimless browsing through a CD-ROM is as unproductive as aimless browsing through a book' (Straker and Govier, 1996, p. 43). The teacher will review the contents of a CD-ROM before it is used by children and will prepare the children. This might involve asking challenging questions or offering advice about how to access information. Alternatively, the teacher might prepare a writing frame or worksheet which will guide the children through the searching process and identify key questions which need to be answered. The questions might be answered by reading text or looking at a video clip or a picture. When children are recording what they have learned, they may write, draw pictures or diagrams and even produce tables or charts.

If the teacher has access to an electronic whiteboard or a large screen monitor he or she might decide to show parts of the CD-ROM to the whole class after they have carried out their own practical investigations. Many CD-ROMs are interactive and he or she could ask the children to demonstrate their understanding by completing the 'experiment' section or the 'quiz' section. At all times the teacher will make sure that children are actively engaged with the subject matter and are given opportunities to express their own ideas and offer explanations.

www.teem.org.uk, www.becta.org.uk and www.ngfl.org.uk are sites which provide useful information about using CD-ROMs and websites and evaluations of some of the software and websites.

Now do the following:

- Select two CD-ROMs which deal with the same subject.
- Familiarise yourself with the navigational tools and explore the learning opportunities.
- Identify some key ideas which you would want the children to understand after working with the resource.
- Show how you would ensure that children were actively involved with the CD-ROM. If necessary, identify the key questions which you would ask. You might like to sketch out a worksheet which would guide the children through the learning process. Would you use an electronic whiteboard to present the materials to the whole class or would you want children to work in small groups?
- Compare the two CD-ROMs and be prepared to present your findings to your group. If you are working alone then prepare a list of 'pros and cons' related to the two resources.

Activity 5   Using the Internet

If you have 'surfed' the Internet you will know how easy it is to spend hours finding the information which you require. Even when you are quite skilled in selecting appropriate keywords, it is not always easy to find what you are looking for. For this reason perhaps it may be wise to use sites which you have chosen when you first introduce children to the Internet. Anyone can set up an Internet site without any checks being made about the accuracy of the information which is read. The teacher will need to check the site, which he or she intends to use, for accuracy and validity before introducing it to children. There are sites which provide evaluations. One such site can be found at www.teem.org.uk. Some subscription sites have been produced especially for children and most of these are easy to navigate and use simple language. Many allow you to have an introductory period free of charge so that you can evaluate the site. It is wise to do this as even subscription sites do not always provide what you are looking for. A very useful and comprehensive subscription site can be found at www.heinemannexplore.co.uk and another at www.livinglibrary.co.uk. Here are some other useful sites, many of which provide links:

www.techniquest.org
www.exploratorium.edu
www.planet.channel4.com
www.sin.fi.edu/biosci
www.izzy.online.discovery.com
www.nasa.gov
www.norcol.ac.uk/nineplanets
www.npac.syr.edu/textbook/
   kidsweb
www.pfizerfunzone.com/
   funzone/index
www.brainpop.com
www.4seasons.org.uk
www.tqjunior.thinkquest.org
www.kidshealth.org
www.saps.plantsci.cam.ac.uk
www.virtualfishtank.com/
   main.html

www.yucky.com
www.bbc.co.uk/nature/programmes/
   tv/blueplanet
www.bbc.co.uk/beasts
www.bbc.co.uk/dinosaurs
www.4learning.co.uk/ict/
www.channel4.com/science/
   microsites/R/robots
www.yahooligans.com this is a good
   search engine for children
http://kids.msfc.nasa.gov/
www.weboflife.co.uk/weboflife/
   species-web/index.html
www.eskeletons.org/
www.virtualcreatures.com
www.sodaplay.com
www.paperairplanes.co.uk
www.technosphere.org.uk/

Now choose one of the following:

(a) www.nhm.ac.uk/education/online/index

Go to the wildlife garden section and click on seasons. You will have the opportunity to answer some questions and to check your answers.

- Would you use this with 10 year olds?
- What would they learn?
- What directions would you give the children as a preparation for using the site?

Activity 5 *continued*

Explore the rest of the site and prepare a brief critique.

(b) www.insecta.com

Go to *bug of the month* and select *ladybugs*. Prepare a list of questions which you might ask children who were looking at the pictures and reading the text. Would you ask the children to write or draw as they answer your questions?

Prepare a brief critique of the site and make reference to the reading level of the text and any words which you feel might be unfamiliar to 10 year olds.

(c) www.askjeeves.co.uk

Ask 'What are ants?' From the selection which appears choose 'ant fact sheet and colouring page'. Prepare a list of questions which you might ask children who were learning about ants. Consider how you would ask the children to respond to your questions. Do you think that this page of the site is suitable to use with 10 year olds? Justify your decision.

REFERENCES

Straker, A. and Govier, H. (1997) *Children Using Computers*, Nash Pollock Publishing.

FURTHER READING

Cross, A. and Peet, G. (eds) (1997) 'Information Technology as essential in primary science', in *Teaching Science in the Primary School*, Plymouth: Northcote House.

Cunningham, F., Kent, F. and Muir, D. (1997) *Schools in Cyberspace*, London: Hodder and Stoughton.

Feasey, R. and Gallear, R. (2001) *Primary Science and Information Communication Technology*, Hatfield: Association for Science Education.

Frost, R. (1996) *IT in Primary Science*, Hatfield: Association for Science Education.

Newton, L. and Rogers, L.T. (2001) *Teaching Science with ICT*, London: Continuum.

Teacher Training Agency (1999) *Using Information and Communications Technology to Meet Teaching Objectives in Science Initial Training*, London: Teacher Training Agency.

Underwood, J. and Underwood, G. (1990) *Computers and Learning*, Oxford: Basil Blackwell, p. 97.

Module 15 The role of external resources in helping children to learn science

MODULE GOALS

- For participants to be aware of the local guidance which applies when we are working with children outside school.
- To consider how the local environment can provide a stimulus for scientific learning.
- To identify the potential for scientific learning by considering a range of environments, both natural and man-made.
- To be aware of the way in which interactive science centres can be used to reinforce the learning which is done in school.

MODULE OVERVIEW

This module is concerned with the learning which takes place outside the school building. Participants are encouraged to think about the planned learning which might take place in the school grounds, in field centres, parks, or in various locations such as woodlands or the seashore. There is some consideration of the health and safety issues and the preparations which need to be made before children can be taken out of school. The use of interactive science centres is also discussed.

The activities in this module involve teachers in considering the issues involved when planning for children to work out of doors or when making educational visits. Participants will do the following:

- consider the risks and other relevant issues which might be discussed in local and government guidance;
- consider how work in the local environment might be organised and what potential learning can be provided by studying in the school grounds;
- identify what scientific activities might be carried out by making visits;
- reflect on the research which has been carried out on learning in interactive science centres.

Timing

Total time: 3 hours

Activity 1	Group work	20 mins
	Feedback and discussion	15 mins
Activity 2	Group work (including the time spent out of doors)	30 mins
	Feedback and discussion	15 mins
Activity 3	Group work	20 mins
	Feedback and discussion	15 mins
Activity 4	Preliminary discussion about the research	15 mins
	Group work	20 mins
	Feedback	15 mins
Activity 5	Group work	15 mins

Materials required

- flip chart and pens;
- copies of the activities for those who do not have the Study Book.

For Activity 1

- copies of the local guidance and government guidance concerning out-of-school visits.

For Activity 2

- clip boards;
- trowels;
- pooters;
- magnifying boxes and containers;
- magnifying lenses;
- plastic gloves;
- coloured pens and pencils;
- tape measures;
- a digital camera and a computer will be useful but are not essential;
- copies of curriculum documents will be useful but are not essential.

INTRODUCTION

Points to make in giving an overview and stating the aims of the module:

- Whether we are aged 8 or 80 we are learning from our experiences. Children can see the relevance of classroom learning if they are given the opportunity to make links with their everyday experiences. Much learning takes place out of school when children are with their parents.
- The learning out of school, which teachers plan, needs to be part of an integrated programme.
- The health and safety of our pupils must always be considered.
- When using interactive science centres we should try to make sure that children have plenty of time to think about the scientific phenomena which are demonstrated by the exhibits.

ACTIVITY 1

Discuss the fact that teachers are *in loco parentis* when they are supervising children out of school. Teachers must take reasonable steps to ensure that any foreseeable risks to the children are documented before the educational visit takes place and have a duty to complete a 'risk assessment' exercise.

Give copies of any local guidelines on health and safety issues. Provide also copies of *Health and Safety for Pupils on Educational Visits: A Good Practice Guide* (1989) which is available free from DfEE Publications Centre. This is advice from the UK government. Other governments will have similar documents. www.nut.org has documentation about safety on school journeys.

Give out copies of the task if participants do not have the Study Book.

Feedback and discussion

Some probable points for discussion might be:

- Issues arising from the risk assessment exercise will probably be concerned with the swinging playground equipment and the misuse of seesaws. Children must be supervised carefully when pushing and pulling roundabouts.
- When considering the preparation for the visit teachers will refer to the ratio of adults to children. This will depend on the local guidelines but will probably be:

  - One adult for every six children aged 6 or 7;
  - One adult for every ten to fourteen pupils aged 8 to 11;
  - The child who is visually impaired should have their own carer.

- The location of toilets.
- How children will be allocated to the supervisors.
- Parents may need to be informed in writing about the visit.
- The head teacher of the school should be informed of all arrangements for the visit.
- All supervising adults should be adequately briefed about the format of the visit and the educational objectives.
- Although some of the adults may not be teachers, teachers have overall responsibility.
- A minimum of two teachers should be involved in the visit.
- There should be a qualified first aider in the party. A small first aid bag should be carried by one of the adults.
- A mobile phone should be carried by one of the adults.
- There should be a person in school who has the contact telephone number for the mobile phone and full details of the children's emergency contact numbers should be easily accessible.
- Children should have waterproof clothing.
- The teachers may need to have notebooks, pencils and clipboards for the children to use.

ACTIVITY 2

Give out copies of the task if people do not have copies of the Study Book. This activity is concerned with working outside the classroom but in the school grounds. Even schools in urban environments will have some areas which could be studied. Give out the equipment which will enable the teachers to dig over soil if necessary. This will enable them to assess the potential of an area which contains living things. The collecting boxes are for short-term use only. It is not necessary to complete a detailed survey of a particular environment at this stage. Participants are merely considering the learning potential. You may decide to allocate different types of environment to different groups. So, for instance, one group might look at the potential of a section of a pathway, others might look at a vertical section of a wall while others might study part of the school football field. Try to be creative in your suggestions about what could be used. The discussion will be more fruitful if you have as wide a variety of environments as possible. Stress that they are looking at a very small area, perhaps a metre square.

Allow about 20 minutes for the field work and a further 10 minutes for the groups to prepare their reports. These could be presented on flip charts or overhead transparencies. Emphasise the fact that they are looking at raising questions for investigation by observing the environment. If a digital camera is used, then photographs of the sites could be used in the reports.

Feedback and discussion

The feedback issues will depend largely on the types of environments which the participants have studied. For instance, if a group has studied a section of the wall, then the focus suggested would probably be materials. Children might learn about the purpose of the dampproof membrane which can be seen at the bottom of the wall. They could investigate which material is best for preventing rising damp. There would be some learning about the bonding of the bricks and perhaps some investigation into the strength of various bonds and the mortar which is used by bricklayers. Perhaps some plant life has been found at the base of the wall and there may be some evidence of weathering. Children could find out about the aspect of the wall and the amount of sunlight which falls onto the wall during the school day. Comparisons can be made with small sections of wall which have a different aspect.

You will have made a preliminary survey of the different environments around your own building and will no doubt have prepared lists of suggestions which might help the less experienced teachers or trainees. There will be some sharing of ideas about how the various sites can be used to teach scientific ideas and skills.

There will be discussion about how the work might be organised with a class of thirty children. If the teacher wants the children to have similar experiences then perhaps they will each have to visit the site in turn and report back on what they have found. Alternatively, the teacher may decide to allocate different sections of similar environments to groups of children who would all make their observations at the same time. However it is to be organised, the role of the teacher and any supporting adults will need to be clearly defined. Children who are left to their own devices might not observe the relevant features of a site, so the supporting adults will have to be very well prepared by the teacher.

It will be useful for the teachers to identify the possible learning outcomes of the work which they suggest and, if there is time, to relate it to the relevant curriculum documents.

ACTIVITY 3

There will be opportunities in this activity to consider the educational visit as a way of enriching the children's experience and making links between the science which they learn in school and science in a wider context. The focus is on planning for learning both in school and during the visit. Perhaps a pro-forma similar to Figure 15.1 could be used to structure the feedback relating to the environments in list A. If any of the participants are planning visits to other environments, then these could be substituted for those in list A. It might be useful, at this stage, to spend a short time sharing details about successful visits which have been made.

Context			
Preliminary activities in school	Activities in the field	Follow-up work in school	Anticipated learning

Figure 15.1 Pro-forma: identifying opportunities for learning outside school

Feedback and discussion

The discussion will be focused on the way in which the school's science scheme of work might be enhanced by the educational visit. For instance, those who have been thinking about the visit to the fire station might suggest that the science ideas and activities which might be linked to this visit could be as shown in Figure 15.2.

The participants may all have different ideas to share with each other. The main purpose of this discussion is to show how the visit should not only be informative in a general way and enrich the children's understanding of the work which the firefighters do, but it should also be linked to the science curriculum so that the learning is integrated into a planned programme.

When considering the puddle and the snow, you will probably want to discuss the way in which teachers make use of the unexpected. It is not possible to tell exactly when we might

Context A visit to a firestation			
Preliminary activities in school	Activities in the field	Follow-up work in school	Anticipated learning
Discussion about the various aspects of a firefighter's role	Discussion about why firefighters smother flames		Fire needs oxygen How to respond to a small fire in the home
	Discussion about how the firefighters use water hydrants Perhaps observation of the fire hoses and the jets of water	Making squeezy bottle 'squirters' and observing the jets Testing different 'squirters' to see which produce the biggest jets of water Playing with hose pipes and observing how the jets of water vary when the pressure of water is increased	Controlling variables, planning a fair test Recording results
			Observing the effects of forces
		Using siphons and pumps	Water moves into the space created when air is sucked out of a siphon
Investigating pulleys and levers	Considering how firefighters use pulleys and levers to free people and animals from dangerous situations		Forces: less force is needed to raise an object if more pulleys are used
Investigating the materials from which protective clothing is made			Certain materials are inflammable. Planning an investigation, interpreting results and drawing conclusions
	Observation of the fire engine and the hydraulic lift	Making hydraulic systems with plastic tubing and syringes	

Figure 15.2 A visit to the fire station: examples of opportunities for learning

have snow or puddles in our playgrounds, but enterprising teachers will make use of these situations. For some children, snow is something which they might see only once every two or three years. It would seem a pity to waste the opportunity for the younger children to investigate what happens to the snow if it is brought indoors in a container, to observe footprints and animal prints, and to look at snow under the microscope and with magnifying lenses.

ACTIVITY 4

Begin by discussing the research. You might find it useful to have your own copy of the article 'Science Centres and science learning' by Rennie and McClafferty (1996) as this is a very comprehensive account of research into behaviours and learning at the centres. The important point to make is that, although children should enjoy the visit, there must be time for them to reflect on the science ideas the exhibits are designed to illustrate. Those exhibits which are designed to give feedback and to include this reflective period will probably be the most successful.

There are some centres such as 'Conkers' which are both field centres and interactive centres. Here children are encouraged to explore various ideas and habitats out of doors and follow up their explorations when they move indoors.

You might also like to consider the way in which museums such as the Natural History Museum encourage children to observe and investigate natural objects. The Investigate centre there encourages the process of scientific exploration.

Give out copies of the task to groups of four or five people. It would, of course, be very useful if the participants could actually use their observation schedules in a centre as they observe children.

Feedback and discussion

Ask two or three people to present their schedules and to justify the inclusion of each of the aspects. There will be some judgement about the 'fun' factor and about what is said and done as the children engage with the resource. Can success be judged? Can challenge be judged? These are questions which you will probably discuss as the feedback is given. The observation schedule should be designed to provide the observer with information about the children's attitudes and learning.

ACTIVITY 5

You will consider the questions which could be asked before the arch in Figure 15.4 is constructed on the flat surface. These could be about the shape of the blocks. There will perhaps be some consideration about asking children to predict what might happen as the board is tilted.

The sense of wonder on the children's faces is delightful to see. You might like to refer to this and discuss how 'wonder' often encourages children's scientific enquiry. The questions which could be suggested will focus on the shape of the curve. Catenary is the name of the curve made by the hanging chain. There may be some discussion about what would happen if we removed one of the blocks in the wooden arch and how the blocks push against each other to keep the structure stable. Children may have seen bridges shaped in this way. Older children might be urged to relate what they notice to the forces involved.

THE ACTIVITIES

As we go through life, we learn something new almost every day. We learn in our homes, when we are out shopping, when we read the newspaper and when we are talking to our friends. If we are put into a situation where we meet a new idea and are given the opportunity to think about the idea, then we are probably going to learn. Education and schooling are not synonymous, indeed, much of children's learning is done out of school.

Although most of the teaching which is provided by schools is carried out within the school building, many links are made to the world outside school. Teachers plan to provide experiences which will reinforce the learning which is done in the classroom. The children may visit a park, a woodland area, a beach, a supermarket, a building site or even an outside area within the school grounds. Many teachers also arrange for their children to visit museums or interactive science centres in order for the children to have further opportunities to think about particular science ideas.

This module is concerned with learning outside school. The activities will focus on the health and safety issues which we must think about when we are preparing to take children out of school, the contexts for learning, the planning and the teaching strategies.

Activity 1 Health and safety

Schools have their own regulations about working outside the school boundaries and these are usually based on the local education authorities' guidelines. Governments also provide advice for teachers who are organising educational visits. Read the local guidance in respect of organising school visits.

Imagine that you are planning to take a class of 7 year olds to a local playground in order to look at the way in which the seesaws, swings and other playground equipment are used. The children have been learning about the forces involved in pushing and pulling and in their design technology lessons they have been thinking about how to make stable structures.

- There are twenty-eight children in the class.
- There is a child in the class who is visually impaired.
- The children will walk to the playground which is half a mile from the school.
- There will be one major road to cross but there is a safe crossing place.

Prepare a 'risk assessment' document for the educational visit and discuss with colleagues the following issues. Prepare a response to the discussion points:

- How many teachers and other adults would accompany the children on the visit?
- Who would be informed of the details of the visit and how would you pass this information to them?
- What would the children carry with them? What would you and the other adults carry?
- Would the children need any special clothing?

Activity 2 Preparing for learning and teaching

Teachers will prepare for educational visits by making a preliminary survey of the area which is to be studied. The purpose of this visit will be to identify any hazards which may be encountered and to assess the learning potential of the site. The nature of the site will, of course, depend on the science which is to be studied. If, for instance, the teacher wanted children to study various habitats, it would be very sensible to start with a relatively small area such as a section of a hedge, an area of land under a single tree, part of the school garden or a section of a pathway. Children are encouraged to focus carefully on the plants and animals which are found in their 'area', the colour and texture of the soil, the amount of sunlight and shade, as well as the sounds and smells which they notice. If children are to have the opportunity to make connections between the features of the habitat, and the living things which are found there, then teachers will need to make sure that the connections can be made. The preliminary survey will provide them with information about the learning opportunities in various parts of the site. If children are allowed to flit from area to area and to dig randomly in a variety of places then their study time could be less than fruitful.

Take a brief walk in your immediate surroundings and select an area for study. This doesn't have to be an area which contains living things. It could be a short section of a street, a path, or a building.

Consider the following questions and prepare to present a report to your colleagues:

- What might be the focus of a study here?
- How would you organise the work?
- What questions for investigation might be raised by observing this environment?
- What specifically might the children learn by studying this environment? (You will need to identify a particular age group.)
- Would you study this area more than once during the year?

Activity 3 Identifying the potential for science learning

Because any environmental setting, urban or rural, man-made or natural, is so highly complex, it is essential to provide a focus for work that might be done in it. It is easy for pupil interest and enthusiasm to be dissipated if they are looking at a wide variety of features and aspects on one visit. The exploration and the investigation will be superficial if the focus is not tightly defined. The school's scheme of work will set down the learning objectives for a particular area of study but teachers will decide how and if learning outside school is appropriate

When teachers arrange for their pupils to work outside the classroom, they have a clear idea about how the resource can stimulate learning. This may not necessarily be confined to work in the science curriculum (see Module 11). However, they must be clear about the anticipated learning outcomes in each of the curriculum areas.

Select one of the environments from list A (larger environments) and list B (smaller environments) in Figure 15.3 and outline the science learning which might develop from a study of the two environments. Make brief notes about the activities which would enable children to learn and identify the specific skills and concepts. Consider what activities might be carried out in the field and what preliminary or follow-up work might be done in the classroom.

List A	List B
A fire station With 7-year-old children	A pile of logs in the school garden With 5-year-old children
A building site With 11-year-old children	A puddle With 6-year-old children
The seashore With 9-year-old children	A blanket of snow in the school playground With 4-year-old children

Figure 15.3 Some suggested starting points

For cross-reference with Study Book see Figure 15.1

Activity 4 Visiting interactive science centres

In recent years many centres have been set up where children can handle exhibits and manipulate them so that effects can be observed. Interaction means more than just touching (Tuckey, 1992). The exhibits in the centres are designed so that children can explore ideas which they may have about various phenomena. 'Science centres are stimulating, they are visually exciting, noisy, active environments' (Rennie and McClafferty, 1996). The best exhibits encourage children to express their own opinions about what they notice and are, at the same time, designed to motivate children's curiosity. Research (Feher, 1990) has shown that there should be a match between the conceptual level of the learner and that, in order to learn from the exhibits, 'pupils must have a store of "suitable" concepts' (Tuckey, 1992).

The centres are not without their critics. Shortland suggests, 'When education and entertainment are brought together under the same roof, education will be the loser' (1987, p. 213). There is no doubt that unless children are given the opportunity to think about the science ideas which are demonstrated by the exhibits then there will be little learning. If children are left on their own, many will move from one exhibit to another without thinking about the science ideas which they encounter.

The centres are popular with both children and adults but the teacher has an important role to play in preparing the children for the visit, working with the children at the centre and in structuring the follow-up work in school. It has been said that teachers should be able to differentiate between 'hands-on' and inter- active exhibits. 'Hands-on' implies that the children touch the exhibit. It may be that they feel something, strike something or assemble something. Interactive exhibits involve the learner in making some sort of response which in turn invites further action. It is the feedback from the operator's action which personalises the experience and it is this which should provoke thinking.

Perry (1989) suggests that a successful exhibit at a science centre should involve the following:

Curiosity	the visitor is surprised and intrigued
Confidence	the visitor has a sense of personal competence by experiencing success
Challenge	the visitor perceives that there is something to work towards
Control	the visitor has a sense of self-determination and control
Play	the visitor experiences enjoyment and playfulness
Communication	the visitor engages in meaningful social interaction

Boisvert and Slez (1994) describe the behaviour of visitors to an exhibit by referring to three levels of engagement:

Level 1 (involved time) Stands in front of and/or looks at the exhibit but does not read instructions or try it; watches another person use exhibit but does not take part; uses exhibit but not as it is intended to be used.
Level 2 (positive interaction) Reads label and directions; uses exhibit as intended; helps another person to use the exhibit by reading instructions, demonstrating its use or manipulating part of the exhibit.

Activity 4 *continued*

Level 3 (instructional time) Asks staff/teacher to explain how to use the exhibit or what the exhibit is about; discusses meaning of the exhibit with staff/teacher; shares own ideas and information about the exhibit with staff/teacher.

Imagine that you are intending to take a class of 11 year olds to a science centre. The children have been learning about sound and you hope that the exhibits at the centre will help them in their understanding.

You are intending to make a preliminary visit to the centre where you will observe groups of children as they play and explore. You will also interact with the exhibits yourself. Use the information provided to draw up an observation schedule which will enable you to make a judgement about the effectiveness of the exhibits.

Activity 5   Helping children to reflect

The teacher cannot be with all of the children during a visit to a science centre. Other adults would be helping to supervise the children and it is for this reason that, during the preliminary visit, the teacher will make notes about how to question children in order to make them think. These notes will be shared with all adults who accompany the children.

In Figure 15.4 you can see an image taken after a group of children had assembled a catenary arch at the Exploratorium in San Francisco. The numbered blocks are laid out onto a horizontal board over an outline of the arch. The board is then tilted slowly until it is in a vertical position. The arch is then standing upright and the base board is lowered.

Figure 15.4 Catenary arch

Source: Photo by S. Schwartzenberg (c) Exploratorium www.exploratorium.edu

For cross-reference with Study Book see Figure 15.2

The arch remains in an upright position. The shape of the arch is the same as a hanging chain. You can see two chains in the picture; one is a thin chain and one is a heavy chain. If the chains and the arch are touched very gently, they will sway.

What questions would you ask children when they have assembled the arch? Write these down so that you are ready to share them with your colleagues. Have you any idea why the arch does not fall? There may be several ideas which you can discuss with your colleagues.

Activity 5 *continued*

Further details about interactive science centres can be found at the following websites:

In the United Kingdom
www.catalyst.org.uk
www.eureka.org.uk
www.gsc.org.uk
www.sciencemuseum.org.uk
www.magnatrust.org.uk
www.msim.org.uk
www.sensation.org.uk
www.techniquest.org
www.visitconkers.com

In the USA
www.exploratorium.edu
www.sciowa.org
www.csc.clpgh.org
www.sciencecenterct.org
www.sciencedetroit.org
www.slsc.org
www.mdsci.org
www.lhs.berkeley.edu

In Australia
www.uow.edu.au
www.questacon.edu.au

In Canada
www.osc.on.ca
www.sciencenorth.on.ca

For information world-wide
Search for 'Hands-on Science Centers Worldwide' www.cs.cmu.edu/cs

REFERENCES

Boisvert, D. and Slez, B. (1994) 'The relationship between visitor characteristics and learning-associated behaviors in a Science Museum Discovery Centre', *Science Education*, vol. 78, no. 2, pp. 137–48.

DfEE Publications Centre (1989) *Health and Safety for Pupils on Educational Visits: A Good Practice Guide*, Nottingham: DfEE.

Feher, E. (1990) 'Interactive museum exhibits as tools for learning: exploration with light', *International Journal of Science Education*, vol. 12, no. 10, pp. 35–9.

Perry, D.L. (1989) 'The creation and verification of a development model for the design of a museum exhibit' (doctoral dissertation, Indiana University, 1989), quoted in L.J. Rennie and T.P. McClafferty, 'Science Centres and science learning', *Studies in Science Education*, vol. 27, pp. 53–98.

Rennie, L.J. and McClafferty, T.P. (1996) 'Science Centres and science learning', *Studies in Science Education*, vol. 27, pp. 53–98.

Shortland, M. (1987) 'No business like show business', *Nature*, vol. 328, pp. 213–14.

Tuckey, C. (1992) 'Children's informal learning at an interactive science centre', *International Journal of Science Education*, vol. 14, no. 3, pp. 273–8.

FURTHER READING

A.S.E. (1994) *Safety in School Science* Hatfield: Association for Science Education.

A.S.E (2001) *Be Safe*, Hatfield: Association for Science Education.

Brooke, H. and Solomon, J. (1992) 'Play or learning? How can primary pupils benefit from an interactive science centre?' *Education in Science*, January, pp. 16–17.

Brooke, H. and Solomon, J. (1996) 'Hands-on, brains-on: playing and learning in an interactive science centre', *Primary Science Review*, October, pp. 14–17.

Hann, F. (1996) 'Science out of school', *Primary Science Review*, December, A.S.E.

Harlen, W. (2000) *The Teaching of Science in Primary Schools*, London: David Fulton Publishers.

Honeyman, B.N. (1995) 'Science Centres: building bridges with teachers', paper presented at the A.S.E conference, Lancaster, January.

Martin, M., Brown, S. and Russell, T. (1991) 'A study of child–adult interaction at a Natural History Science Centre', *Studies in Educational Evaluation*, vol. 17, pp. 355–69.

Module 16   Evaluating classroom practice and providing effective feedback to teachers

MODULE GOALS

- To consider the various ways in which classroom practice can be monitored and evaluated with particular reference to the quality of teaching and learning.
- To consider the strengths and weaknesses of each method.
- To consider how feedback is given to practitioners after observation and the relationship between the observer and the observed.
- To consider the role of the senior management team and governors.

MODULE OVERVIEW

This module is designed to support teachers, in particular co-ordinators, in some aspects of monitoring and evaluating science provision. Activity 1 is concerned with examining pupils' work as a tool for monitoring and evaluating provision. Activity 2 is about classroom observation and the feedback provided to practitioners and more widely. It will also show how this can inform a range of issues such as standards, the quality of teaching and learning. Activity 3 involves looking at standards achieved by pupils and how these compare with national standards and Activity 4 is about talking with pupils about their learning.

Timing

Total time: 2 hours 35 minutes

Introduction		10 mins
Activity 1	Group work	30 mins
	Feedback and discussion	15 mins
Activity 2	Group work	20 mins
	Feedback and discussion	15 mins
Activity 3	Group work	20 mins
	Feedback and discussion	15 mins
Activity 4	Group work	15 mins
	Feedback and discussion	15 mins

Materials required

- flip chart and pens;
- copies of the activities for those not having the Study Book.

For Activity 2

- OHT of some indicators of effective teaching and learning.

INTRODUCTION

This module is concerned with monitoring and evaluating classroom practice. It builds upon a number of previous modules. There are a number of different ways to monitor and evaluate provision, some of which are easier and less costly than others.

Planning is an essential prerequisite to successful teaching. In England there are national schemes of work upon which teachers can draw. Continuity and progression are secured by making sure conceptual difficulty and the progressive acquisition of skills in scientific enquiry are planned for appropriately. The monitoring of planning is an important part of ensuring children have appropriate learning experiences. Assessment for learning is similarly essential and integral to good planning.

A view of the standards that are appropriate for pupils of differing ages is important to ensure children are achieving levels of attainment which reflect that which would be expected, bearing in mind their prior attainment. The monitoring of standards and trends in standards are important, but account needs to be taken of such factors such as size of cohort, which, for small cohorts could cause significant fluctuations from year to year.

Work sampling, display and talking with children give a valuable picture of attainment and progress. Analysis of test questions and pupils' work generally, can provide useful information on areas of strength and weakness which can then inform planning.

The quality of teaching and learning is vital to raising standards and it is important that this is monitored and evaluated and that routine reflection on participants' practice should be the norm. There are cost implications to this in terms of releasing teachers to observe.

ACTIVITY 1

Work sampling

This activity considers the importance of work sampling in monitoring and evaluating science provision in school.

Teachers discuss in pairs which aspects of provision could be monitored and evaluated by work sampling and then pool ideas. The facilitator records responses on a flip chart. Teachers then return to their pairs to devise a series of questions that will help them to work sample with a purpose, so that key judgements can be made. Pairs can then report back on specific aspects and questions under each heading can be collated for the group and distributed subsequently. Finally, the group can consider how useful work sampling is in monitoring and evaluating different aspects of provision and what the limitations of this method are for each aspect.

Feedback and discussion

Aspects of provision that could be monitored in this way include:

1 General compliance with school policies, e.g. marking and presentation.
2 If whole school planning/schemes of work are being followed.

3 Standards of attainment (in general and of particular groups of pupils, e.g. girls, boys, able pupils, different ethnic groups).
4 Achievement or progress (in general and of particular groups of pupils, e.g. girls, boys, able pupils, different ethnic groups).
5 Continuity and progression.
6 The balance between experimental and investigative science and knowledge and understanding.
7 Teaching.

It may be worth pointing out that work sampling is more manageable if there is a particular focus. This could be in response to a whole-school issue, for example, the use of formative assessment or the extent to which work is differentiated for pupils with differing prior attainment, or a subject specific issue, for example, the extent to which pupils' investigative skills are being developed. Different foci can be covered on different occasions, so ensuring all aspects are monitored and evaluated.

Possible questions include:

1 General compliance with school policies, e.g. marking and presentation:

   (a) Is work neatly presented?
   (b) Is work completed?
   (c) Are corrections or teachers' questions responded to?
   (d) Is a range of recording methods evident?
   (e) Is the work marked?
   (f) Do teachers make corrections?
   (g) Are comments made which indicate why work is good and what needs to be done to help pupils improve?

2 If whole school planning/schemes of work are being followed:

   (a) Does the work in different year groups correspond to that indicated in the planning?
   (b) Is the amount of depth appropriate or are some teachers over-/under-estimating what is required resulting in either possible mismatch of work to pupils, repetition in subsequent years or of work already carried out, or gaps in coverage?

3 Standards of attainment:

   (a) Are standards of attainment by the end of Key Stages appropriate taking into account pupils' prior attainment? (It is worth reminding teachers that the baseline assessments made as pupils enter the school are important, as are factors such as mobility.)
   (b) Are there any differences in attainment of boys and girls?
   (c) Are there differences in attainment of different ethnic groups (where this is an issue for the school)?
   (d) Is the attainment of able pupils sufficiently high?
   (e) Is the attainment of SEN pupils as good as it should be taking into account their prior attainment?
   (f) Is the attainment of EAL pupils sufficiently high taking into account their stage of acquisition?

4 Achievement or progress:
   Are pupils making the progress they should? Similar questions to those in the previous section can be posed. It may be that given their baseline, SEN pupils are making good progress despite not reaching nationally expected levels. Similarly, higher attaining

pupils could be achieving beyond the national average but not making as much progress as they are capable of.

(a) Is progress better in some year groups or Key Stages than others?
(b) Consider mobility factors. How does the progress of pupils who have been at the school all their school life compare with pupils who have spent less time at the school?
(c) Is progress in experimental and investigative work comparable with that in knowledge and understanding?

5 Continuity and progression:

(a) Does the content in one year build appropriately on that in previous years?
(b) Are there sufficient opportunities for revisiting and reinforcing?
(c) Is there any evidence of checking children's ideas at the outset of a topic, or of assessing their knowledge and understanding at the end to inform future planning?
(d) Is there evidence of progression in the development of children's investigative skills?

6 The balance between experimental and investigative science and knowledge and understanding:

(a) Are sufficient opportunities evident for pupils to learn investigative skills?
(b) Are sufficient opportunities evident for children to carry out a scientific investigation independently (or for younger children, with an appropriate degree of adult support)?
(c) Are investigations used to develop children's knowledge and understanding?
(d) Do children use their knowledge and understanding during investigative work?
(e) Is there an appropriate balance between different areas of knowledge?

7 Teaching:
While the best way to judge teaching is by observation, a number of indicators of the quality of teaching can be found through work sampling. Questions may include:

(a) Is the work sufficiently differentiated for pupils of differing prior attainment?
(b) Is there evidence of teaching investigative skills in a progressive way?
(c) Is the work marked to enable pupils to understand what they have done well and how they may improve?
(d) Is there variety in the recording methods used?
(e) Is there evidence of a range of teaching and learning styles?
(f) Are pupils with SEN sufficiently supported to enable them to demonstrate attainment?

ACTIVITY 2

Lesson observation

This activity is in two parts. The first is for participants, in pairs, to list key features of effective teaching and learning, starring those that they feel particularly relevant to science. They can then share these and compile a list from all participants and compare these with other sources.

The second part of the activity is to read the summary of the two lesson observations and, in pairs, plan the feedback they would give to the teachers concerned. This is then shared with the group and general issues arising are noted.

Feedback and discussion

Observation of teaching and judgements of the quality of teaching and learning are now routine in most schools. This is carried out on a regular basis in England by an independent team of inspectors in national inspections, and by headteachers, senior management teams and subject co-ordinators as part of the routine monitoring and evaluation of the quality of teaching and learning in schools, and also as part of performance management procedures. Most schools have a specific form that is used for lesson observation. These are often generic containing typically sections for standards, teaching, learning and pupils' response. Others can be more detailed or subject-specific, an example being found in Newton and Newton (1998, p. 161). Many schools also have protocols for observation of lessons, often as a result of the introduction of performance management and it is important to recognise and work within these. The DfES publication *Embedding Performance Management 2002: Training Modules* (2002) also have sample lesson observation forms and helpful guidance.

The first part of the activity involves participants reflecting upon what they perceive are essential characteristics of good quality teaching and learning. Many texts can be used to supplement their ideas. The OFSTED *Handbook for Inspecting Primary and Nursery Schools* (2000) (used in inspection in England) contains guidance on making judgements on the quality of teaching and learning. These include for teaching:

- the ability to plan effectively;
- setting clear objectives;
- a good subject knowledge and the ability to select methods and activities to enable pupils to learn effectively;
- the ability to manage pupils well and insist on high standards of behaviour;
- the ability to assess pupils' work effectively and use homework effectively, and
- to use resources including support staff, ICT and equipment effectively.

These are generic and are important indicators of effective teaching. Effective learning is seen as the extent to which pupils

- acquire new skills, knowledge and understanding;
- are productive and work at a good pace;
- understand what they are doing, show interest, maintain concentration;
- can work independently.

It will be useful to have some of these on an OHT for reference. Two further useful publications are *Co-ordinating Science Across the Primary School* (Newton and Newton, 1998) and *The Primary Co-ordinator and Ofsted Re-inspection* (Gadsby and Harrison, 1999). The former contains a chapter on monitoring and evaluating science teaching and learning and the latter contains a chapter on monitoring your subject area that covers generic and subject-specific issues. In particular there is a very detailed set of questions that will prove useful in classroom observations of teaching and learning.

The second part of the activity involves looking at a brief report of two lessons following an observation. These are deliberately purely descriptive rather than to any prescribed format. Ask participants to work in pairs to identify the positive aspect of teaching and learning they would wish to identify and those areas for development. Depending upon the experience of participants it may be necessary to first discuss the features of successful feedback and how this should be carried out. Again this may be outlined in a school policy for performance management, but for initial teacher training some guidance will be needed.

Some general points to include should be:

- This is not an inspection and the purpose of the observations should be part and parcel of the school focus for observations, be it on general teaching and learning or very specific aspects of science teaching identified as needing investigation as part of raising standards in science.

- To be helpful it should be a genuine dialogue between the observer and the observed. It is always important to ask the views of the observed. Often from an observer's point of view, there are many issues requiring clarification, for example, why the course of a lesson was changed, why certain decisions were made.
- It is therefore important to decide the most appropriate questions to ask to help to evaluate the lesson, often these can only be decided during the observation, but generic guidance is available in the DfES training package on *Embedding Performance Management 2002*.
- Note the positive points first, since almost invariably these will outnumber any development points unless there is a problem.
- Agree the discussion so that both parties feel an appropriate summary of the observation has been made.
- It may be that in some instances concerns with respect to the teaching have been identified which need discussing with a member of the senior management team or the headteacher.

ACTIVITY 3

This activity assumes knowledge of the previous Modules 6 and 7 on assessment. Two examples of summative assessment are outlined and have been included in Module 6. First, the example of summative assessment which may occur at the end of a unit of work to assess the degree to which pupils have made appropriate learning gains, and second, the summative assessment which may occur through national testing or teacher assessment at a particular age.

Ask participants to work in pairs or threes to consider which questions they would want to ask to decide, first of all, if appropriate progress had been made through a unit of work and, second, if appropriate standards were being met compared with other schools.

Feedback and discussion

In discussing whether appropriate progress has been made in a particular unit of work, a range of issues may arise. It is important that participants are aware of the need to assess where pupils are at the beginning of a unit of work to check if progress is appropriate. Good planning should address issues of continuity and progression (see Module 12), so that work planned is broadly at a level appropriate for a particular age. Records of pupils' prior attainment will be useful; however pupils retain information to varying degrees dependent upon a range of factors such as length of time since the same area was taught and the degree of understanding at the end of the last block of teaching on that topic. It is good practice therefore to have some strategies for finding out pupils' existing ideas (see Module 1). Planning should address match of work to pupils, so that there are differentiated learning objectives and learning outcomes for pupils. Clear difference in the attainment of pupils would be expected where there are differences in the level of prior attainment, rather than outcomes that are broadly similar, but it would be hoped that there was good value added for all groups of pupils.

Issues which may cause concern might be:

- those associated with inclusion such as the attainment and progress of different groups, for example, lower attaining pupils or gifted and talented pupils, girls or boys;
- attainment and progress in different aspects of science such as investigative work compared with knowledge and understanding;
- whether attainment is broadly what would be expected in terms of the proportion of pupils attaining a threshold level.

In considering if standards at a specified age are high enough, the importance of baseline needs to be stressed so that value added is considered and not just the final outcome. National data is available in England in the 'Autumn Package' and comparisons of school test results with national data and similar schools (based upon the proportion of pupils eligible for free school meals) in the form of the 'PANDA' (Performance and Assessment Data). Some discussion of the proportion of pupils reaching a threshold level, how the numbers of pupils attaining different levels compares and the significance of average points scores would be needed. Trends over time are important. For Key Stage 1 statistics are based upon teacher assessment, so the importance of accuracy of judgements and moderation needs to be considered. Other factors which need to be taken into account include mobility (now recognised as having a significant impact on pupils' attainment) and the size of cohorts and the extent to which importance can be attached to variations from year to year. Many education authorities are providing statistical data to help schools to analyse how well they are doing compared with other schools in their area. It may be worth looking at the anonymous PANDA that OFSTED have produced so that students are familiar with the format of these, while teachers can examine their own school's PANDA.

ACTIVITY 4

Talking with pupils

Two activities are envisaged, one for 7 year olds involving finding out their knowledge about materials and some investigations they have carried out about these, and the second is involved with finding out about pupils' understanding of dissolving and the factors which may affect how quickly or how much substance dissolves.

This activity is involved with deciding the sort of questions that would be effective in determining how much pupils know and understand, and in making an assessment of standards generally.

Get participants to work in pairs or threes to list the questions they feel would give them the information they need.

Feedback and discussion

It is worth emphasising the rather unnatural nature of the discussion, particularly if the children are not well known by the interviewer. Some general questions are advisable to place pupils at their ease, such as about those activities they especially enjoyed. Young pupils are invariably forthcoming and keen to show how much they have learned. It is often helpful for younger pupils to have some concrete materials to explore and to focus discussion around. A selection of different fabrics or rocks may be useful. Typical questions may include the following.

For 7 year olds:

- What is the same about these materials?
- What is different about these materials?
- What do the materials feel like?
- Can you describe the different materials?
- Which sense are you using to describe them?
- How can you sort the materials?
- What are the materials used for?
- What makes them useful?
- Where do the materials come from?
- Can you change these materials?
- What would you like to find, or have you found out about these materials?
- How would you decide which rock was the hardest?
- How would you decide which fabric was the warmest?

For 11 year olds:

- Can you tell me what happens when you add sugar to water?
- Why do you think this is happening?
- How is this different from when you add flour to water?
- Do you think there is a limit to the amount of sugar that dissolves in water?
- Can you keep adding sugar to water and it will always dissolve?
- Will a larger amount of water dissolve a larger amount of sugar?
- Does the temperature of the water make a difference?
- Do you know what soluble/insoluble means?
- How would you plan an investigation to find out how the temperature of the water affects how quickly a substance dissolves?

A number of subsidiary questions are likely to arise, for example:

- Which substances would you want to use to dissolve?
- Why?
- How hot would you want the water to be?
- What do you think will happen to the amount of substance that dissolves as the temperature of the water increases?
- If the temperature is warmer will more dissolve?
- What range of temperatures would you wish to use?
- Why is this a good choice of temperatures?
- What will you measure?
- What will you change?
- What will you keep the same?
- How will you decide what effect the temperature has on how quickly the substance dissolves?
- What sort of table would you have to record your results?
- Would you draw a graph? What sort of graph?
- What shape do you think your graph would look like?

Activity 1 Work sampling

Work sampling can provide some very useful insights into many aspects of science provision in schools. It is routinely carried out as part of the inspection process in England. A range of work needs to be examined covering all age groups in the school and a sample of different attainment needs to be represented within each year group including those pupils with Special Educational Needs. Which aspects of provision could be monitored and evaluated in this way? For each aspect try to devise a series of questions you would be asking yourself, to ensure your examination of pupils' work provided the evaluative judgements you need.

Finally, consider the limitations of work sampling for providing evidence for each aspect of provision.

Activity 2 Lesson observation

Teacher A

A class of Year 5 children have been studying habitats and this has led to a lesson on food chains. The teacher begins the lesson with questions about what the children's favourite foods are. They then talk about the different types of food and revisit previous work on healthy eating. They move on to consider which foods their pets eat.

The teacher's questions are effective in revisiting previous work. Pupils are eager to answer questions and many express the view that foods they particularly enjoy are not always those most healthy. Most recognise that this is not a problem unless their particular preferences are taken to excess. Higher attaining pupils can recall there are major food groups (carbohydrates, proteins and fats) but need help in remembering the scientific terms. Once prompted, however, they remember these. The majority of children can express, knowledgeably, the sort of foods that would make up a healthy packed lunch and recall work they have done in Design Technology in making packed lunches and pizzas.

In discussing the food their pets eat, many are not aware of what is contained in the various foods – 'we just open the packet and feed them!' More are aware of the food wild animals eat and can explain, for example, that lions and tigers eat meat whereas other animals, for example, rabbits and mice, eat plants. Most recognise that humans eat meat and plants, but few appreciate that some humans choose only to eat plants. When the teacher introduces the terms carnivore, herbivore and omnivore many of the higher attaining pupils have been introduced to these and are familiar with them.

The main activity involves sorting pictures of animals into carnivores, herbivores and omnivores. The teacher has differentiated primarily by recording method. Higher attaining pupils record independently by listing the animals under the three headings and writing a definition of each term. They quickly complete their work. Other groups stick pictures in sets and complete definitions in cloze procedure exercise. The lower attaining group are very confused by the terms and flounder.

Teacher B

A class of Year 6 pupils are carrying out an investigation on friction and which shoe sole will have the best grip. They discuss different types of surface – rough and smooth and which, from personal experience, they have found to have the better grip. Some pupils are familiar with the term friction. They examine the different shoe soles and discuss what they look like and which they feel will provide most friction. Most pupils predict that the rougher and more ridged the surface, the greater the friction. A variety of methods to test out which shoes are suggested, including pulling the shoes along the floor with a Newton meter and placing the shoes on a slope to see which are least likely to slide as the slope is made steeper.

The teacher has provided a range of Newton meters and a good range of different shoe soles as well as some different types of surface to pull the shoes along. Most pupils choose to pull the shoes using a Newton meter and see which are 'hardest to pull'. One group becomes confused as they try the same shoe on different surfaces and lose sight of their original question. Another group uses

Activity 2 *continued*

too smooth a surface so that little difference is observed between the force needed to pull the various shoes along. The teacher intervenes with some good questions to focus pupils on the difficulties they are having, and how they may overcome these, such as trying a rougher surface or putting a mass in the shoes to simulate weight. Some pupils are able to explain that the greater the force needed to pull the shoe, the greater the friction. Most can draw a conclusion about which shoe sole has the best grip. One shoe sole took a lot less force to move it than was expected but the opportunity was not taken to speculate on why this was so.

Activity 3   Looking at standards

'How well are we doing?' and 'How do we compare with other schools?' are important questions to ask. In order to have a view on this, teachers need to be secure in their judgements about standards and if they are high enough. Summative assessment is required (see Module 6). This can be in the form of teacher assessments for a specific part of the curriculum covered to find out if pupils have made appropriate gains in learning, or tests and teacher assessment which compare pupils' performance with other pupils nationally, typically at specified points in a pupil's education. For the former it is important to know what the pupils knew and understood before teaching occurred, in order to judge whether they have made appropriate progress. For the latter, in order to become secure in judgements, teachers need to examine a range of pupils' work and come to decisions about the particular level that the work represents as defined by the National Curriculum, the Scottish 5–14 Guidelines or other locally used curriculum document (see also Module 7).

In deciding how high standards are in the school, what questions would you wish to ask (a) to decide if appropriate progress had been made in a particular unit of work; and (b) if standards at a specified age were high enough?

Activity 4 Talking with pupils

Discussion with pupils is very helpful in establishing the degree of their knowledge and understanding as well as some other aspects of learning such as their attitude to science and what they need in order to improve.

Imagine you are talking with a group of 7 year olds about the work they have been doing on materials. List the sort of questions you would ask to find out the extent of their understanding. Include questions to find out what they understand about scientific enquiry.

Now extend your list of questions to those you would ask of 11 year olds to determine their understanding of dissolving and the factors likely to affect how much or how quickly a substance dissolves.

REFERENCES

DfES (2002) *Embedding Performance Management 2002: Training Modules*, London: DfES.

Gadsby, P. and Harrison, M. (1999) *The Primary Coordinator and OFSTED Re-inspection*, London: Falmer Press.

Newton, L.D. and Newton, D.P. (1998) *Coordinating Science Across the Primary School*, London: Falmer Press.

OFSTED (2000a) *Handbook for Inspecting Primary and Nursery Schools*, London: HMSO.

OFSTED (2000b) *Inspecting Subjects 3–11: Guidance for Inspectors and Schools*, revised edn, OFSTED website (www.ofsted.gov.uk).